THE
FOUGHT
ALONE

MAURICE BUCKMASTER

THEY FOUGHT ALONE

THE TRUE STORY OF SOE'S AGENTS IN WARTIME FRANCE

Biteback Publishing

This edition published in Great Britain in 2014 by
Biteback Publishing Ltd
Westminster Tower
3 Albert Embankment
London SE1 7SP
First published in Great Britain in 1958 by Odhams (Watford) Ltd.
Copyright © Maurice Buckmaster 1958

Maurice Buckmaster has asserted his right under the Copyright, Designs
and Patents Act 1988 to be identified as the author of this work.

All rights reserved. No part of this publication may be reproduced, stored
in a retrieval system or transmitted, in any form or by any means, without
the publisher's prior permission in writing.

This book is sold subject to the condition that it shall not, by way of trade
or otherwise, be lent, resold, hired out or otherwise circulated without
the publisher's prior consent in any form of binding or cover other than
that in which it is published and without a similar condition, including this
condition, being imposed on the subsequent purchaser.

Every reasonable effort has been made to trace copyright holders of material
reproduced in this book, but if any have been inadvertently overlooked the
publishers would be glad to hear from them.

ISBN 978-1-84954-692-8

10 9 8 7 6 5 4 3 2 1

A CIP catalogue record for this book is available from the British Library.

Set in Garamond by Soapbox
Printed and bound in Great Britain by
CPI Group (UK) Ltd, Croydon CR0 4YY

To the brave men and women of the Resistance who gave their lives for the liberation of France

Contents

	Introduction	ix
	Map of France and F Section Circuits	xiv
Chapter 1:	'Set Europe Ablaze!'	1
Chapter 2:	Matchbox	18
Chapter 3:	Recruiting and Training	45
Chapter 4:	The Match	75
Chapter 5:	Suspicion	102
Chapter 6:	First Flames	118
Chapter 7:	Cradle of the Resistance	132
Chapter 8:	Blackmail	162
Chapter 9:	Check	181
Chapter 10:	Traitor	204
Chapter 11:	Kindling	225
Chapter 12:	Flame	242
Chapter 13:	Aftermath	262
Appendix 1:	Report of Sabotage and Guerrilla Warfare, October 1944	270
Appendix 2:	List of SOE and Resistance members run by Buckmaster's F Section	282
Index		300

Introduction

The role played during the Second World War by the French Resistance and by the British Special Operations Executive (SOE) officers and agents who worked alongside them is widely understood. But their critical role ahead of D-Day is only rarely recognised and is certainly far less known. There were a number of Allied special operations forces on the ground in France, of which those run by F Section of SOE were by far the most numerous. Indeed, F Section was the largest individual section within SOE, running more than eighty 'circuits' or groups of resistance fighters, each with an organiser sent in from the F Section headquarters in Baker Street, London, based just a few yards from the supposed home of fictional detective Sherlock Holmes.

The head of F Section was Maurice Buckmaster, who was thirty-seven at the start of the war and had been a teacher, a merchant banker, the head of the first French office of the Ford Motor Company and then head of its European operations. Buckmaster was commissioned into the Intelligence Corps and in 1941, being fluent in French, was appointed head of SOE's independent French section. There was a separate French section designated RF which worked with the Free French led by Charles de Gaulle. Relations between the two sections were often difficult.

In recent years, it has become fashionable to blame Maurice Buckmaster for the deaths of SOE agents who were killed as a direct result of German infiltration of F Section's 'circuits'. There is no doubt that F Section suffered substantial losses and that a relatively small number of its 'circuits' (eight out of a total of eighty-six) were penetrated and turned back against the British under German control. Buckmaster cannot entirely escape blame for that, although he was certainly not solely responsible. But the losses need to be kept in perspective. F Section had at least 425 agents in France, of whom 104 died, with only around twenty dying as a direct result of the German penetration of the eight 'circuits'.

Those sent in from England were told before they went in that their life expectancy, in a country where Nazi surveillance was far more intense than it was in any other country in occupied Europe, was just six weeks. In such circumstances, it would have been odd indeed if the Germans had not managed to track down some of the SOE agents, even if they had not been assisted by Henri Déricourt, an SOE agent who passed details of some of his fellow agents to the *Sicherheitsdienst*.

The original revelations of the German successes, made in the late 1950s by the writers Elizabeth Nicholas and Jean Overton Fuller, led to the commissioning of an official history of *SOE in France* by Professor M. R. D. Foot and it is worth quoting his conclusions: 'Not only did F Section staff do all for the best; they did all that could be reasonably expected of them, given whom they were up against. There was far too much going on at once for every circuit to get the minute care it deserved.'

It has been argued that Buckmaster failed to pick up telltale signs from the radio communications with his agents that they had been captured. The omission of important security checks which ought to have been seen as signs that the agents had been captured and were being played back against the British were missed. Certainly they were, but not by Buckmaster. Spotting those issues was not his job. The more pertinent criticism is that when told of such problems by Leo Marks, the head of SOE coding, he ignored them. While there is substance to such claims, it is clear from Marks's admirably honest *From Silk to Cyanide* that the reality is more nuanced.

It is true that Buckmaster was sometimes reluctant to accept that an agent had been blown, but not always without justification. Even the best agents occasionally failed to send security checks or sent the wrong ones. But it is clear from the Marks account that Buckmaster's failing was more a reluctance to give up on any one of his agents and in the case of at least two of the better known casualties, Gilbert Norman and Noor Inayat Khan, Buckmaster recognised they were blown but insisted on continuing to communicate with them in the hope that it would keep them alive. Marks noted that no matter how late he called the F Section head with a message from an agent in the field, 'he was always waiting in his office, and his first concern was for the safety of the agent. Not all country section directors shared that attitude. To some of them, agents in the field were heads to be counted, a tally they could show CD [SOE Chief Colin Gubbins]. But Maurice Buckmaster was a family man.'

Notwithstanding the failures, there were fifty active circuits in place, all under Buckmaster's control, when it really mattered ahead of D-Day. Co-ordinated from London via the *messages personnels* broadcast by the BBC, they mounted a campaign of sabotage of railways, bridges, and German supply and ammunition dumps. They also destroyed telephone exchanges, an important element which ensured that German communications had to be sent by wireless transmissions that could be intercepted by the British and deciphered at Bletchley Park.

The work of the Communist *Maquis* in mounting guerrilla attacks on German troops, delaying their arrival in Normandy and thereby enabling the allies to establish a vital bridgehead, has never been properly recognised, not even in France where they were airbrushed out of history because they were not part of the Free French forces. None of these vital operations would have been possible on such a scale without F Section's operations and support.

At the end of the war, when the failures were already well known to his superiors, Buckmaster was described as 'an excellent officer with great powers of inspiring other people. It was owing to his wide knowledge of the French and his personal drive and enthusiasm that a large part of the French Resistance was successful.'

He was appointed an Officer of the Most Excellent Order of the British Empire, a Chevalier de la Légion d'Honneur by the French government and awarded the Legion of Merit by the US government. He wrote two memoirs, *Specially Employed* (1952) and this book, *They Fought Alone* (1958). It is a true classic but was written a dozen years after the war and before the official files were released, and as a result included a number of mistakes which have been edited out of this book. In addition, agents whose identities had been disguised have been named to ensure that their bravery is recognised. I am very grateful to David Harrison for his assistance in helping to ensure that it is now as accurate as possible.

Michael Smith
Editor of Dialogue Espionage Classics

Map of France and F Section Circuits

The map on the opposite page contains references only to those who are mentioned in the text of the book. There were many other leaders and thousands of Frenchmen who do not find mention here.

HQ Staff

Colonel Maurice Buckmaster	Section Head
Vera Atkins	Intelligence and PA to Section Head
Lt Col Robert Bourne-Paterson	Planning
Major Jacques de Guélis	Briefing
Major Lewis Gielgud	Recruiting
Major Gérard Morel	Operations
Captain George Bégué	Signals
Major Louis Huot	US liaison officer
Mr Park	Janitor

These are just some of the more than eighty F Section circuits across France with their organisers. There were around fifty circuits operating ahead of D-Day.

1 – Pierre de Vomécourt – Autogyro Circuit
2 – Ben Cowburn – Tinker Circuit
3 – Francis Suttill – Prosper/Physician Circuit
4 – François Basin – Urchin Circuit
5 – Peter Churchill – Spindle Circuit
6 – Richard Heslop – Marksman Circuit
7 – Virginia Hall – Heckler Circuit
8 – Claude de Baissac   Scientist Circuit
9 – George Starr – Wheelwright Circuit
10 – Michael Trotobas – Farmer Circuit
11 – Gustave Biéler – Musician Circuit
12 – Harry Rée – Stockbroker Circuit
13 – René Dumont-Guillemet – Spiritualist Circuit
14 – Amédée Maingard – Shipwright Circuit
15 – Philippe Liewer – Salesman Circuit
16 – John Farmer – Freelance Circuit
17 – Frank Pickersgill – Archdeacon Circuit (Pickersgill was sent out as controller of the Archdeacon Circuit in June 1943 but was captured soon after landing. The Archdeacon Circuit became German-controlled for the next eight months.)
18 – Pearl Witherington – Wrestler Circuit
19 – Henri Peulevé – Author Circuit

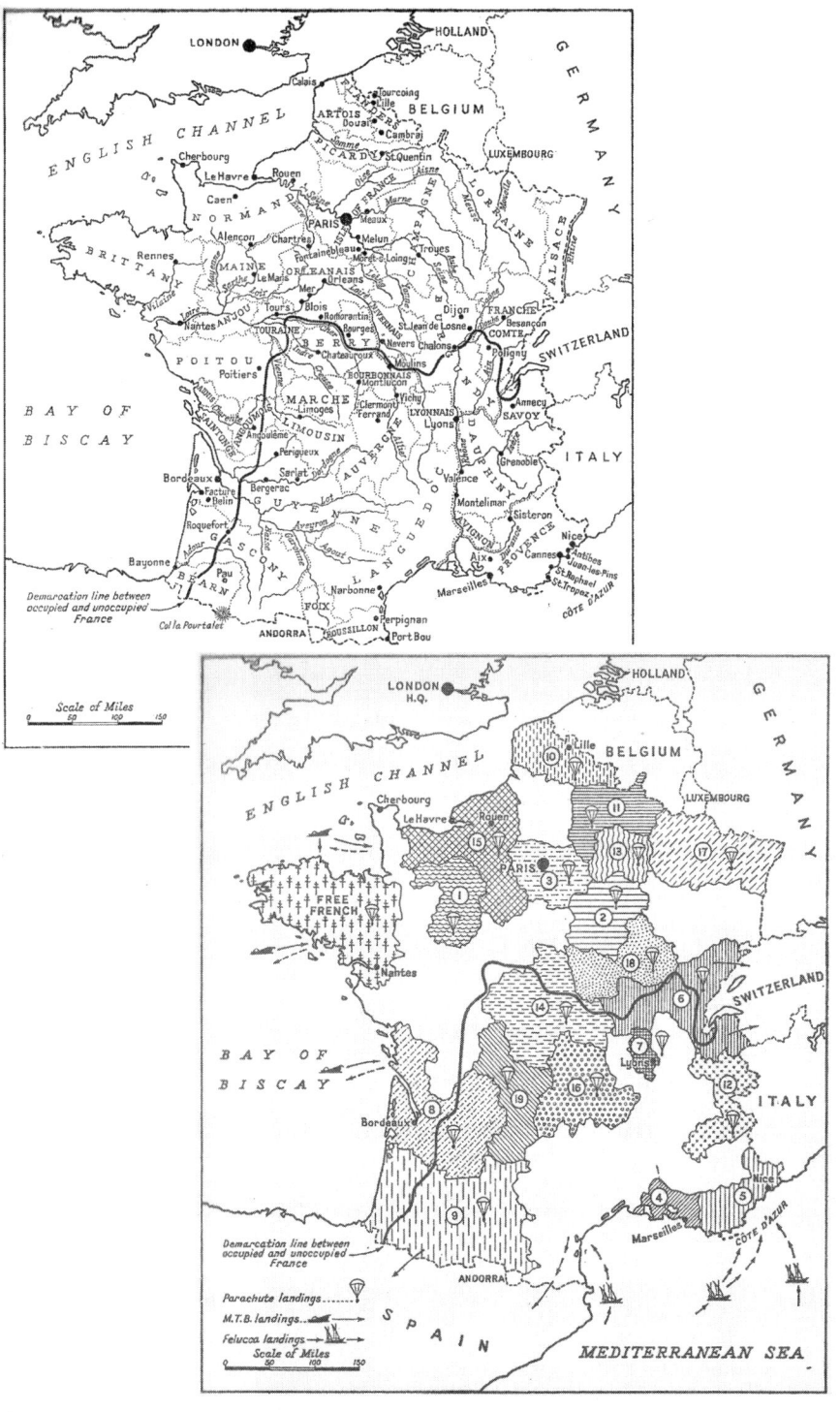

Chapter 1

'Set Europe Ablaze!'

'Yes, Buckmaster, what is it?' The voice of the General commanding the 50th Division was curt, but not unfriendly.

'I wondered whether I might come in and see you for a moment, sir.'

A pause was followed by the words 'Yes, come in.'

It was a March day in 1941 and the 50th, to which I was the Intelligence Officer, was stationed somewhere in the south of England. An electric fire was burning in the General's office and he stretched his hands to it as he growled, 'Well, Buckmaster, what's the trouble?'

'I don't exactly find this easy to say, sir—'

'Come on, man, out with it.'

'Well, sir, it's about the division's move to Libya—'

'What of it?'

'I believe that Italian's likely to be the language for Prisoner Interrogation there.'

'That's the general idea, yes.'

'I think you know, sir, that Italian's not really one of my languages and I'm sure you'd be better off with an IO who spoke it.'

The General warmed his hands. 'There might be something in that,' he conceded at last, with a smile. 'But assuming we get someone else, what are we going to do with you? I suppose you've got some ideas on that too, eh?'

'I did have one or two thoughts.'

'Quite.'

'If, for instance, there were a post where my French could be of use—'

'Like that Dakar show, what?'

I smiled wryly; even today I cannot recall the Dakar expedition without a certain annoyance. Calculated to be the first sign that we had recaptured the spirit of offence, the combined operation had been hardly impressive. I myself had very little part – except for the fact of my physical presence – in the affair; my clearest memory of it is our sitting in the bay of Rufisque and being bombarded and dive-bombed for twenty-four hours, as well as being torpedoed, without being able, owing to the strategic objective of the expedition, to return or parry the fire of the Vichy French whom we were seeking to recruit to our side.

There's nothing more unpleasant to any soldier, including strictly non-professional ones like me, than to be 'straddled' regularly by fifteen-inch shells without any chance of taking cover. My whole being longed for a nice slit trench and they don't have slit trenches on battleships. Many conflicting accounts exist of the political wranglings and the tactical misfortunes of the episode; for my part, I was concerned only to help in winning the war and had been deeply disappointed at the touchiness – a touchiness which the years have apparently aggravated – of de Gaulle and some of his colleagues who seemed more suspicious of England than aware of the purpose of the sortie. I was never, throughout the war, very much concerned with politics and I cared more for harrying the Germans than apportioning the credit to respective persons. I had been attached to the Dakar force simply because French-speaking officers were, naturally, at a premium on such a joint Anglo-French operation. I must have allowed something of my impression of the matter to become known to the General: hence his sally about the 'Dakar show'.

I said: 'I wasn't exactly thinking of anything in that line again, sir.'

'I understand,' he grinned. 'Look, I'm pretty pushed at the moment with the division about to go overseas—'

'I fully realise that, sir.'

'Can you come up to London with me on Wednesday morning? I've got to pop into the War Office and you might care to be on hand.'

'Thank you very much, sir,' I said, rising.

'All right, Buckmaster.'

I left feeling very much relieved. It may seem that I was taking rather a high-handed line in asking for a change simply because the 50th Division was going to an area which I did not greatly fancy, but only those who are actually aware of our situation in 1941 will realise how keen I was to make the fullest possible use of whatever special qualifications I had. I have always loved France and I lived there for many years before the war, first as a tutor to a small boy, later as a reporter on the French newspaper *Le Matin* and finally as Assistant Manager of the Ford Company which I had joined in the meanwhile; I was eager to serve Britain by helping France.

On Wednesday morning we drove in the General's car up to London. It was a London dented and buffeted by the bombardment she had suffered. Daylight raids were largely past, but the nights were still filled with the wailing of sirens and the explosion of bombs; people still made their way to work through the rubble of last night's damage. Though the country stood firm and even now was beginning to try and turn the fight, disruption was inevitable; viewed from today it seems that victory was certain, even in the darkest days: in the darkest days, it seemed far from certain.

'Come on,' said the General. 'This is where we get out. I've got a meeting which will take about an hour. Meet me back here at – eleven. All right?'

'I'll be here,' I replied. I walked away, up Whitehall to Trafalgar Square. Of all the countries of Europe, England alone was free, free and alone. I shall never forget my deep pain when I thought of France in the grip of the Boches; I thought of the many friends I had made there and of how they must be feeling at the collapse of their France. I was with the 50th Division (the first Territorials to land with the BEF) throughout the campaign which ended for me with Dunkirk and for France with occupation.

Promptly at eleven I was waiting for the General at the place he had said. When he came down the steps, I saluted and as he returned the salute he growled, 'Sorry to keep you waiting. Come along in.' The General strode along the passages of the War Office with a brisk determination while I followed him with long and persistent strides. As he came to each door he would look up at it with a snort of inquisitiveness. The first we came to had a card with the name of a Field Marshal on it; to my surprise he banged authoritatively on it with his swagger stick. 'Come on,' he called to me, as he opened the door and marched in. I followed diffidently.

'Brought a young chap to see you,' my General said to the Field Marshal when he had gained admittance to him. 'Buckmaster, excellent fellow. Speaks French. Intelligence chap, you know.' He rattled off several other maliciously flattering references and then suggested that the Field Marshal should find me a post. Politely, we were shown the door. 'On second thoughts,' the General said when we were back in the passage, 'you wouldn't want to work for him in any case. We'll try someone else.' We tried several others (including another Field Marshal); if our reception was courteous, my rejection was firm. I became dispirited and, by this time, somewhat embarrassed. I suggested we persist no further; I would go to Libya with the 50th.

'Nonsense! We wouldn't have you. There're lots more Generals yet, my boy, lots.'

'It's very kind of you, sir—'

'Of course. I know the very man! Stupid of me not to think of him before! Come on.' He set off at a great pace down the passage and up some stairs and down another passage while I struggled to keep up with him. 'First-rate fellow this,' he was mumbling, 'he'll fix you up, you see.'

A minute later I was being presented to yet another General. 'Templer, I want you to meet a young officer of mine – Buckmaster.'

'How do you do, sir?'

General Templer listened attentively while my General again retailed my abilities and my qualifications. This time, to my surprise, I was not so quickly rebuffed.

'You know something about Intelligence work, Buckmaster?'

'A certain amount, sir. I was on the first Minley course.'

'And your French is really good?'

'I think I could fairly say that, yes.'

'We've recently formed a new organisation to deal with something that sounds very much up your street – subversive warfare in France. It's something quite fresh. They need an Information Officer. You sound the man for the job. How about it?'

I looked at them both and smiled: 'I'll have a shot.'

'When could you start?'

'When would you want me?'

General Templer said: 'Tomorrow?'

I looked at my General. He nodded.

'Tomorrow,' I said.

II

The next day I reported to the headquarters of the French section of Special Operations Executive at 64 Baker Street. As I walked in through the plain entrance and rode in the lift up to the fifth floor, I wondered what my duties would be exactly. There was, I found, little exactness about the routine of the fledgling organisation in which I found myself.

'The fact is, Buckmaster,' my commanding officer told me, 'everything's highly embryonic here.' The bare office and the deserted atmosphere of the place confirmed this gloomy observation. The man on the other side of the desk was a civilian, whom we knew by his initials, H. M., who had experience, as I had, of working in France. He seemed rather dispirited to me and indeed he was soon to retire because of illness. However, I could not know this and I asked rather brusquely what my job entailed.

'The general idea,' H. M. explained, 'is to see what we can do about getting information about occupied France. We want to find out what's going on there, what sort of targets we should concentrate on attacking – when we're in a position to attack them – and so forth.'

It seemed to me that the man was either being cryptic or rather vague.

'What sort of information is available?' I asked.

He shrugged. 'Very little. There's hardly anything to go on.'

'What about Secret Service reports?'

'Oh, no, we don't get those. Can't get hold of them.'

'Well, what can we get hold of?' I demanded.

He smiled wanly: 'That's for you to discover.'

It seemed that there was nothing further to be gained, so I took my leave. My elation at the new job was fast disappearing. I telephoned a Colonel in the Intelligence Corps on the 'scrambler' and asked him what the whole set-up was about.

'Subversive activities,' he explained.

'I've gathered that, sir, but what kind of subversive activities?'

'I'm not too clear myself, but I think the idea is to sabotage industrial installations in France which have been or might be put into service for Jerry.'

'This isn't a Secret Service affair then?'

'Heavens no, old boy, Special Operations.'

'Well, what're we under?' I inquired. 'The War Office?'

'Doubt it. MEW, I should think. Ministry of Economic Warfare. I should try them.'

'Thank you, sir.'

It is not easy to contact a Ministry and since I had no idea who, if anyone, in the MEW was responsible for SOE (French Division), I decided to waste no further time in attempting to find out what I should do or what information I was supposed to procure. I sat in the bare office with which I had been provided, staring into the empty wire out-tray. There was no in-tray.

On reflection, it seemed to me that the best thing I could do was to try and remember what I could about French factories which I had visited when I was working, during 1932–6, for the Ford Company of France. My information might be out of date, but at least it was information. I drew a pile of typing paper towards me.

Day after day, for three weeks, I dredged my brain for knowledge, noting down every conceivable thing I could about the potential, the staff and the lay-out of French industry. In spite of my hard work, however, I could not conceal from myself the haphazard and incomplete nature of my notes. There was no system, save a vague geographical ordering from north to south. If only there were an alphabetical list…

'The Bottin,' I said, aloud. 'Of course, the Bottin!' It was exactly what I had been looking for – an alphabetic thesaurus of French industry and commerce, department by department, from A to Z. It only remained to get hold of a copy. I telephoned confidently to my chief.

'I'd like a copy of the Bottin,' I told him.

'You are our Bottin,' I was reminded.

'Somebody must have one.'

'That may be; I haven't managed to get hold of it.'

'Do I have your authority to try and get a copy?' I demanded.

'Certainly, but it won't do you any good.'

I got through to my Colonel in the Intelligence Corps.

'Bottin? Haven't got one in the place, old boy,' he announced cheerfully.

'Do you mean to say that in the whole length and breadth of Military Intelligence there's no copy of the Bottin?'

'If there is, I haven't seen it,' the Colonel said, putting down the receiver.

I thought of getting through to de Gaulle's people, but my earlier experiences of them, together with my instructions not to do anything to upset them, dissuaded me. I tried the booksellers: nothing. With some hesitation I rang through to General Templer's office. I explained my difficulty in procuring a copy of the Bottin and was given another extension in the War Office where it was thought they might help me.

'Colonel Denvers here.'

'Oh, this is Major Buckmaster, French section of SOE.'

'Of what?'

I explained roughly the nature of SOE in so far as I knew it myself and then said: 'I need a copy of the Bottin very badly if I'm to get on with my work.'

'Who told you that we had a copy?'

'General Templer suggested I ring you.'

'We're not allowed to release any of our secret material.'

'Why should the Bottin be secret material? The Germans have got as many copies of it as they want. What's the point of keeping material from your own side that's freely available to the enemy?'

'Look, old man, that's not my worry.'

'Well, it is my worry. Your name was given me and I really would be most grateful if you could help me.'

'My instructions are not to let my copy of the Bottin out of my sight.'

'You have got a copy then?'

'Possibly, possibly.'

'Well, sir, can I come round to your office and use it there? It would still be in your sight.'

'Mm, that's a thought.'

I went round to the War Office and managed to present myself to Colonel Denvers.

'I can't have you working actually in the room with me, Buckmaster,' he told me. 'I've put you in the little office my secretary uses for keeping her coat.'

'Thank you very much, sir,' I replied. He showed me into the fawn partitioned office. It was quite bare except for a desk and a chair, but on the desk was a copy of the Bottin. I sat down and began to go through it; to my delight I discovered, as I had hoped, a preface to each chapter which detailed the industries of the *département* with which it dealt. The first which really interested me was the Timken Ball Bearing Factory, Quai Aulagnier, Asnières, Seine. I happened to know that particular factory well.

Each day I returned to the Colonel's secretary's cloakroom in order to pursue my researches, comparing them with the notes I had already made and adding new details of which the names of various manufacturers and factories reminded me. After I had been working in this manner for some weeks, undisturbed either by inquiries from my CO or liaison activities from other members of the SOE organisation, I chanced to meet a man I knew who had something to do with the War Office library.

'Are you working here now?' he demanded.

'I have to,' I complained, and went on to tell him about the Bottin.

'What do you mean you can't take it out of the building?'

'I gather it's the only copy in the place.'

'Come along with me.' I followed him to a large and dusty storeroom which was piled high with various out-of-date handbooks and French guides. Under the window-sill was a stack of Bottins. 'Help yourself,' he suggested.

I helped myself.

That was the end of the only work I ever did in the War Office. I thanked Colonel Denvers for his kindness, informed him deferentially where he might replenish his slender stock of Bottins and repaired to Baker Street. As usual, things seemed pretty quiet there. In spite of my industrious tabulation, I was still unable fully to understand what SOE was all about or when it was going to start doing whatever it was supposed to do. Patiently, I continued my study of the Bottin; I had reached 'P' by now.

III

One night in May 1941, when I happened to be Night Duty Officer, I heard somebody moving about in the corridor outside the NDO room. Since my job made me responsible for the security of the building, I went out to investigate. A figure was standing in the lighted doorway of one of the rooms. It was no member of the staff I had ever seen. A voice said: 'Good evening.'

My eyes narrowed in an effort to see the man's face. 'Who are you?' I demanded. 'What are you doing here?'

'My name's Hambro,' he replied.

'Is it just? Would you kindly step into the NDO room?'

'Willingly.' The stranger strolled past me into the bright room. He walked over to the window and checked the blackout curtain before turning to me with a smile. 'You seem to be cosy in here.'

'I'm sorry but I must ask to see your identity papers.'

'Of course.' He smiled and handed them across.

I read the name 'Sir Charles Hambro' and handed them back: 'I still don't quite see—'

'I happen to be the number two in this SOE set-up,' he informed me gently, producing another piece of paper.

'I'm very sorry, sir, I had no idea.'

'Ah!' He sat down in the armchair behind the desk. 'What's all this?' he asked, looking at my Bottin researches.

I attempted to show him the lines on which I was working.

'You're just doing this off your own bat, are you?'

'I'm afraid I am, yes. I thought as Information Officer, I'd better try and get some information.'

'What does this mean?' Sir Charles indicated a symbol against the name of a proprietor of a big motor car plant.

'That means that I think the man will co-operate with us in any operation we might plan against his factory – if it's put to him in the right way.'

'And this?'

'Those factories are the ones likely to be producing war material for the Germans.'

'And this?'

'There are likely to be collaborators there, sir.'

'Well, well, this is all very interesting.'

'I'm glad you think so, sir. You see, I've been rather working in the dark—'

Sir Charles smiled. 'We're very much in the first stages still,' he explained. 'You see there's never been a situation quite like this before and that means that it takes a long time to persuade people to see just what's needed; they always want to build on what already exists and when a new situation presents itself they prefer to ignore it rather than make a few innovations. Churchill's told us what our job is – it only remains to persuade the high-ups that we know how to go about—'

'What is our job, sir?' I asked. 'I've never been told.'

Sir Charles looked up and blinked mildly. 'To set Europe ablaze,' he said.

'I see.'

'You don't see, do you?'

'Not exactly,' I confessed. 'I mean – what's being done?'

'Well,' he said, 'we've got a small nucleus in training already, including about ten men preparing to get back into France and see what it's all about. Naturally our information is very poor – apart from newspaper analyses and that sort of thing. The chiefs of staff are very keen to know what sort of active support we can hope for when we're ready to start going in again. That's why I was so interested in what you're doing; it ties in very well with the general scheme. The important thing is to move fairly slowly at first—'

'Well, we certainly seem to be doing that,' I observed.

Sir Charles said: 'I know it seems slow but there'd be little point in encouraging rashness on the part of the French; we don't want a lot of people shot and repressive measures taken until the reasons for them are sufficient compensation for the fall in French civilian morale that would result. What we want is co-ordinated action and co-ordination takes a long time.'

'All the same the sooner we get someone into France to take the temperature of the French so to speak, the better we'll be able to plan future action.' Sir Charles nodded. 'Has anyone gone yet?' I went on.

He said, 'They're in training.'

'Good Lord,' I said, 'it's nearly a year since we were chucked out of France—'

'Now look here, Buckmaster, these things take time. In 1940

we had to concentrate on real essentials – defensive essentials – we're only just beginning to get our breath back. If SOE is to have any justification it must be as a military operation, properly planned with a definitive object. We must build an organisation and have it ready for use when it's most needed.'

'But why are our numbers so small? Surely there are plenty of Free French?'

'We can't use the Free French. They've got their own set-up. That made recruiting a bit slow to start with. You see we can only use British citizens to train as agents who happen by some good chance to speak French like natives. Those people aren't easy to find.'

In the face of Sir Charles's quiet and logical exposition of the aims and difficulties of the organisation I began to temper those criticisms of it which had been germinating in my mind for some time. Our conversation continued till the early hours of the morning and in the course of it I became much better acquainted both with the tactical hazards and strategic objectives of the organisation. I realised the immense difficulties that faced us and became aware of the fact that the kind of analysis which I had been making with the aid of the Bottin could be extended, with the aid of Michelin guides and railway maps, to cover every aspect of French industry and communications, so that when the time came we would have a comprehensive and cross-indexed dossier on France. In order to know the most vulnerable length of line and the most easily blocked section of road, it would be necessary merely to turn up the relevant card. The shape of future operations grew in my mind as my eyes sought to detect from the dry statistics the nerve-centres of enemy industrial and economic planning.

IV

In May 1941, a solitary aircraft was reported to have dropped leaflets on a town in the centre of France. Leaflet raids were not very common and the inhabitants of Nevers were somewhat surprised. So were the Germans, and they spent a great deal of time collecting the leaflets and fining those who kept them. On the way to Nevers the plane had passed over a large private property.† As the plane flew over the middle of it a single parachute opened and a solitary figure floated down. The plane droned on to its mission over Nevers. The parachutist landed and undid his harness. He did his chute in a ditch and walked up to the great house. The man was George Noble, the first SOE agent to land on the soil of France. The house he entered belonged to a close personal friend of a certain Major Maurice Buckmaster.

V

Sir Charles Hambro rang me up in July 1941, and asked me to take over temporary control of the Belgian section of SOE. Accordingly, I left my indexing in the hands of my secretary, Yveline, and started working on a similar scheme for the Belgian side of things; naturally I felt less at home there, for though the language was still French I was less acquainted with the industry and national temper of the Belgians. There were, of course, separate departments of SOE for each of the occupied countries, each of them concerned with measuring the power and the will of their inhabitants actively to assist

---

† At Valençay, now the site of a memorial to the 104 members of F Section, 13 of them women, who gave their lives for the liberation of France.

in the discomfiture of the common enemy. I still managed to drop into the fifth floor office and see what progress Yveline was making with our index system and I never really considered my link with the French section broken. I was amused to notice, on one of those visits, that my office had recently been issued with an in-tray; there was, however, as yet nothing in it. No information had yet come into the office.

In September 1941, I was working in the office of the Belgian section when a phone call came through to me from Sir Charles Hambro. 'Buckmaster, how do you feel about a change of job?'

'Another one, sir?'

'Well, this isn't exactly a change so much as a reversion. H. M.'s health has finally proved too much for him and he's decided to retire. We want you to take over.'

'In what capacity, sir?'

'As head of the French section, of course.'

'Permanently?' I inquired.

'Permanently.'

The next day I took over. I was at once conscious of the immense amount of work with which I was faced. As yet we had no organisation, few means of having our agents received by friendly patriots or of accepting messages from them once they had landed. France was without means of speaking to us. So far we had landed only three or four agents whose job it was not to make contact but to obtain information; they were much more 'spies' than were our later agents. They included a Lancastrian named Cowburn whose code name was Benoit.

If our actual impact on France was still negligible, however, our London organisation was recruiting with modest zeal. My staff now numbered about eight at headquarters: my secretary, my personal assistant (the indispensable Vera Atkins), recruiting officer, briefing officer, escorting officer (for observing and reporting back on the training behaviour of our agents), signals officer and planning officer. We used every possible means of discovering likely material for recruiting men (at first they were all men) of character, of courage and of resolution whose French was perfect and whose nationality was not French.

Two months had passed and we had still heard nothing from Cowburn. We wondered if he had been picked up by the Germans. It would not be a good omen. Already questions were being asked by inquisitive Generals about the usefulness of our organisation and the efficiency of its staff.

One day in late September my secretary came into my room where I was working on a recruit's report and did the most extraordinary thing. She dropped a sheaf of papers into my information in-tray. For the first time we had information direct from France.

Chapter 2

Matchbox

Benoit's report contained much valuable information, both about the oil installations which he had been sent to reconnoitre and about the conditions in France. He himself had been over the demarcation line which at this time still existed between occupied and unoccupied France and he gave us details of petrol stores and oil dumps all along the French coast from Marseilles across and up to Bordeaux, Le Havre and Dunkirk. Benoit had contacts of his own in France (as I said, he had worked there for many years) and he managed to proceed on his business with great freedom and confidence. Furthermore, to our immense delight, he reported that nearly every Frenchman to whom he had spoken was almost recklessly willing to help our organisation and had hardly been restrained from indulging in some act of foolish defiance to prove his eagerness. This was precisely the fillip we all needed so badly and it gave us tremendous zest for our work. The reason we had not heard from him for so long was that he had had difficulty in getting back to Marseilles and a certain house in the *Vieux Port* where a wireless operator had now been installed in an attic above a brothel.

By now we had landed, by devious means, several more agents on the coasts and lonely plateaux of unoccupied France. I called in my briefing officer, Major de Guélis.

'At last things seem to be happening,' I observed. 'Benoit's report is pretty encouraging. I thought things would be far tougher than they are.'

He glanced through the report. 'He seems to have got across the demarcation line easily enough. What I can't understand is why we haven't heard from any of the others.'

'It takes time for them to find their feet, you know. We must be patient. At least we know the Marseilles house hasn't been blown.'

'How many men have we got in the field now?' de Guélis asked.

'Ten, including Georges and Benoit.'

'Well, we should hear something more soon.'

The house in Marseilles was the vital link with us. At the scheduled times (skeds) our operators listened, gave the call signal and listened again. At Baker Street we waited, day by day, for the information which should be coming in.

Meanwhile our recruiting officer, Major Lewis Gielgud,[†] was busy detecting more bilingual British of the right calibre for our work. De Guélis, the briefing officer, went through Benoit's thin report to glean as much information as he could about conditions on the other side. I went down with him to the blacked-out airport where our next batch of agents were to leave from and saw them vanish into the night, bound for Gibraltar whence the trusted feluccas (Portuguese coasting vessels) would ferry them to the deserted Côte d'Azur.

About this time we extended our premises to include a flat in Orchard Court which, among other amenities, sported a black tile bathtub which was to become a legend in the service. Here

---

[†] Elder brother of the actor Sir John Gielgud.

we conducted our briefing operations under Major de Guélis, taking care to segregate the various agents (they were more numerous now) the one from the other so that, even if they knew each other – they had probably been at training school together – they would have no idea of the nature or region of each other's mission.

In early October I called in one of them, Harry Morgan, and explained the particular task I wanted him to do.

'How are you feeling, Harry?'

'Pretty good, sir.'

'All set to go?'

'Rather.'

'Look, apart from the things briefing have told you, I want you to pay particular attention to finding out what's happened to communications from Marseilles. We haven't heard a word from anyone for over two weeks. Go slowly, but if something has gone wrong or the equipment's got captured or something, let me know as quickly as ever you can. I can't believe there can have been trouble in Marseilles. After all, it's in the unoccupied zone.'

That night Harry, having checked his orders, was on the plane bound for Gibraltar. Already Pierre de Vomécourt had been parachuted into the Loir et Cher with his wireless operator, and taking into account Jacques Poulain, Harry Morgan and those others whom we had already landed, we should be getting some news shortly. Like a man who has backed many horses, we were confident that one of them would come up. Each day I looked up hopefully as my secretary came into the room. Each day she came empty-handed. I remained calm (there was no point in being anything else), yet anxious for results.

II

Pierre de Vomécourt and his wireless operator Gaston[†] had landed in France in August. They had instructions to proceed to Paris and pick up certain personal contacts there. At the beginning we were forced, in order to create our system of safe houses and trustworthy co-operators, to recommend those friends we possessed upon whom we knew we could rely. This was risky but the risk had to be taken.

Pierre and Gaston buried their parachutes with some trepidation, wondering what they might meet in the way of security police or German troops – for their landing-point was very near the demarcation line.

'Everything seems to be quiet,' Pierre observed as the aircraft zoomed away from them back towards England.

'So far,' agreed Gaston.

'Come on.' They picked their way across the fields in the direction which de Guélis had told them in their briefing and soon found a deserted hut in which they were able to clean up their shoes and check their equipment. The heavy wireless set was disguised – in so far as it could be disguised at all – as a suitcase.

Pierre carried a large sum of money in another cheap fibre suitcase. To look at, the two men were shabbily yet respectably dressed as two *petits bourgeois*; you might have taken them for commercial travellers and it was as such that their papers (carefully forged in a grey stucco house on the Kingston bypass) revealed them to be.

It was dawn by the time they walked into Tours. No one paid them the smallest attention. They saw no Germans. Soon

---

† Code name for Noël Burdeyron.

they were inextricably mixed with the crowds in the centre of the city on their way to work. De Guélis had told them to catch the 8.48 to Paris. They still had an hour before the train was due to go, so they went into a café and ordered coffee, croissants and butter.

'No butter, messieurs,' said the waiter, looking at them curiously.

Gaston laughed. 'You don't have to tell us.' It was against this sort of mistake that our men had to guard incessantly – the tendency to let things slip out so automatically that they were said by the tongue before the mind had time to check them. They ate their dipped croissants and gulped their ersatz coffee and left the café for the station. They still had over half an hour to waste and they had no desire to loiter around the station where there were certain to be Germans and *Milice* (members of the Vichy police), so they lingered on the quai along the Loire until it was time to go to the station.

At 8.40 they presented themselves at the booking office and Pierre said: 'Two to Paris, please, third class.'

'But, Monsieur, the Paris train has left.'

Pierre said. 'But 8.48—'

'That train is cancelled, Monsieur. It has been for several months.'

'My timetable is out of date,' Pierre said. 'When is the next train?'

'The next *rapide* is not till 4.21 this afternoon,' the man replied.

This was typical of the sort of snag into which our first agents were continually running; certain foods were unobtainable on certain days, others had vanished altogether, trains were cancelled and timetables altered. An agent required to keep his sangfroid if he was to avoid betraying himself by a detail so trivial as almost to be laughable were not the penalties for capture so dreadful.

Gaston and Pierre reached Paris at ten that night, only one hour before curfew. They had only one address, in the Rue des Sts Pères.

'If we have any difficulty in getting there,' Pierre said as they left the station, 'we may find ourselves out after curfew. I think it would be safer to find a hotel and get on to our contact tomorrow.'

'I don't like walking around the streets with this sewing machine,' Gaston said.

'Come on, we can't waste time. Let's try the hotels.'

'Perhaps we should separate?'

Two German officers in their smart, arrogant uniforms swaggered past. The streets were beginning to empty as people hurried home before curfew. Pierre saw there was no time to lose and quickly set off across the boulevard into a maze of side streets where many hotels, some of them highly disreputable, clustered about the approach to the station.

'I still think we should separate,' Gaston said. 'It looks so obvious – two of us—'

'What's obvious?' Pierre snapped.

'I insist on separating,' Gaston said.

There was no time to argue. 'Meet me at the entrance to the métro Rue du Bac at ten tomorrow morning. Failing that I shall be there every hour on the hour till one. Be punctual. Good luck.' Pierre clapped his friend on the shoulder and left him. He himself hurried on and went into a small dingy hotel where a sign pointed up the tile stairs: *Bureau – Premier étage.*

The *patron* was a fat, heavily jowled man with a half-inch of black whisker. He was very sleepy and allowed Pierre to fill in his *fiche* without even bothering to inspect his papers. At this time the Germans were confident of their ability to control France and were not jittery enough to bother about using their troops to check papers and peruse hotel registers. The time was to come when they were to be made so: that was our job, or part of it.

The next morning Pierre rose early and left the hotel before any inquisitive official should come round. The *patron* was still dozy and still unshaved, and Pierre left without yet having to put his forged *Carte d'Identité* to the test. He decided to make his way to within striking distance of the Rue du Bac so that he could make his rendezvous with Gaston at precisely ten o'clock; he had been impressed during training with the vital importance of punctuality. No agent was allowed to loiter at a rendezvous; loiterers were always likely to be picked up, perhaps on suspicion of being black marketeers, and there could be nothing so harmful to the organisation as the running of senseless risks.

At one minute to ten Pierre, having had his coffee and rolls in a café in the Boulevard St Germain, turned into the Rue du Bac and walked down towards the métro entrance. Two German field police walked incuriously past him. A man in a beret emerged from the métro, stared at him and strolled away down a side street. It was exactly ten o'clock. A girl came up from the métro. A man in a blue mackintosh and with a briefcase went quickly, confidently, down the grey stone steps. A bus stopped at the red light and the conductor allowed two men to descend from it; neither of them was Gaston. It was five past ten. Pierre walked quickly down the street, crossed it and came back up the other side, keeping the métro in sight. It was ten past ten.

At a quarter past Pierre left the Rue du Bac, walking confidently as if he had somewhere definite to go; but if his steps were certain his mind was not: he wondered whether he should go straight to the address in the Rue des Sts Pères and deposit his suitcase which contained, among other things, over £2,000 in French notes. If he should be stopped, that might not be so easy to explain. On the other hand he wanted to be at the Rue du Bac at eleven when Gaston was due; obviously for some reason he had been unable to make the ten o'clock rendezvous. Probably he had overslept.

Pierre bought a newspaper and sat down in a café to read it. Of course the press was controlled by the Germans and it was full of assurances to the French about the speed with which the war would be finished; further it assured Parisians that France had never been more contented or more honestly managed than it was now under the Marshal. At one minute to eleven Pierre turned once again into the Rue du Bac. A man was waiting at the top of the métro steps. But it was not Gaston. Pierre walked straight past him. A girl ran up to the man and they walked off briskly together. Abandoning his circumspect approach, Pierre ran down the métro steps to see whether Gaston had perhaps misunderstood his instructions. The white tiled corridors leading down to the trains were deserted. Now, at ten past eleven, Pierre could no longer restrain the fear which earlier he had suppressed: something had gone wrong. Unless Gaston had made his way for some reason straight to the address in the Rue des Sts Pères.

Pierre hurried to the Rue des Sts Pères. He buzz-clicked the front door of the tall, narrow apartment building in which his contact lived. The *concierge* came out and looked at him: 'Monsieur?'

'Monsieur Arpiège?'

'The third floor, monsieur, number ten.'

Pierre bounded up the stairs. A small white-haired woman in an apron opened the door of number ten in answer to his ring. 'Monsieur Arpiège?'

'What name shall I say?'

'Monsieur Germain.'

Monsieur Arpiège was a distinguished looking man with a goatee. He had been a solicitor and was now retired on a small pension; he had been a friend of de Guélis, our briefing officer, before the war. Pierre quickly explained who he was and how he had got the lawyer's name. 'I must confess to you, monsieur,' Pierre continued, 'that my friend also has your address and may possibly arrive here during the morning.'

'I understand.'

'Your housekeeper, monsieur, is she trustworthy?' Pierre asked apologetically.

'She has been with me many years. She has no reason to love the Boches. Her husband was killed in 1917.'

It was arranged that Pierre should leave his suitcase with Monsieur Arpiège while he returned to the Rue du Bac in the hope of meeting Gaston. It seemed to him, as he walked quickly to the métro St Germain, that Gaston was certainly in some sort of difficulty and he cursed his luck that such a misfortune should have occurred so quickly.

'*Vos papiers, monsieur.*'

Pierre looked up to see that he had walked into a control. There was nothing for it: he produced his forged *Carte d'Identité*, not knowing whether it would be convincing or not. At this stage we were not too well informed of the regulations in force in the occupied zone.

'This is no longer valid, monsieur.'

Pierre looked the policeman in the eye and shrugged. The gendarme stared at him. After a moment he handed the *carte* back to him. 'I should get a new one,' he suggested.

Gaston was not at the Rue du Bac at noon.

At 12.30 Pierre, dispirited and apprehensive, returned to the flat in the Rue des Sts Pères. All seemed quiet. He hurried upstairs to Monsieur Arpiège.

'There is no sign of my friend in the Rue du Bac,' he reported.

'He has not been here,' the lawyer replied, tugging at his goatee with a nervous thoughtfulness.

'It looks as if he must have been picked up by the police – or the Germans. In which case the sooner I get out of here the better; they may force him to say where he was making for.'

'Yes,' said the lawyer, 'you'd better leave now.'

Pierre saw that there was no point in hesitating; equally there was no point in asking Monsieur Arpiège to recommend him somewhere to go, since if the Germans were to arrest him they would surely extract from him the address to which he had sent Pierre.

'Goodbye, monsieur. I'm sorry to have caused you this trouble.' Pierre shook the lawyer's hand, snatched up his suitcase and quit the flat in the Rue des St Pères. It was now nearly one o'clock. In spite of his fears, Pierre made his way once more to the Rue du Bac, in case Gaston should make their last rendezvous. He waited till twenty past and then gave up. He was not the sort of man to lose his nerve in the situation in which he now found himself, yet he could not but curse the luck which had deprived him so suddenly of Gaston and, with Gaston, of his only link with London. He went to a restaurant in the Boulevard St Michel where, at an inflated price, he was able to enjoy a meal of almost pre-war standard.

Pierre's cover story made him out to be a traveller in stationery and pencils and he had been carefully briefed on some of the aspects of the business before he left England, yet he had never been intended actually to earn his living by this means and his instructions were (this was standard) that he should furnish himself with up-to-date papers as quickly as possible, preferably genuine ones. His first aim was to make contact with people who might help him to attain this object; the memory of the gendarme's 'This is no longer valid' remained with him.

On the left bank at this time there were marooned a large number of people of various nationalities, students, writers, artists and intellectuals, whom the fortunes of their countries and the fall of France had first exiled and then trapped; Pierre decided to go to earth among them; in the honeycomb of rooms and studios of the *Quartier Latin* there were so many shifting and shiftless people that it was safe to assume that the authorities could not keep track of them all. Pierre had the advantage over these people of having plenty of money and accordingly he had no trouble in finding temporary accommodation in a student hotel in the Rue Grégoire de Tours. He silenced all questions by paying a week's rent in advance. He went straight up to his room, pushed the bolt across the door and lay down on the bed. He lit a cigarette and took stock; being the first of our agents in the Paris area he had no organisation into which to integrate himself: it was his job to lay the foundations of just such an organisation. There was little hope of getting news of Gaston, for if he was captured that was an end of him, while if he was free the odds were a thousand to one against meeting him now. There was only one thing to do – to proceed with his mission as far as he could. But first he would contact his old friend, Bertrand, who lived near the Jardins du Luxembourg; Bertrand might be able to give him a safe address where he could live undisturbed as long as he was in Paris. Pierre felt uneasy about staying for longer than absolutely necessary in this hotel; he did not know how trustworthy the *patron* was nor could he tell when the police or the Gestapo might elect to make a sweep through the Latin quarter.

Pierre pushed the button on the call-box phone.

'Hallo, Bertrand?'

'Who is this speaking?'

'Pierre. Pierre de Vomécourt.'

'Pierre? But I thought—'

'Never mind, my friend. I must see you. Can you meet me at the Dupont Latin in half an hour?'

Half an hour later, Pierre and Bertrand walked into the café together. Pierre wasted no time in explaining to his old friend the rough purpose of his mission and the difficulty he was in: 'I must find somewhere to stay before anyone at the hotel gets suspicious.'

'I daren't have you to my place,' Bertrand said. 'My mother-in-law is staying with us and I don't trust her to keep her mouth shut.'

'I understand.'

'Meet me at the Café Mabillon at eight-thirty tonight. I'll try and fix something by then.'

III

The bottom of the rowing boat grated on the deserted beach. Harry Morgan narrowed his eyes as he inspected the line of dunes for signs of the *Milice* or other unwanted visitors; there was no one. He gave the boatman a wave and vaulted, case in hand, onto the soft sand. At once he drew his revolver from his pocket and strolled warily up the beach. If the captain was to be relied on, he should be a mile or two from the town of St Tropez on the Côte d'Azur. At this time, October 1941, this coastline was still unmolested by the Germans and Harry expected a trouble-free trip. It was now three in the morning. He passed through the cactus-infested dunes on to the harsh gravel of the foreshore. Within a few minutes he could see the outlines of a farmhouse; he decided not to approach it to avoid the howling of dogs which he particularly feared. Instead he cut up through a pine grove and soon found himself a pine-board hut where the cork-cutters kept their tools. He lay down there to rest for a couple of hours, not wanting to enter the town at so conspicuous an hour.

Bearing in mind my instructions to find out what had happened in Marseilles, Harry decided to make his way straight to that city. Later that day he was sitting comfortably in a second class compartment as the train bore him along the rugged Provencal coastline.

'*Vos papiers, Monsieur.*' A member of the *Milice* stood in the door of the compartment.

Harry handed up his papers.

'Where are you going?'

'To Marseilles.'

'For what purpose?'

'Business.'

The policeman handed back his papers. *'Bien, Monsieur.'*

Upon reaching Marseilles, Harry decided to go carefully. He took a room in a commercial hotel in the business district under his cover name of Monsieur Nulli, wine salesman. Casual travellers were, of course, quite unremarkable in so busy a port as Marseilles and a feeling of security soon reassured Harry. He spent a certain amount of time loitering around the tabacs and bars of the old quarter which had added to its reputation for toughness another for defiance. Already its narrow and ill-smelling streets hid many refugees on the run from the Nazis in the occupied zone and it was a brave member of the *Milice* who dared to venture into the quarter alone. Occasionally an over-zealous *sous-officier* attempted some kind of a search, but a pail of slops might inadvertently be tipped over him or a wardrobe slide unaided down a steep staircase at him. The *Vieux Port* remained strictly Free French. Eventually, exasperated by its continued resistance, the Germans were to blow it up, but that was not yet.

Nagged by a small pain in his side which he discounted as mere nerves, Harry began cautiously to question various contacts – the small lawyer whose practice was in the poorer quarter, the railwaymen who worked the shunting service along the quays and similar trustworthy people – about their willingness to participate in a clandestine ring; this ring was later led by a group who took the corporate name of the Palestine Express by virtue of their common Jewish origin. They did valuable work and remained undiscovered till after the liberation. Harry was somewhat surprised that those whom he approached were at first very suspicious of him and when he was able to win their confidence he asked them what made them so apprehensive. They answered, cryptically, 'Rumours'.

The house where our wireless operator was supposed to be working was at number twelve bis Rue de la Colline Noire. Harry scouted round the area, largely at night, taking drinks in the tiny *bistros* of the quarter and keeping his ears open. He had to exercise the greatest tact in his inquiries, for he knew that if anyone suspected him of being a police spy – whether counter-espionage or routine detective – the people of the *Vieux Port* would give him short shrift.

Soon it became clear that he would have to abandon his circumspect approach and make boldly for the wireless operator's den. If he had been blown, there was nothing for it: Harry would have to take his chance that the *Milice* had abandoned their watch on the house.

The Rue de la Colline Noire was a dark alley between cliffs of black houses, the entrances to which were up narrow stairs beside the shops forming the ground floor. Prostitutes hung about the doorways and seamen of many nations and origins moved silently up the street. The pain in his side was really worrying Harry now and he pressed his hand to it as he pushed through the knot of whores at the door of number twelve bis, ignoring the cries of 'Hallo, cheri,' which greeted him. A very fat woman a-jangle with cheap jewellery met him on the first landing. '*Bonsoir, monsieur,*' she said in an inquisitive tone.

'*Je viens de la part de Monsieur Pierre,*' Harry said.

The woman looked sharply up the dark stairs which led to the second floor.

'Send him up,' a voice said.

Suspiciously, the woman removed her body and allowed Harry to pass. He hesitated, somehow alarmed by the tempo of the words which had just been spoken, and then went up the stairs. He looked back over his shoulder and saw that the fat woman had resumed her massive station barring the way down.

In the shadows on the top floor was a man. Harry had left his revolver with the lawyer, who had put it in his strong box. Once the danger of the actual landing was completed an agent might well find his revolver an embarrassment, since the times when, engaged on jobs of this kind, he would have to fight his way out, were outnumbered by those when he might be searched. A revolver would, of course, betray him when otherwise he could expect to bluff his way out.

The man in the shadows said: '*Tu viens de la part de Pierre?*'

'Yes.'

'Come in, please.'

Harry went past the man through the door into the attic. It was in darkness.

'I'll turn on the light,' the man behind him said, clicking the switch.

Three members of the *Milice* with drawn machine-pistols faced Harry across the narrow attic.

IV

Pierre was still without any means of contacting us in England and of keeping us informed of the results he had obtained and the work he was doing. Already we had had several signs that the French would rally to our cause, but we were desperately anxious to get first-hand information from our men actually in the field and the complete silence from France was a strain on our nerves and a dam to our progress. There was nothing we could do but wait. We waited.

At the beginning of December, Pierre was talking with a contact in a flat in the Boulevard Raspail when another visitor was admitted. This was a tall, narrow-faced man with black brows and black hair whose eyes burned in their deep sockets with a compulsive fervour.

'This is my friend Stanislaw Raczynski,' Pierre's contact said. 'Stanislaw, this is Félix, a British officer.' Pierre was used by this time to these gross breaches of security and he knew it was useless to protest about them. He shook the Pole's skinny hand, surprised by the strength in the bony fingers.

'I am pleased to meet you,' the Pole said. 'I like working with the British.'

'Oh, have you worked with us before?' Pierre inquired. 'I am working now with you,' was the startling reply. 'Our wireless operator is British.'

Pierre knew that there were no other members of the organisation in Paris, so he could not resist the temptation to discover who this other Briton was; at the same time he had the fear that the man might be a German decoy, in which case the sooner he was exposed the better. On the other hand, if he was a genuine wireless operator, this might be a chance for regaining contact with us in England; it was a chance that had to be taken. Pierre was there to use his initiative.

'Really?' Pierre said. 'I should like to meet this other British officer.'

'But naturally. Come to the café des Beaux Arts tonight at nine o'clock. I will take you to him.'

Pierre talked to Lucie about the proposed meeting and she begged to be allowed to accompany him. He insisted on going alone, for he feared that the rendezvous might be a trap.

Stanislaw Raczynski was there in the café des Beaux Arts, but he brought disappointing news: the British officer had positively refused to meet Pierre unless he could be sure that he could be trusted.

'I simply must meet him,' Pierre replied. 'I'm sure I could convince him.'

'He wants proof.'

'What sort of proof can I provide?' Pierre snapped. 'I haven't got my passport with me.' The prospect of making contact with London was so close that he could scarcely restrain his impatience, even though his mind told him that the wireless operator's caution was perfectly justified.

'I will talk to my friends. Meet me on the far side of the Pont de l'Alma at six o'clock tomorrow evening.'

A series of rendezvous followed as Pierre was shuttled back and forth between the various members of the Pole's organisation. There seemed to be a vast and involved mesh of officers. Interviews took place in dark cellars in front of people who were addressed as '*mon Capitaine*' and '*mon Colonel*' and even, on one occasion, '*mon Général*'. It seemed to Pierre that so intricate a set-up must eventually be permeated by the enemy, for its very rigidity made it vulnerable. In all our operations we strove to eliminate unnecessary red-tape, both at home and in France; at times we were to be censured for it, but the men in the field were thus able to feel that their own initiative mattered while they were in France and that we in England would do everything we could to help them, no matter how unpopular it made us with other branches of the service.

At last Pierre was able to meet the British wireless operator; by now it was almost Christmas. The Briton was working in a tiny upstairs room in the Gobelins district, a poor quarter beyond the Jardins du Luxembourg. Snow lay on the ground and it was very cold. The wireless operator was lying in bed when Pierre was admitted by a Polish member of the organisation who nodded meaningly at the operator and sat himself on the stairs outside the room, the woollen collar of his canvas jacket turned up about his ears.

'*Mon Dieu*, am I glad to see you!' Pierre said.

The other drew his eiderdown up to his neck. Pierre knew that there was a pistol pointing at him under it.

'You know this is all strictly against orders?'

'Yes I know. But I must get a message back to England. You were the only hope; that's why I insisted on seeing you.'

'Whom do you work for?'

'I'm afraid I cannot tell you that.'

'Look, don't be a fool, how can I send a message if I don't know who to send it to?'

'How do I know you're really what you say you are?' Pierre said.

'You'll have to trust me. Now then.'

Pierre said: 'The message would be for DLYM 299047.' This was a code call-sign which de Vomécourt had been instructed to use.

'What do you want me to tell them?'

'I want instructions. I think I ought to get back to London, but they'll know what the best thing is. The important thing is to let them know that I'm alive and have information for them—'

'Ah!' The other shifted the eiderdown and smiled. 'Tell me, do you go to the theatre at all?'

'Yes, a bit,' Pierre said with a frown.

'Did you ever see that thing of Sheriff's they did at the Windmill in 1938?'

'The Windmill? You must have the theatre wrong.'

'I don't think so, my friend.' The eiderdown was pulled aside to reveal the expected revolver.

'Look, what is this – they only do leg shows at the Windmill—'

'All right,' the other suddenly smiled. 'I'll send your message.'

V

Harry Morgan was quickly handcuffed. He had the presence of mind to protest most vigorously at this treatment.

'I will call my lawyer,' he shouted. 'I'll have the law on you. You won't get away with this.'

'We are the law,' said the chief of the *Milice*. 'Take him down.'

As Harry was led away through the streets of the *Vieux Port*, there were boos and catcalls from the inhabitants. '*Sa-lauds! Sa-lauds! Sa-lauds!*' they chanted at the *Milice*.

Harry was driven in a Black Maria to the police headquarters.

'Now then, Monsieur Nulli, what were you doing in that house?'

'I refuse to answer any questions until I have spoken to my lawyer.'

'There will be time for that,' sighed the detective.

'I am a sick man. I need a doctor. My friend Pierre told me I could find one in the Rue de la Colline Noire – suddenly I am arrested. Should a man be arrested for being ill? I will write to the Marshal himself about this. It is an outrage. Have you the Marshal's permission to detain me?'

'We do not need—'

'I demand to see my lawyer. I am a sick man. I need a doctor.'

'We will telephone—'

'I am losing my faith in the Republic—'

'What did you want in the Rue de la Colline Noire?'

'A doctor. I am a—'

'You are a sick man, we understand that,' the detective shouted. 'How are you sick? What is wrong with you?'

Suddenly Harry remembered the pain in his side; at once a twinge went through him. 'Here,' he said, 'feel this.' The detective apprehensively placed his hand on Harry's side. 'Can you feel it? The palpitation. It's terrible.'

By this time, Harry had everyone in the police station rushing about, phoning the lawyer in the *Vieux Port* and trying to get hold of a doctor. Nevertheless, in spite of having somewhat distracted the interest of his captors, Harry knew that sooner or later they would begin to interrogate him in earnest; the quicker he could get away from them the better. For the moment, however, no opportunity presented itself. At this time Vichy had a number of plainclothes Gestapo men working for them; Harry knew he must clear out before he was handed over to them.

The 'palpitation' seemed to have impressed the detective, for within half an hour a doctor was shown into the cell where Harry had been locked. He examined Harry and a frown came over his face when Harry explained about the pain in his side. 'We must get you to hospital at once,' was the verdict.

'That is impossible,' said the detective. 'This man is a terrorist.'

'He must go to hospital. I will phone about a bed. He must be operated on at once.'

'I refuse to allow him to go to hospital in Marseilles,' persisted the detective. 'He has friends here. He might walk out of the hospital.'

'My dear sir,' replied the doctor, 'if this man walked out of hospital he would not get very far. He has appendicitis.'

Harry listened to this diagnosis with considerable trepidation; he seemed unwittingly to have brought more on himself than he had bargained for. Within an hour he was in an ambulance with the detective and the doctor on the way to Aix-en-Provence. The doctor told him that the hospital there was excellent. Harry lay on the stretcher in the ambulance and closed his eyes, thinking; he knew that Aix also contained the headquarters of the *Milice* for the district. The people in Marseilles had told him of men being taken to Aix for questioning. They arrived in Aix at four in the morning. Harry was put to bed in a private room with a guard on the door.

'We'll soon have you right,' the doctor assured him. 'We'll have that appendix out in no time.'

At eight they came for him. He was put on a trolley and wheeled down the corridor to a waiting room outside the operating theatre. He was wearing pyjamas with his mackintosh over them instead of a dressing gown. The guard had been refused entry to the operating theatre. 'Do you think he will walk away in the middle of the operation?' the doctor snapped indignantly.

When the trolley had halted, the doctor and the surgeon went into the vestibule for a short consultation. Harry could see them talking through a round observation hole, their backs to him. He was alone. He knew it was now or never; once he had been operated upon he would have to lie powerless while the *Milice* checked his papers and found them to be forged. He might well go straight from his convalescence to his death. Silently he swung his legs to the ground and slipped out of the room. He could not go back the way they had come for fear of the guard, so he took a passage which ran at right angles to it. He must find some clothes. Now he had a stroke of luck – searching with frenzied calm for signs of discarded clothing, he saw through an open door a room which the painters used to keep their overalls and equipment. Within seconds he had slipped on a paint-stained overall and paint-drenched espadrilles, snatched up a pot and a ladder and hurried on his way. So far there was no outcry, but it must come any second. He realised that the front door would be alerted. He must find the back stairs.

'Stop him! Stop the assassin!' There it was. Harry heard running footsteps behind him. The passage along which he was walking seemed endless. He turned and began to walk back towards his pursuers. Not recognising him, the detective and the doctor and the guard and a nurse came tearing past towards the front stairs. He made room for them to pass and proceeded to the service stairs. A few seconds later, still with his ladder and his pot of paint, he walked out of the hospital into the streets of Aix. Stabs of pain bit into his side as he boarded a tram for the suburbs of the town.

Finally, he managed to get aboard a train for Narbonne, through the agencies of a railway employee who smuggled him into the engine's fuse-box. Throughout the history of the Resistance the railwaymen were, almost 100 per cent, the keenest and most resolute resisters. Their strong sense of comradeship and their fierce independence were alike unquenchable. At Narbonne, Harry's railwayman put him in contact with a dentist who was already involved in an escape-route, and from there he was taken down to the foothills of the Pyrenees. In mid-December, in the company of a Pyrenean guide and still suffering the agonising pains of appendicitis, Harry Morgan walked over the Pyrenees into Spain.

VI

From September to the end of December 1941 we were completely cut off from France. By then, none of us at headquarters in Baker Street was in a very Christmassy mood. I was continually being asked by inquisitive Generals what I was doing, and my persistent reply that Rome wasn't built in a day became more and more hollow. In spite of the disappointing silence, however, we were recruiting with great success and more agents were being landed by a variety of means; we had not yet settled down to the parachute dropping which later became the rule, for we were handicapped by the lack of reception committees to accept the agent and to guide the planes.

We landed men from MTBs and from feluccas, by Lysander aircraft as well as by parachute. The missions of these men were still strictly exploratory; they were not to make any bangs until we gave the word. For our part, however, we were co-operating with the Ministry of Economic Warfare in an endeavour to plot the right targets for attack when the moment came: we had to deduce what the Germans would particularly need in six months' time and place those targets first on our list. Even at home we had always to be one step ahead of the enemy if our work was to be fruitful.

The New Year started as gloomily as the old one had ended. Then, at four o'clock in the afternoon of 1 January 1942, my telephone rang.

'Is that Major Buckmaster?'

'Speaking.'

'This is Colonel Smee. I don't suppose you know who I am. You certainly shouldn't. Look, the point is we've had a message on our wire from one of your chaps. The whole thing's a bit peculiar, because strictly speaking your chaps shouldn't know that our chaps exist at all.'

'What's the name of the man you've heard from?'

'Code name is Félix.'

I knew it was de Vomécourt. 'How the hell did he get hold of your operator whoever he is?'

'That's what worries us. It looks as if something may have gone wrong and that's why I hesitated before I rang you. We're a little bit suspicious this end about just how trustworthy our bloke's messages are.'

'What does Félix say?'

'His message reads: 'Gaston blown mission completed best possible await instructions suggest time come home Félix.' Our man's expressed willingness to take any message you want to send back. Frankly, we're not very keen on this sort of thing, but we'll send anything you want sent – always bearing in mind that the whole set-up may be a German blind.'

I was faced with the first of those tremendously difficult decisions which were to continue and proliferate themselves as the scope of our operations grew. If we were to act on the assumption that Félix's message was genuine, we might run the risk of giving the Germans an insight into the way in which we were organised. On the other hand, if we were to ignore it we might be losing one of the best men we had and a source of information which at this time we vitally needed. On consideration, it seemed to me that there was every chance that the message was in fact genuine: the loss of Gaston would explain de Vomécourt's long silence and it was indeed time for him to come back to England. I rang Colonel Smee back and told him that we would accept his offer and use his operator to contact our man.

Meanwhile in Paris, de Vomécourt waited impatiently for a reply to his message. He was now rather nervous about what he had done, for though he had faith in the operator himself, he was uncertain about the security of the organisation into which he had blundered.

So were we, but I decided that we must get Pierre out. I sent a message to him that he should leave Paris at once and go to Sarthe, about 150 miles from Paris. I arranged that a Lysander should pick him up from a field near Le Mans. We had to arrange the whole operation before he left Paris, for there would be no means of contacting Pierre once he had left the city. The date and place and time of the pick-up were fixed and it was up to us to stick to the arrangement.

On the evening of the agreed date I was very worried. Should the flight be cancelled we might never see Pierre again and not only would a good man be lost but vital information about conditions in occupied France would remain unheard. The RAF had to succeed.

The Lysander was spotted by the German ground defences just as it came in to land. Pierre, crouched in a hedge, praying the plane would spot his torch signals, saw a great star shell go up, giving the general alarm to German troops in the area. The plane seemed to stutter in mid-air, as if the pilot was thinking of pulling out. Pierre held his breath. The plane straightened and came in to land. The star shell drifted slowly down in a shower of phosphorescence. Pierre ran to the plane. A rifle shot cracked from the gate of the field. The plane moved off bumpily across the field.

'Halt!'

The plane rose slowly and made off through the curtain of flak which now blossomed in the sky. Looking down, Pierre could see the lights of Gestapo cars on the road from Le Mans. He turned to the pilot. 'Thanks,' he said.

'You're welcome,' was the sardonic retort.

Chapter 3

Recruiting and Training

Throughout our years of battle with the Germans, our objective was to do them active harm. Our role at Special Operations Headquarters was not that of spy-masters, but of active and belligerent planners of operations to be carried out in advance of the Allied landing. The usual picture of an agent is of a man lying up and watching enemy movements and reporting them back to his home base, in short an essentially passive undercover man. The agents of SOE were essentially active. At the beginning, we were, naturally, not absolutely certain which kinds of men would make the best agents and sometimes we made mistakes. For instance, I remember early on a chap called Nigel Low was sent to our office by a well-meaning person in another branch of the service to whom Nigel Low had spun an attractive yarn.

Low was a very plausible chap, tall and good-looking, and his plausibility was, at first, very pleasing; it seemed to me that this confident and easy man with his slightly worn charm and his thorough knowledge of French and of France, particularly of the Riviera, would be of great service to our embryo organisation. I questioned him thoroughly about France and told him about the sort of thing he would have to do.

'Of course,' he said, 'you know all about me, don't you?'

'Yes,' I said, smiling, 'I know.' The fact was Nigel Low was a professional gambler and he was not above a spot of confidence trickery if things were not going too well for him at the tables. All this I had found out from Scotland Yard when I first heard about Low.

The Yard were at all times at our service and they were immensely helpful in a number of ways: not only did they provide us with a thorough account of the history of possible recruits to our work, but they also put at our disposal experts whose job it was to detect enemy agents in this country and who were therefore able to help us protect our own men against mistakes which might make professional counter-espionage men suspicious. With their help we searched every agent before he left the country, checked laundry marks and tailors' labels, brushed English tobacco out of jacket pockets and added French dust (and dust appropriate to the area in which the agent was due to work) to the turn-ups of French-tailored clothes.

The Yard had not failed to tell me that Nigel Low had a long record of convictions in this country, yet by a stroke of what I thought was good fortune he had never been convicted or apprehended in France, hence he would not be known to the Sûreté; plainly his method of operation had been to draw his funds in England and try his luck in France. I decided he should be given the chance to try his luck there once more. After much heart-searching, we resolved to use him. He was, after all, a man accustomed to playing a part and he knew all the tricks of the underworld as far as concealment and bluff were concerned.

I explained to him in some detail what sort of things we wanted him to do. In these early days, this was largely to get as much information as possible about the day-to-day routine of living in an occupied country – ration books, permits, controls, train services and so forth were to be checked and reports sent back to us at Head Office. In this way our briefing of future agents would become more and more exact. I told Low that since he was going, so to speak, into the blue, it would be up to him to bluff his way through where our lack of information led him into difficulties.

'Sounds right up my street,' was his comment.

'The important thing,' I said, 'is to get the information back to us.'

Low went down to the country house which we had commandeered for our training centre and there went through all the courses we had devised. These courses were very thorough and were based, of course, on the routine 'spy school' model. The use of codes, unarmed combat, fieldcraft, shooting, sabotage (which included the use of explosive and the knowledge of where to use it to inflict the maximum damage on specified targets), methods of contact, psychological tests were all included in the curriculum.

Often I would go down together with others from headquarters and would cross-question recruits, taking on the roles of Gestapo men, in order to try and break their cover stories. By this means the story itself would become ingrained in their minds and they themselves would gain some small idea of the rigours of interrogation. If they survived without cracking, their confidence would be greatly increased and they could face the thought of genuine German interrogation in the knowledge that they had already withstood a similar grilling successfully. These rehearsals were grim affairs and we spared the recruits nothing. They were stripped and made to stand for hours in the light of bright lamps and though, of course, we never used any physical violence on them, they certainly knew what it was to go through it by the time we had finished.

If they cracked badly under the strain, it was tolerably sure that we would not send them, for it was clear that a man who caved in when questioned by HQ staff, in however realistic conditions, would be only too likely to wilt in the face of the Boches. A minor slip would not be held against a man, but too general a collapse most certainly would; we derived no pleasure, I need hardly say, from those occasions when our cruel jibes, our reiterated and shouted questions and our implacable persistence broke a man's spirit, but we could console ourselves with the fact that his cracking at a rehearsal might well have saved his life – and others' – by preventing the possibility of his doing the same thing with the enemy. We were not playing a game.

Nigel Low passed all these tests with credit and it seemed to us that he had found a vocation admirably suited to his talents and one in which he would be able finally to prove himself. In the spring of 1942 he went to France by MTB. He had with him a largish sum of money in old French notes, for at this time we had no other way of financing our men. Low reached the Riviera and from that day to this we have never heard of him again. He had worked his greatest confidence trick. As usual, it may be noted, he had raised his funds in this country and had taken them with him to France. He was, so far as we know, never caught and certainly he betrayed no one. I suppose he is knocking around somewhere in one of the world's gambling centres, but he must be doing better for he has never set foot in this country again in search of further funds.

We learned our lesson with Low and we never again employed any of those who, according to many fictional accounts, are qualified by virtue of their underworld lives to carry out espionage activity. The training courses took careful account, in all future cases, of the gambling habits of recruits. They were also primed with spirits to see how they behaved under the influence and whether their tongues were loosened in agreeable company. Everything that the men did they had to do in the French manner, whether it was combing their hair or leaving their knives and forks on their plates (or removing them from them), answering the telephone or calling for a waiter. Often a man could give himself away by using an incorrect idiom in French, even though his accent and the individual words of a phrase might be perfectly correct.

For instance, when on the telephone the French never say *Tenez la ligne* (hold the line) as we do; instead they always say: *Ne quittez pas l'écoute* (literally: 'Don't quit listening') or more simply: *Ne quittez pas.* The use of any other phrase would automatically make a Frenchman suspicious – and if that Frenchman were a supporter of Vichy, so trivial an error might lead to the death of an agent. Similarly, we would keep watch on a man to see if he talked in his sleep – and if so, in what language and about what.

We could never be sure that a pattern of behaviour would be repeated or that a new one would not develop and we had (as always) to act on probabilities, not certainties. Probabilities can go wrong and so did we. All we could do was to keep the number of errors to a minimum. For instance, it might have been that another confidence man would have done better than Nigel Low did, but we took no further risks – the next one might do better, but he might also do worse; that was a risk we dared not take.

I decided against any further attempt to employ those whose records were not in every respect first-class; sometimes a man's personal qualities might lead me to override this ruling if I thought that the blot on his copybook was due to the prejudice or undue rigidity of the man or service which had marked it against him: I did not feel myself bound to worry too much about a man's proficiency on the parade ground, for example. General slovenliness was quite another matter, however, for a man who was a slack soldier might very well become a slack agent. One could not risk a man who might forget to burn used codes or whose memory was liable to let him down or force him to take notes of secret orders. I tried to judge each man on his merits, but there was one thing we could never afford to do – give a man the benefit of any doubts.

General de Gaulle tended to discourage contact between his officers and mine and he never lost his dislike of the fact that our agents were working in France. He felt that their presence, no matter what their individual merits, infringed the sovereignty he was so eager to preserve. As I have said, I managed to make personal friendships with some of his staff, but the General himself never relented and never really brought himself to a realisation of our common objective – the conquest of the Germans and the liberation of France.

On several occasions we found that dropping grounds which our men in France had already scouted out and which we had incorporated into our operational maps became the subject of dispute because the Free French considered that they had a right to them. De Gaulle's insistence on French sovereignty gave him the idea that he was entitled to the best dropping grounds regardless of our prior claim on them.

On one occasion we arranged a drop to some partisans in the Gironde area. The planes returned without dropping the supplies. I was naturally very alarmed when I saw the ops report. The captain of the plane concerned reported that they had seen lights in the dropping zone designated but that they had failed to give the pre-arranged signals and had replied in a totally wrong way to his own attempts to make contact. He thought it wiser not to drop the supplies and had turned for home. This was the kind of hitch that was doubly worrying to me. We had failed to arm our men and we were faced with the possibility that the *Réseau*[†] had been permeated by the enemy. It was necessary to check up as quickly as possible.

The next day I sent a message to the *Réseau* leader to report fully on the hitch. We would probably be able to tell from the tone of the reply whether or not the Germans had rooted them out. The reply was not long in coming. The explanation was perfectly simple. Our men had arrived on the dropping ground to find another party of *résistants* already in control of it. Rather than risk the possibility of these men being agents provocateurs my men had withdrawn with all speed. The next day my *Réseau* chief made contact with the head of the Free French *Réseau* which was acting, of course, quite independently and the muddle had been cleared up at their end. I managed to get onto the Free French HQ in Dorset Square and put it to them that as our chaps had scouted out the dropping ground first it was only fair that we should have first use of it. De Gaulle would not concede this point at all and we were forced to come to an amicable arrangement about it without the General knowing.

---

† The French name for a Resistance group's base, literally a 'nest'.

This kind of coincidence was inevitable and we found it rather amusing; what was less amusing was the effort necessary to sort it out. There was never any clash in the actual field of operations. In France all the various *résistants* did their best to co-operate as far as they could without infringing each other's secrecy.

The conflict between de Gaulle's *Réseau* and ours was also a factor which had to be taken into account when we were planning operations in France. We did our best to turn these rivalries to good purpose and we hoped that the competitive element in our relations would lead each group to outdo the other. This may not have been the ideal way of running things, but it did make the best of conditions as they actually were. What liaison did exist between us at Baker Street and de Gaulle was conducted unofficially by individual officers whose tact and charm was the only weapon against jealousy and intransigence.

Another executive headache was the fact that there was, in the first year or two, some confusion in the minds of my superiors about the exact role which they wanted SOE to play. At one moment they would doubt the value of having us exist at all, while at another they would ask of us much more than, at that time, we could possibly encompass. They demanded miracles and when we failed to work them they became disillusioned and sarcastic. Perhaps their scepticism as to our efficiency served a good purpose, for it spurred us on to fresh efforts.

If at home there were problems, my task soon became clear as far as France itself was concerned. Co-ordination was a vital part of the sabotage picture. We had to convey and pass on information about targets, synchronising the attacks and briefing the different *Réseaux* about German dispositions. Then we had to plan the actual operations with a view to doing the maximum harm to the Germans while occasioning a minimum of reprisals against the civilian population. One of our ways of doing this, when aircraft became more readily available to us, was to arrange that the RAF should pass over a given target area at a given time so that the detonations which took place on the ground could be attributed to the aircraft which were flying over it. Strangely enough, the Germans would always co-operate in ascribing the damage to the bombers for this helped to hide from the French the presence of so active and powerful a resistance force in their midst.

It might seem that the RAF could just as well have done the job if they had to be overhead anyway. The answer is that the men on the ground were able to be much more accurate (in spite of the RAF's amazing precision) and so could cause more vital, though less widespread, damage. Apart from this, the RAF would in this way be able to do two jobs on the same night, one sham, one genuine.

The actual planning of an operation, for example, the destruction of a power station, might be done in two ways: either we would construct a dummy replica of the station in this country and train a man or group of men especially for the mission, or we would pass the order, together with every detail we could discover about the lay-out, sentries and so forth, to a group already in the field. In the latter case, I would ensure nothing was omitted which might make the saboteur's job easier; we might, for instance, arrange for a diversionary action in the same *Kommandantur* area, so that the German security forces would be split and indecisive. Speed was essential and our men were trained to get in and out before the Germans knew what had hit them. Large-scale operations were usually planned in London by our staff but there was also a good deal of individual enterprise on the part of the *Réseaux* chiefs who often had special knowledge of tempting targets.

Planning combination also worked between men in the field and ourselves at Baker Street. Information was filtered to us through a series of post-boxes which took messages from Paris all the way down to the Spanish border, over the mountains and so to our various agents in neutral capitals. It would not be discreet for me to explain exactly how these worked. The messages reached us largely through the efforts of our men who carried them with them over the border. They might arrive some months after they were written but their strategic value would not necessarily be impaired. One such message came from a foreman at the airscrew factory at Figeac. It was a detailed explanation of how an attack could be mounted against the factory. There was a plan of the installations and an account of the security arrangements.

I asked our planning officer to arrange for a large-scale replica of the factory to be made. Aerial photographs were used to supplement the foreman's drawings. The replica was exact to the smallest detail and almost filled one of the rooms at our briefing flat at Orchard Court. One of the best men whom we had in training at that time, an agent who went under the name of Maxime,[†] was now brought in to be in charge of the operation. He had under him an explosives expert called Eustache.[‡] These two would form the nucleus of a team whose other members

---

[†] George Hiller. Field name Maxime. Code name FOOTMAN.
[‡] Cyril Watney. Field name Eustache. Code name FORGER.

would be recruited in France. Maxime and Eustache were taken over the whole lay-out and planned the best means of wrecking the plant. When they were thoroughly familiar with the whole lay-out and adept in the use of the plastic explosive they would be using we prepared to mount the mission. The foreman was alerted to stand by. The *Réseau* chief in the Figeac area was told to expect two 'bods'.

Maxime and Eustache dropped in the next moon period. Within two days they had met with the foreman and his gang who were all set to go. The foreman was able, through his friends in the factory, to smuggle Eustache and Maxime into a disused storeroom where they were able to lie up when the rest of the workers went home for the night. The factory was completely blacked out, of course, but their experience with the model now proved its value: Eustache and Maxime were able to move through the darkened factory with complete confidence. They made their rendezvous with the foreman who showed them exactly where their explosive would do the most damage – in fact on the valves which connected the power presses with the generating plant – and within minutes the charges were in place and the fuses set. Maxime and his men left the factory, led by the foreman. Half an hour later the charges went up. The mission was a complete success. It set the pattern for co-operation between planners at home and informants in the field. The pattern was followed many times subsequently.

Rehearsals reached a very high standard. The LNER lent us several old engines and we had the use of a disused branch line in the Midlands where our railway saboteurs practised derailing and knocking out the old engines. A railway engine is a pretty hardy affair and it needs exact knowledge of where to put a charge of explosive if it is to be put out of service for good. LNER engineers provided that knowledge. We provided the explosives. In the end, the Germans had a large number of engines out of service.

As the number of our agents – and of the *Réseaux* which they founded – increased from a meagre seven in 1941 to fifty by the middle of 1942 and 120 by June 1943, so we in Baker Street were able to plan more and more ambitious and destructive raids against the German supply machine. By February 1944, at the stage of some of our most important work, we had 200 agents in the field – many of them veterans of more than one tour of duty – all either in liaison with large sections of *Maquisards* or acting as wireless operators. On D-Day itself, there were 220 agents putting into effect the plans which we relayed to them from headquarters in Baker Street. In all, 480 active agents were employed by the French section of SOE. From uncertainty even as to its purpose, the section grew to be a confident and deadly fighting force.

By the beginning of 1943 we had managed to organise ourselves in a manner which was to set the pattern for the duration of the war. We had our headquarters in Baker Street where all operations were planned and where intelligence was collated and filed and where new reports from agents in the field were received. We held our briefing sessions at a flat in Orchard Court, not far away. Here men who were about to be dropped into France were given the latest details about conditions, both generally and as they affected their own particular districts. It might be that a certain operator was suspected of working with the Germans. We would warn the outgoing agent and tell him in what circumstances he should take appropriate action to silence the man. This flat in Orchard Court was the one which contained the famous 'black bathroom'.

This bathroom contained a black tiled bath in which from time to time Peter Churchill might be found, fully clothed in the dry tub, his feet resting on the taps, doing *The Times* crossword.

The Orchard Court flat was presided over by Park. Park had been a bank messenger in the Paris branch of the Westminster Bank and he had a prodigious memory. He knew every agent by his training pseudonym and made each one personally welcome when they arrived at the flat for briefing. His cheerful countenance was beloved by all the members of the French section and his tact was responsible for avoiding many awkward meetings between men who were not supposed to know each other's appearance.

We wanted to discourage our men from meeting each other in the field and the best way to do that was to see that they did not meet each other in England more than we could help. Park would spirit people from room to room in the nick of time. Of course people did meet each other and we were not silly about forbidding it – our agents were far too intelligent to need petty regulations of that kind; but there was one thing which was absolutely against orders, that was to tell anyone where one was going. There was a particular danger of this happening when two agents met in the flat and knew that they were due to be sent off at the same time. Park tried his best to stop them knowing this. In general he succeeded admirably, his tact and popularity enabling him to move people from briefing room to briefing room (and into the bathroom) with the agility of the characters in a French farce.

No device of spy literature was used. There were no hollow fountain pens or detachable heels, for we thought them, on the whole, more trouble than they were worth. One man did ask for a suitcase with a false bottom. He was quite insistent that he could not go without it. I eventually conceded that he might have one but I was equally insistent about its use. 'I don't mind you having the case,' I said, 'but I forbid you absolutely to carry anything in it.' The Abwehr were trained CID men. They would rumble a false bottomed suitcase in no time at all. It was no use having secret devices, for once they were discovered the game was up. It was much better to carry messages folded in a newspaper, for instance. In a tight spot the paper could be chucked away and no one would think anything of it. In principle, of course, nothing should have been written at all, but this was not always possible: one's memory can only absorb so much.

On the other hand, immense pains were taken to ensure that the agent looked to the very last detail the part he was supposed to be playing. This applied not only to the appearance but also, for instance, to a man's accent. It is easy to speak perfect French and yet still retain traces of a foreign inflection. If this were so, we would account for the deviation by a Canadian background or a Belgian education or whatever was most appropriate in the cover story which the agent was given to learn.

Once the agent was absolutely clear on the purpose and the background of his mission he would be passed on to an escorting officer who would stay with him until the very moment when he boarded the plane. This officer was responsible for making sure that no English cigarettes or money were slipped into a pocket at the last moment – for such a small lapse of memory could cost a life and wreck weeks of careful planning. For my part, I always made a practice of seeing each officer personally before he left and I always tried to have some memento to give to each one – a pair of cuff-links or a cigarette case or something of that sort – so that when he was alone in France he might be reminded of the fact that we at home cared about him and were thinking of him. I tried as often as my work at the office allowed, to accompany the men to the aerodrome, for this moment before take-off was the most upsetting to the nerves; it was then that melancholy or morbid presentiments could most easily assert themselves.

One group had been trained for a raid against a munitions factory in the Lyons area. They were all keyed up and ready to go when, on the actual runway, the flight had to be cancelled. This was but the first of many cancellations. That particular group was doomed. Whenever they got to the aerodrome the weather would close in or something would prevent them from taking off. If they took off, then the reception committee would not show up and the aircraft would return with them still aboard. After three months, the leader of the group came to my office.

'I am sorry, *mon Colonel*,' he said, 'but my men cannot go on with this mission. Their morale is gone.'

'You're sure?'

'I'm sure.'

'Yes, well, I quite understand,' I said. 'It's not your fault. I'm glad you came and told me. Don't blame yourselves.'

I arranged for the men to be returned to their units. I meant what I said: it was no one's fault. It was just one of those cases of waiting finally exhausting men's patience and confidence.

When the agent had finally gone, we could only wait to hear from the RAF that they had dropped him and eventually from the man himself that he was in contact with those whom he had been sent to meet.

The messages from France came to a large country house which was situated near Sevenoaks in Kent. Over 500 men and women were stationed there whose business it was to send and receive wireless messages, working with agents in all the occupied European countries. Each operator in France had his own 'godmother' or 'godfather', usually the former (a FANY) at Sevenoaks. She would always be on duty when her own particular operator was due to come on the air. The FANY would take down the message and would be better able, by virtue of her knowledge of the agent's 'fist', or morse technique, to detect any irregularities or impostures.

If an agent was doing skeds at fixed times and was having no difficulty in adhering to them the FANY would come on duty about half an hour before the sked was due to begin and would set about listening to the wavelength on which her man might be expected, perhaps oscillating slightly from side to side in case something was slightly off beam. One does the same sort of thing when trying to get exactly on a station when tuning-in one's radio at home. It was this need to tune-in which sometimes led a FANY to miss the very first part of a message, a section of the code call-sign for instance, and she would then have to make up for lost time and get down the rest of the message as best she could. At other times, only a fragment of a message would be audible at all, owing to interference. We always insisted on being sent the mutilated portion and we at headquarters would make what we could of it.

It was this lack of precision which occasionally led us – and some other sections of SOE – to accept as genuine messages which were in fact German-controlled. It has been suggested that we should have known that an operator was warning us that he was being controlled by the Germans because he left out the first part of his call-sign; in other words, he gave his name (his code name, that is) as, for instance, Master instead of Buckmaster.

Such mutilations were everyday occurrences; had we suspected all such minute deviations as indicative of attempts to warn us of German control we should have been quite hamstrung. Furthermore we should have had a large number of irate agents demanding to know why we ignored their messages and doubted their loyalty. Morale would have plummeted. In secret wireless work under far from perfect conditions, we were quite unable to ask for repetitions of doubtful passages and to employ all those aids to accuracy and checks of sources which are so easy in peacetime radio work.

The FANY who had taken down the message had no idea of the meaning of the coded groups she had written down on her pad. She passed the encoded form, including any mutilated or incomplete groups exactly as she had written them, to the decoding officers. They worked in a separate wing of the same house. They decoded the groups of coded letters and passed them in sealed envelopes to a dispatch rider who signed for them. He then came as fast as he could to Baker Street and handed the envelopes to us.

We did not like using the telephone, though at times when we were desperate for news of the outcome of some mission or anxious to know if a certain job of sabotage could be handled by the group we had contacted, we would use the 'scrambler' for added speed.

I always insisted that the decoded groups were sent to me exactly as they had been taken down, regardless of any apparent 'mistakes.' The decoding officers started off, in the early days, by airing their skill at textual emendation; they changed words which 'obviously' should have been different. For instance, the message as they had decoded it might read 'HAVE PREPARED ONION WITH GASNOT.' The decoding officer, in an excess of scholarly zeal, would interpret this as, 'HAVE PREPARED UNION WITH GASTON.' Now while he was probably right to put GASTON for GASNOT it might be that UNION for ONION was totally wrong ONION might be a code name for a particular operation or a dropping ground, of which the decoding officer knew nothing. At Baker Street we would be flabbergasted.

'What the hell is Armand doing 'preparing union with Gaston?' I would say. 'We told him Gaston was no good. He was supposed to make everyone sever contact with him.'

We would then check back and Vera Atkins would find that severing contact with Gaston was to have been known as operation ONION. We would have to check back with our decoding officer and then we would find that it had been ONION all along. Nerves were frayed and time was lost. If the situation were more complex, it might take hours to unravel and hours were precious. We might even have to refer back to the agent on his next sked. He would then lose confidence in our ability to understand his code and become jittery and unsure of himself and of us. Therefore I insisted that all messages, however ridiculous they might superficially appear, should be sent to us at headquarters exactly as they had been taken down. The decoding officer was very firmly discouraged from using his wits.

As a result of this, messages used to come to us which appeared to be totally and irrevocably indecipherable, even though they were in fact 'in clear,' i.e. decoded. They should have been ready to read. Instead they might look like this (a simple example):

IMI THMRY SAYG ABLE TAKE TWHGVE CONTTTN?S G??U?D AFFLY BBR MASSAGE MIEUW TORT KUE???IIS.

The question marks indicated letters the operator had been unable to take down.

Now for the interpretation: IMI was a code device showing that a request was being made. The rest of the message could be read off by us at Baker Street to the following effect:

IMI TOMMY SAYS ABLE TAKE TWELVE CONTAINERS GROUND APPLE BBC MESSAGE MIEUX TARD QUE JAMAIS.

The last part is, of course, a French phrase meaning, 'Better late than never,' and it was the phrase which our man wanted the BBC French service to broadcast when the operation was about to be undertaken. You can see that there are several places where the decoding officer could have gone wrong – he might have taken AFFLY to be APPLY, not realising that we had given various dropping grounds in a certain area the names of fruits. As a result of this, he might then change the last part of the message to accord with the 'correction' he thought he had already made. Chaos would follow. Equally, BBR MASSAGE might have been intended to be read as just that, in which case a correction to BBC MESSAGE would have given quite the wrong sense to us who were 'in the know'.

The example which I have given here is a simple one. Often the messages were so garbled that you might think sense could never be made of them. Yet we became so adept at unravelling their meanings that we would be able to read off jumbles of letters at sight, much to the astonished admiration of any top brass that might be in the office at the time, for the unpractised eye was quite unable to make anything of them at all.

On occasions, when an operator was, for instance, on the run or could not keep to exact sked times owing to increased German control or detector-van activity, the 'godmother' would work, alternating with another operator, on a non-stop, twenty-four-hour basis, so that the agent would be able to come on the air at a moment's notice when the coast was clear, knowing that his message would be received.

Speed was essential in the relaying of agents' messages to us at headquarters. If I was particularly worried about a certain agent I would ring through to the commanding officer of our wireless station and tell him that any news from that agent was to be phoned through direct to me. On other occasions, a decoding officer might sense from what he had deciphered that something was very urgent, in which case he would go to his CO and tell him that he thought it should be phoned through. We hesitated to use the phone too much for fear that an enemy agent (if any existed) might get wind of something or even through the accident of a crossed line hear of some secret information.

Further, we feared the possibility of distortions and misunderstandings; when you had something in front of you in black and white it was much easier to make sense of jumbles and detect the point of a message.

Sometimes the urgency of a message would be alarming. I remember on one occasion receiving a warning that the Germans had suddenly moved a large number of troops to the vicinity of a factory which our men were due to attack that very evening. The report was put on my desk at 7.10. It read: 'GERMAN TROOPS GESTAPO REINFORCING CAMBRAI ALSO SOME TANKS'. The report came from one group in the area who did not know that another in the same district was due to attack a plant in Cambrai upon the receipt of a BBC message: PIERRE EMBRASSE YVETTE. That sentence was in the script of the French service announcer and was due to be broadcast at 7.30. If the message went out our men would probably walk straight into a trap. There was no time to be lost.

I tried to get through to our liaison officer's room. He was not there. He had already left for the studio. I tried to get through there. I could not be put through. It was too late.

I rushed out of my office and down the stairs into Baker Street. Luckily, a FANY driver was waiting.

'Bush House,' I yelled. 'And drive as fast as you can go,' I added once I was in the car.

She did. I leapt out of the car at 7.25 and ran up the imposing steps to the front door. A commissionaire barred the way. 'Out of the light,' I cried, barging past him and flinging my pass at him as I did so.

I dashed into the lift and demanded to be taken to the studio floor. Luckily I knew where the broadcasts were made and I was able to run along the passage and into the studio just as the announcer was starting the *messages personnels.* As I entered the studio and scampered across the floor to him, I heard him say in his measured, quiet way: *'Pierre Embrasse Yvette.'*

It was among the very first messages. I grabbed him by the shoulder and shook my head fiercely. 'No,' I mouthed. 'No.' There was an endless pause as he tried to make out what I was attempting to convey. Then, to my immense relief, he got the point. In his firm, unruffled voice he said: *J'annule* (I deny or retract) *Pierre Embrasse Yvette. Je repète J'annule Pierre Embrasse Yvette.*'

I sank into an armchair and thanked God. If I had been a minute later it would have been certain that our men would already have switched off their set, for they would not listen to the BBC a moment longer than was absolutely necessary, for fear of detection. Even as it was I could not be sure that they would have heard or realised the import of the announcer's denial of Pierre Embrasse Yvette.

We waited nervously for the next sked from that particular section. It came the next day – all was well. The message had been fully understood and the operation called off. This was the closest call we had, but there were several other occasions on which the Bush House liaison officer had to cross off a message just as the announcer was about to read it. The latter's voice never wavered.

Sometimes it was not the BBC messages which had to be cancelled but a flight which we had to stop because there would not be a reception committee waiting for an agent who was going to be dropped. Then there would be frantic calls to the air station and midnight rushes down the runway to halt aircraft whose engines were already warming up.

There were other unpredictable factors that might come into play at a moment's notice: perhaps the RAF would be unable to fly a sortie owing to bad weather or a new flak battery and we would have to warn the reception not to assemble; perhaps a double agent was suspected and an outgoing agent prevented from falling into a trap. We had continually to be alert and ready to change our plans at the very last second.

German espionage was not, it need hardly be said, anything like on the same scale as our own in the occupied countries, for they had no friendly civilian population on whom to base it. We could never have functioned at all had it not been for the brave and unflinching support which the ordinary French civilians rendered to us. The Germans had no one on whom they could rely. As a result, I was never the victim of any assassination attempt nor were any of my staff. Though the Germans did in fact know my name they never sought me out.

It may be wondered how the Germans found out my name. The truth probably is that someone told it under interrogation, for to give my name would endanger no one and that was precisely the sort of information which, under agonising torture, a man would give to stave off further pain. Though it was against strict orders, I do not think that anyone could be blamed for giving the name of a CO who was beyond the reach of the Gestapo. Certainly it was preferable to giving the name of a local *Réseau* leader. I myself discovered that the Germans knew my name through a piece of information which reached us through Spain. This consisted of a secret document spirited out of Gestapo HQ which purported to give the British Secret Service set-up. The plan was highly fanciful and contained almost every famous name the Germans could think of as well as those, like my own, which were really associated with secret work. My name became known to Hitler himself and he is reported to have said: 'When I get to London I do not know who I shall hang first – Churchill or this man Buckmaster!' No enemy agent ever tried to walk into my office, though several did try, without success, to come over to this country through our escape lines and join our organisation. These attempts somewhat underrated the efficiency of our security arrangements and they were frustrated without much trouble.

Our office in Baker Street was not known to many people and even my wife never discovered it until one day in 1943 when she was on her way to visit a friend in the company of our bull terrier bitch, Misty. It so happened that I had taken Misty to the office with me several times so that she should not be left alone during the raids when my wife was on duty at a First Aid Post and her intelligence led her to remember the place. Accordingly as she passed the door of the building she turned in. My wife called her but she paid no attention and, wagging her tail agreeably, she led the way up to the commissionaire. She got no farther, but it was not too difficult for my wife to deduce the reason for the dog's sudden detour and the secret was out.

I think that was the biggest breach of security which ever occurred in our office, though there was another time when a friend of my wife's happened to hear a FANY saying to one of her colleagues that she had come to Baker Street to drive Colonel Buckmaster, for whom she was now waiting. This friend was later able to tell my wife that she knew where I worked, but she sensibly refused to share the information until Misty's misdemeanour unmasked me.

My own working day was determined by what was going on during any particular phase of our operations. In general, I would arrive early at the office, either by bus, in a taxi or in the car of one of our FANY drivers. To avoid my being seen leaving in her car I would usually meet the FANY at South Kensington Station or at a bus stop. I avoided routine, though, to be quite frank, I never considered very seriously the possibility of anyone on the enemy side trailing me or wanting to kill me. Nor did anything even vaguely disquieting ever happen to me.

If things were reasonably quiet at Baker Street around supper time, I would go home to Chelsea for dinner with my wife and then perhaps leave again around eight o'clock and cycle (on her bicycle – one of those high-seated angular ones) back to Baker Street where I might stay till four in the morning, or, quite frequently, all night.

My average working day was one of about eighteen hours. Even when I had managed to get away from the office, messages would follow me. Often the phone rang in the middle of the night and a coy voice would say: 'Two umbrellas have been seen in Hyde Park.' This conveyed to me that two parachute drops had been made in the Jura. If one was a bit fuzzy from tiredness these things took a bit of working out. The conversation might proceed:

'Red umbrellas or blue ones?' (Was it men or material we had succeeded in dropping?)

'Two blue ones – with handles.' (Two agents with their wireless sets and equipment.)

'Well, I hope they've rolled them up and taken a nice stroll down the Mall.' (I hope they have got rid of their chutes and moved off to their rendezvous.)

This kind of conversation might seem a little arch and it may be thought that any enemy agent could decipher its import without much trouble, but actually the idea was not to hide anything from the enemy but rather to prevent that kind of careless talk which might lead an inquisitive telephone operator to listen in so that later he could show off to his friends how much he knew about the secret war. He could not possibly know where 'Hyde Park' was.

Another time I might be told that 'Two frogs are croaking in the lily pond.' From this I could divine that two wireless operators had made contact with us from the Lille area. If their messages were urgent I would get up and cycle over to Baker Street to see them. (Incidentally this nocturnal cycling enabled me to discover that you can freewheel nearly all the way from Marble Arch to Chelsea, something for which, after the exhaustion of an all-night session, I was often not ungrateful.)

While I was out, the phone might ring again and my sleepy wife would be informed that 'Three redskins have touched wood.' Blearily she would take down the message and when I got home I would know that three members of the Resistance had crossed a neutral border to safety.

At the office we did not, of course, use this abstruse terminology and the progress of each agent and each *Réseau* was plotted with the greatest care. We did not, however, keep elaborate records, for the more there was on paper, the greater the chance of something going astray. It was therefore our policy to destroy all records after an appropriate time had elapsed. Until then, not one message was thrown away, and that included the jumbled versions as well as the finally deciphered editions. So we were able to check up on the style and value of the information each operator had sent us. Thus we could determine whether any of our men or those they had recruited was being suspiciously unforthcoming or whether he seemed (by the falseness of any messages he had sent) to be responsible for the frustration or destruction of others.

To decide whether a man was working for the Germans was not easy from London. Yet, at times, we had to make that decision, for we were in the best – though not the ideal – position in which to judge. We could not afford to risk our men being betrayed and we severed contact with all wireless operators and section heads who seemed to us to be suspect. When this happened we warned all interested parties.

How could we test the loyalty of an operator? The easiest way was to check first whether he was who he said he was. To do this we might send him a message asking: 'HAVE YOU CONTACTED NICOLE AS ORDERED?' where Nicole was a fictitious person and no such order had been given. The tone of the reply would give us a clue, 'WHO THE HELL IS NICOLE AND WHAT ORDER?' would suggest that our man was genuine, but such replies as 'WHERE SHALL I MEET HER?' or 'AM ARRANGING IT SEND FURTHER DETAILS' or simply 'WILL DO' made us more doubtful and we would then continue to ply the man with trap messages, knowing well that any genuine agent would soon ask us to explain ourselves or shut up.

One had to be careful about jumping to conclusions, for it might be that a newly recruited operator's inexperience would look like deceit and we had to beware against being too subtle and Sherlock Holmes-like in the detection of minute sins of omission and commission. It is tempting to suggest that we should have been able to detect false agents by their 'fist', since the experts told us that they could distinguish one fist from another as certainly as a handwriting expert can distinguish one script from another; but we knew that agents often had to send their messages in the most difficult conditions – it might be in a central-heating plant in a loft or in the freezing cold of an outbuilding – and cramp or other afflictions could radically alter their methods of keying.

We at home had to be flexible and one cannot hide the fact that at times this flexibility led us to give the benefit of the doubt, at least for a while, to an operator who later turned out to be false. That was the fortune of war. We were not so rich in operators that we could afford to ditch them for the tiniest indiscretion; had we done so, the confidence of the agents in the field in our competence and our common sense would have been speedily destroyed. War is no exact science.

SOE's activities grew in scope as the war progressed and in 1942 we added a psychological side to them. This took the form of spreading 'sibs'. A man now prominent in the world of literature and broadcasting had an office in our building where he sat all day inventing dangerous rumours. These rumours or 'sibs' were designed for circulation among the people of France and, in particular, among the German occupying forces. Lawrence would try to think up what a service man likes least to believe about conditions at home and about his own status.

One day Lawrence came into my office and in a conversational tone asked me: 'Have you heard they've discovered you can have VD for several months without knowing it?'

'I can't say I have.'

'No, don't suppose you would. Still, it might make some of the Boches in the garrison towns a bit nervy, eh?'

It did. By simultaneously spreading the rumour that all the prostitutes in a certain town had VD we succeeded in having all the Germans there confined to barracks for several weeks. The troops grew disgruntled and practically mutinous.

Other 'sibs' would concern such things as the virtue of wives left too long alone in distant Germany with only Nazi party officials for company. Other rumours concerned German food supplies. Lawrence would try this one on the office staff: 'Well, chaps, it's dehydrated mules' brains for lunch.' If enough of us looked sick, the word would go out that the sausage supplied to German cook-houses was made from the quoted recipe. We attacked morale from every possible angle and nothing was too low if it hurt the Germans.

Immediately before D-Day we spread the message that animals' blood was to be used for transfusions in German military hospitals in the event of an invasion. We also put it out that two train loads of German ammunition had had to be returned to Germany because it was found to be the wrong size. It was suggested that ammunition was desperately short in France because the High Command did not really intend to put up any resistance to the British and American forces.

The important thing was to surrender as quickly as possible before the Russians arrived.

These rumours were heard at garden parties in neutral countries where the Swiss chargé d'affaires would hear them from a British consular official and pass them on, quite innocently, to the Germans. The reports would get back to Germany through the letters written by the German embassy officials to their families and their relatives in the forces. Merchant seamen in Lisbon would pick them up from our agents in dockside cafés. Collaborators would repeat them at official receptions in Paris. The word would go round in a thousand different ways.

Chapter 4

The Match

I think I ought to say before I go any further that from the beginning of 1942 onwards our activities were greatly increased, so much so that I shall be quite unable to recount more than a handful of the personal adventures and successes of our men in the field. We were getting men into France now with much greater confidence, for we were better able to gauge the staunchness of the co-operation we were likely to receive there; this knowledge was gained from the researches of our earlier and exploratory agents, like Harry Morgan and Pierre de Vomécourt, and the groups they had formed. From their reports, we were able to piece together a picture of conditions in the field which, as the months passed grew increasingly, though never sufficiently, comprehensive. Some agents felt that we did not give them adequate briefing before their departure, but in the main we were able to give them enough detailed information to prevent them committing small acts so anachronistic (for instance asking for cigarettes that were no longer obtainable) that they would give themselves away before they had time to find their feet at all.

'Still no sign of anything from Harry Morgan,' I observed to Major Bourne-Paterson, our planning officer.

'Looks as if he's had it,' B-P agreed unhappily.

'We haven't been using Marseilles at all, have we?' 'Nobody's been given the address since Harry left.' 'Good. If the Boches are using our man there I should think they'll soon get tired of waiting. I don't think we need give up hope of Harry. He's got his wits about him—'

'I know.'

'I think he'll turn up. We've got Churchill in Antibes.' Peter Churchill was here, there and everywhere – testing methods of introducing our men into France, recruiting new units and encouraging existing ones – in short, doing the work of ten men. The story of his work has been told; its value cannot be too highly estimated.

'Yes, and Rake's due to go any day now.'

'You don't seem too happy about him, B-P.'

'You know I'm not.'

'I think he'll do a good job,' I said.

I had to admit that we had taken a bit of a risk with Rake. He was rather older than the rest of our agents and lacked certain of the qualities which were present in them.

Denis Rake was born in Belgium and came to England between the wars. He went on the stage and appeared in *No, No, Nanette* and a number of other musical comedies. He went into the army as soon as war was declared – he had been a Territorial before – and went to France with the BEF. After Dunkirk he did a number of jobs where his French made him useful, including that of interpreter and wireless officer on a Free French minesweeper. He was not particularly happy in this work, however, for he wanted something in which he could feel that he was doing a job which really tested his mettle. He was stationed in Portsmouth on this minesweeping job, and as he was rather depressed he spent a fair amount of his time around the pubs. One day in late 1941 he was sitting in the saloon bar of a big and deserted pub in Southsea when a cluster of RAF men came in.

'I don't think I shall have anything to do with it, old boy,' one of them said. 'Sounds a damn sight too risky!'

They laughed. 'Getting windy, Ginger?'

'Jumping out of a kite isn't what I joined the RAF for, old boy.'

Denis went up to the bar. 'Half a pint of beer, please.' Seeing he was alone, the RAF men asked Denis whether he would care to join them. He did. Carelessly and indifferently they continued to discuss the 'parachute job' they had been talking about when they came in.

'Let's face it, it just isn't our cup of tea,' they concluded.

'Have you any idea what the job entails?' Denis asked.

'Thinking of volunteering, old boy?' one of them asked, in a joking voice.

'Yes,' Denis said, 'as a matter of fact I am.'

II

A month later, after devious enquiries through his solicitor, Denis was put in touch with Major Lewis Gielgud who was at that time our recruiting officer. Afterwards Gielgud came in to see me.

'Any useful chaps?' I asked.

'I'm not too sure,' Gielgud replied. 'I've just been talking to this fellow Rake who was put on to us by the War Office.'

'What's he like?'

'Well, he's very keen and his French is all right. He says he wants to do a worthwhile job and hasn't been able to find one yet. Apparently he's a qualified wireless operator.'

'Good Lord, that's just what we're short of—'

'Yes, I know, but—'

'If he's really a qualified W/T boy, I don't think we should turn him down,' I said. 'Let's put him through the training course anyway and see how he shapes up.'

Denis Rake was sent to our training school near Guildford. At first the reports we received of him were far from encouraging; he hated explosions and refused to have anything to do with assault courses which contained them or with demolitions in which the use of dynamite was necessary. He even refused to do revolver practice, maintaining that a wireless operator would not need to use one. Our escorting officer's report was that Rake was 'hopeless'. If he had been recruited in the later years of SOE, when we could be more selective, it is doubtful if he would ever have got past the first few weeks of his training. (Incidentally, there was no disgrace in failing in this way; many brave men who were to prove themselves tough, resourceful and heroic in other spheres found the work which we demanded of them called for something they could not provide.) Rake insisted, and I saw his point, that all this explosive work was quite beyond anything he was likely to be called upon to do in France. I allowed him to remain at the training school. We were able to exercise a much greater flexibility in our attitude to our men than were other branches of the service: to us they were always individuals and, in return for the hazards of their work, we felt they deserved the trouble which such treatment sometimes entailed. For instance, I remember one man on the point of leaving coming to me and saying that he could not go. Of course we were neither able nor wished to force a man to go against his will; he would probably fail and might bring disaster on those who met him.

'But why not?' I demanded, concealing my slight annoyance that at the last minute the man was going to ruin our timetable.

'My code name is Alphonse, is it not?'

'That is correct.'

'Then I cannot go.'

'But why?'

'I have a cousin Alphonse. He is a traitor. I cannot take his name: it will spoil my luck.'

'How would it be,' I asked quite seriously, 'if we were to call you Alain?'

'Alain!' His face broke into a smile. 'That would be different.'

Alain left on the same plane that would have carried Alphonse.

One day, Bourne-Paterson came into my office and said: 'Well, your good friend Rake's really done it this time.'

'What is it now?'

'Last night he refused to do his balloon jump. I think we'll have to RD† him.'

'They're crying out for wireless men,' I said. 'Surely there's another way of getting him in.'

'Look, forgive me for putting it this way, but I don't see how we can rely on the courage of a man who won't even pull the trigger of a revolver.'

'Let's have a word with the trick-cyclist,' I suggested.

'Oh Lord!'

In spite of Bourne-Paterson's disgust, I talked to our psychiatric expert. On the whole, I must confess, I did not find his opinions over-helpful, for while they were careful and explicit

---

† Return to Duties.

and often profoundly interesting, they equally often seemed to me to miss the points with which we were specifically concerned. I never reached that stage of proficiency where I was able to evaluate the importance of the presence or absence of a mother-fixation in the selection of an agent for a particular mission. On this occasion, however, perhaps because he said what I had hoped he would, I was impressed by what he told me. 'Lots of people are nervous of jumping out of balloons,' he said, 'where they could fairly easily be persuaded to bale out of an aircraft. The fact that there's a cable attached to the ground often brings on an attack of vertigo which would never occur if the drop were from an aircraft totally unconnected with the ground. I wouldn't attach too much importance to this incident at all.'

'What about the explosion fear?'

'Is he going to do any demolition work?'

'Not if I can help it,' I said.

'Why worry then?'

'You don't think he's going to be in a blue funk over everything he does?'

'From what you've told me, he sounds a thoroughly dedicated sort of person who wants to do the job he's volunteered for and isn't prepared to do a lot of things he considers outside his range. He'll play his part but he doesn't fancy understudying all the others as well.'

'That's exactly my view,' I said.

'All the same,' the psychiatrist went on, 'I shouldn't persist with the parachuting. Isn't there any other way of getting him to the target area?'

'That's a thought,' I said.

Three days later we heard that one of our wireless operators in Lyons had been caught and shot. I gave de Guélis the word to have Rake ready to leave for Lyons in two days. He came straight up to London for his briefing. This was done in the flat in Orchard Court. Rake came into my office immediately after he had finished with de Guélis. 'Feeling all right, Rake?'

'Yes, sir.'

'I hope de Guélis told you all you wanted to know.'

'Well, he told me all he knew, I think,' Rake smiled.

'Anything else you want?'

'No, sir, I don't think so. It all seems pretty clear.'

'I'm sure you're going to do a first-rate job. You're really needed out there and we've got a fine lot of people for you to work with.'

'I know that, sir.'

There was a knock at the door and Jerry Morel, our operations officer, came in. 'I've got the money from the bank, sir,' he reported.

'Good stuff. I hope it's in old notes, as we asked.'

'I haven't looked yet, sir.' He opened the case which contained the money and emptied it on my desk. Bundles of gleaming new notes cascaded out. 'Just what the doctor ordered,' Morel commented sarcastically.

'We shall have to do something about this,' I said. 'Call in anyone who isn't vitally tied up. Dirtying notes detail!'

Bourne-Paterson, Gielgud, Vera Atkins and my secretary Yveline came into the room looking very suspicious. I sent Yveline off to get some oil and some grease, meanwhile I undid the elastic bands round each bundle and flung the 1,000 and 5,000 franc notes abandonedly into the air. 'Get busy,' I ordered.

'Rub them in your hands, scribble on them, fold them and generally muck them up. We've got to have old notes for new.'

Yveline returned and we all set to, spattering the notes with ink, bending the edges, greasing them, rolling them into tight little balls and then trying to straighten them out. The work seemed lighthearted, but the purpose was deadly earnest; there was nothing so suspect as new notes and if Denis – or any subsequent agent – were to be caught with a bundle of them he would certainly be detained and, if the investigation were thorough, revealed.

All the time we sought to protect our men from being betrayed by trivialities: they faced enough danger without being revealed by so small a detail as a tailor's tab or the fact that they were carrying a British pencil. Before being sent off they were searched by an ex-Scotland Yard expert – trouser turn-ups were emptied, linings examined and cigarette cases brushed out to eliminate the presence of Virginian tobacco. We even had our own dentist who excised British fillings (neat and silver) and substituted French ones (bulky and gold). Some agents thought that we were going rather far in our precautions, for they doubted whether the Gestapo would bother with investigations of a kind likely to discover such microscopic evidence.

In London, however, we felt it our duty to give our men every possible assistance that we could think of, no matter how niggling. Often, I agree, the Gestapo adopted methods so brutal and so summary that nothing could protect our men from them; what people forget, however, is that quite frequently our men were able to bluff themselves out of awkward situations and here the presence of, for instance, a London bus ticket in a top pocket, might make all the difference between release and death. If this was the case on just one occasion, all our precautions were justified.

The kind of thing against which we were powerless to protect an agent was instinct, or actions which had become so automatic as to rank as instinctive. One of our girls landed in France in 1943 and successfully reached the large town where she was due to rendezvous with a local Resistance man. In the middle of the town she was obliged to cross a very busy main road. As she went to cross it she looked right to check that the road was clear; this is, of course, the natural thing to do if the traffic drives on the left-hand side of the road. Seeing the road clear, she started to cross; a howl of brakes and the curses of a lorry driver revealed her mistake. She fell back on to the pavement, tripping heavily on the kerb. At once she was the centre of a crowd of towns people to whom the lorry driver was expostulating furiously. It was her bad luck that a Gestapo agent was among the crowd. With cruel speed he deduced the real reason for the girl's accident and arrested her before she could scramble to her feet.

At length we had dirtied all the money with which we had been supplied and Morel handed Denis Rake the bundle of now grubby notes to which he was entitled. The next day he was put on a grey, camouflaged trawler, bound for Gibraltar and the south of France. Denis spent most of his time in his tiny cabin, rehearsing the cover story which he had been given; he came to the conclusion that it was rather slender. He had been told to say that he was a Belgian businessman who was seeking contracts in France. It was still difficult for us to give really credible and watertight cover stories to our men and we relied on them to improve their stories once they were in the field and had been able to procure genuine papers as they often were through the friendly mayors of small towns.

At Gibraltar, Denis was moved from the trawler to a felucca carrying the Portuguese flag. Two nights later a small rowing boat landed him on a beach near Juan-les-Pins. He carried two suitcases, one containing a wireless set, the other with his personal belongings and a large number of dirty notes. Denis made his way through the town. He found that he felt much more confident now that he had landed than he had ever done during training. He had been given the address of a certain Dr Lévy in Antibes whom he was to contact; the password was, 'Do you know where I can buy some good oysters?' The doctor would then reply: 'No, but I have some shrimps you would like.'

Denis lay up for the rest of the night in a vacant lot on the road to Antibes and did not enter the latter town until the sun was up and there were plenty of people about. There was a faded atmosphere in the place, for the hotels were nearly all closed and the memory of carefree pre-war days remained to blight and mock the sorry present. Denis had been well briefed on how to find the road in which Dr Lévy lived, for we were particularly careful to warn our men against asking directions in the centre of a town where a policeman or the *Milice* might overhear them.

The doctor's house was number eight, Boulevard du Maréchal Foch, a secluded road of detached villas. Denis had been warned that, if there was danger, the statues on the balcony facing the street would be turned towards him and he should not enter. There were no statues at all on the balcony of number eight, Boulevard du Maréchal Foch. Denis turned and walked quickly back out of the front gate of the villa. He hurried on up the road, looking for any house which had statues on the balcony. There was none. He tried to recall his briefing: he was certain that de Guélis had said number eight. He went back to it and walked boldly up to the front door. On it was a small brass plate: D. Lévy, Medecin et Chirurgien. Reassured, Denis rang the bell. A maid opened the door.

'I have come to see Dr Lévy; I believe he lives here.'

'What is the name, please?'

'I have a personal message for him. I must see him myself.'

'Dr Lévy is not here. Will you wait?'

'No, I cannot wait,' Denis replied. 'I'll – I'll telephone him later. What time are you expecting him?'

'He will be back from his surgery at ten o'clock. If you telephone then you will catch him.'

Denis took the number from the maid and left the Boulevard du Maréchal Foch. He was getting slightly nervous about time now, for he was due to rendezvous with Clément,[†] another of our men, in the Bar Sportif in Antibes at noon that day. If he missed that meeting, he would have to wait till noon the next day. Denis walked down into Antibes. This waiting about between appointments when one had nowhere to go and nothing to do and only the most hazy sort of cover story was always a trial to our men; Denis wisely spent it reading all the local and national newspapers on which he could lay his hands, taking care not to buy more than two at any one kiosk. A box on the front page of the local paper warned people against the possibility of terrorists landing on the beaches and reminded them sternly that it was their duty to report any suspicious loiterers or strangers.

It is one of the most remarkable qualities of the French that

---

[†] Field name of Philippe Liewer.

they are able to pick out strangers with the greatest facility; the smallest accentual difference, the slightest unfamiliarity with the prevailing slang is sufficient clue. Often an agent would be surrounded by curious – and, thankfully, on the whole friendly – locals, all of whom had within seconds of his entering a restaurant or bar detected his alienness, this in spite of the fact that our men spoke perfect French and wore clothing indistinguishable from Frenchmen. It was for this reason that we liked to drop agents into zones of which they were in fact natives, but this was not always possible, either because they might be known too well or because they were needed elsewhere; in these cases they had to assimilate themselves quickly.

Denis, with his suitcases, felt very conspicuous. He noticed that there were a fair number of uniformed *Milice* men on patrol; ten o'clock could not come soon enough. These *miliciens*, who wore uniforms aping the SS, were at this time extremely officious; the men of Vichy sought to alleviate the natural sense of guilt with which defeat burdened them by that zealous discipline which defeated nations so often impose upon themselves in an effort to associate themselves with their conquerors.

Most Frenchmen regarded these attempts with cynical derision, but at first they were unable to do anything about them; later, however, when the Resistance took shape and gathered substance, the bumptiousness of the *miliciens* changed into a kind of arrogant impotence; they no longer tried to control the French but allowed the French to control them. To be fair, many were half-hearted in their allegiance to Pétain and even at the beginning did their best to turn a blind eye to our activities whenever they could do so without incurring punishment themselves. They sensed earlier than the Germans that the Boches had lost the war and took what steps they could to retrench themselves in the affections of their fellow-countrymen. The Resistance permitted them to think that they were being successful in this and on the promise of post-war immunity secured many valuable favours and lives.

In 1941, however, Vichy was at its most repressive and we started by underestimating both the efficiency and the ruthlessness with which the *Milice* performed its duties. In effect we came to fear them more than the Gestapo or the Abwehr. Their cleverest tactic – and the one most difficult to detect – was to lay *souricières* (mousetraps) such as the one in the attic at Marseilles which trapped Harry Morgan. Because their agents were Frenchmen and indistinguishable from local people, they were able to permeate our organisations with a confidence impossible to the Gestapo and they had the power, like dry rot, of spreading their corrupting influence, among both the discontented and the timid. Thus they could take over whole subsections of our organisation and an agent might fall into one of the traps before we could know that it was not safe any more. Often our suspicions were aroused only after an arrest had been made and, as a result, our man had not contacted us as he should. In that case, we would assume the contact was either blown or treacherous and would give it to no more of our men until we had a thorough report. All the same, the *souricières* took their toll.

At ten o'clock Denis went into the Post Office and got through to Doctor Lévy's number.

'Hullo,' a woman's voice answered immediately. 'I was expecting you to call.'

'Good, may I speak—'

'It's about the Siamese cats, isn't it? Well, they're beauties this time and I'm letting them go really quite cheap. I know you won't be disappointed. Tiburce's[†] produced a beautiful litter, really beautiful—'

'I wanted to speak—'

'I know you're a friend of Yvette's and—'

'Doctor Lévy – I want to speak to the doctor—'

'Isn't that Monsieur Isnard?'

'No, I'm afraid it isn't,' Denis said.

'I wish you'd told me,' the voice said. 'I'll call the doctor.'

'Lévy here.'

'This is a friend of Grégoire's. I need your help. I wonder', Denis spaced the words carefully, 'do you know where I can buy some good oysters?'

There was a stunned silence. 'I beg your pardon?'

'Do you know where I can buy some good oysters?'

'Is this a joke? Oysters? How should I know anything about oysters? Who are you?'

Denis replaced the receiver. It seemed to him that something had gone seriously wrong, for he had been taught that if there was any possibility of a contact being blown he should sever all connection with it. In a mood of great despondency he caught the bus to Antibes, still carrying his suitcase containing the wireless and the other containing the money. Just one control and he would have had it. He reached the bar in Antibes without any alarms. He had been told that Clément, who was to accompany him to Lyons, would be sitting at a table at the

---

[†] Field name of Albert Browne-Bartroli, organiser of the DITCHER Circuit.

back of the room reading a copy of the *Nice-Matin* and smoking a short black cigar. He would be wearing a beret. Such a man was sitting at the table farthest from the door.

Denis went and sat at the next table. 'May I have a look at your paper,' he asked, giving the password, 'I left mine on the bus?'

The other man replied, 'I bought this one in Nice this morning.' It was Clément all right. He went on: 'I was beginning to wonder whether you were going to turn up. Jacques, let's have another bottle of red. Well, did you have a good trip?'

'Yes, thanks.'

'Good stuff. Are we all set to go to Lyons?'

'I think the contact in Antibes has been blown,' Denis said. 'I phoned him and he didn't know what I was talking about.'

'I don't suppose he's been blown. Probably got your wires crossed. I should try and go and see him.'

'I don't think he'll see me.'

'Give it a try; this sort of thing's always happening. If you think he really has been blown, come back here this afternoon. I'm usually here till about three-thirty.' There was a casual air about Clément which at once reassured and troubled Denis; it was all very well to find that one's colleague was confident, but Denis could not but be uneasy at Clément's lackadaisical manner. He talked in a loud voice which almost invited people to listen to what he was saying. Denis was happy to take his leave of him – still lugging the two suitcases – and start on the way back to Antibes. The bus was again unmolested by controls and he reached Antibes by early afternoon. He started to walk up the road past the station on the way to the Rue de la Sainte Marie when he saw ahead of him a crowd of people, halted at the top of the road where a bridge crossed the railway line. He stopped in an arcade on the pretext of tying up his shoelace and tried to see what was going on. He soon realised: all travellers were being forced to open their cases. Denis turned and started to walk with leisurely indifference back the way he had come. He watched anxiously for further police blocking off the other end of the street, for we had warned him that this was a common move. He turned left down a broad street running parallel to the sea. At the far end of it was a knot of *miliciens*, idly patrolling the centre of the road and stopping all those who came that way. He turned again and started away from the town centre towards St Raphael. Down a street leading to the sea another band of *miliciens* were advancing. With dazzling suddenness the place was swarming with them. Denis kept his head, though the two fatal suitcases hung like lead weights on either arm. He thought of going back to the station and putting them in the consigne, but he realised that the police, if they were being as thorough as it seemed, would probably go through everything that was there and, when they discovered the wireless, would wait for him to come and claim it. He knew how precious it was to the organisation. He kept walking. On the outskirts of the town he looked for a road which led back to bypass the town centre (there is generally such a road looping most French towns, for *poids lourds*) and, finding it, was able to outflank the controls and reach the Rue de la Sainte Marie once again. By this time he was tired and anxious.

'Doctor Lévy cannot see anyone at present,' the maid told him. 'He is out on a call.'

'May I speak to his wife then?' Denis asked desperately.

'What name shall I say?' The maid was very suspicious.

Denis had a thought: 'Say it is a friend of Yvette's,' he said, 'interested in buying a cat.'

The maid returned to say that if he went round to the back where the kittens were being kept, Madame Lévy would see him. Thankful to be out of sight of the main road, Denis went round and knocked on the door of a small shed. Madame Lévy opened the door. When she saw Denis she looked extremely surprised.

'I thought—'

'Madame, forgive me for intruding in this way, but I am desperately keen to see Doctor Lévy.'

'Who are you?'

'I have come from England,' Denis said recklessly. 'I was given your husband's name and told to contact him.'

'But you should have been here four days ago,' Madame Lévy said in a mildly hurt tone.

'But when I gave him the password he did not understand. Is his phone tapped? Is he in danger?'

'We are always in danger, Monsieur,' said Madame Lévy with a sudden dignity which made Denis blush.

'I quite understand, Madame. Forgive me. It's simply that I am rather worried – you see, the *Milice*—'

'Of course. My husband is not here now and will not return till after surgery. If you come back—'

'May I ask you a favour, Madame? If I go and see your husband at the surgery I'm sure he'll know who I am. Meanwhile, may I leave my cases here?' Denis felt unable to make the doctor's wife see the urgency of the situation. 'I really don't want to carry them all over Antibes.'

Madame Lévy looked at the cases apprehensively. 'All right,' she said. 'I'll put them at the bottom of the garden. If they are discovered for any reason – I shall say you brought them. I don't know what's in them and I don't want to know.'

Denis managed to secure the address of the doctor's surgery and set off at once, much relieved at having disposed of the suitcases. There were several patients in the waiting room and Denis perceived that the best thing he could do was to join the queue.

'Next.'

Denis rose and went into the surgery. Doctor Lévy was sitting at a small desk covered with papers and bottles, for he did his own dispensing.

'Yes, what can I do for you?'

'Doctor Lévy, I have been trying to get in touch with you all morning. I phoned you at your house at ten o'clock—'

'Ah, so you're the mysterious stranger who called. Well, what do you want?'

'I have just come from England.' The doctor did not change expression at Denis's words. 'I was told your address and the password I gave you—'

'I don't know what you're talking about. I don't know anything about it.'

'But your wife said you were expecting me.'

'We were expecting some friends,' the doctor admitted cautiously, 'but how can you prove that you are one of them?'

'The password—'

'Do not keep talking about passwords.'

'Perhaps this will convince you,' Denis said, pulling from his pocket a small pill-box. In it were two lethal tablets. He showed them to Doctor Lévy. The doctor inspected them and then looked at Denis.

'Very well,' he said, slowly removing his glasses in a tired gesture. 'Come back here at three o'clock. We will look after you.'

III

At home, we had decided to reverse our previous principle of infiltration without sabotage, and when Ben Cowburn, still in the field, got in touch with us in February we gave the go-ahead on a plan he had to blow up some engines which were used to haul munitions trains from the German border.

He was a man of the greatest determination and resource and it seemed to us only just to give him the chance of making the first bangs. We had sent him his own wireless operator at the end of 1941 and so were able to keep in the closest contact. He had transferred his attentions to Troyes in Eastern France where the rail depot was, and in February we gave him the word. He had recruited a number of tough helpers from among the railwaymen who provided, as I have said, one of the most fertile recruiting grounds we had; Ben, a dour north-countryman, had also recruited a reception committee to whom we were able to drop explosives and detonators and small arms. The drop we made to Ben was one of the first and presaged the enormous mass drops which we were later to make to the *Maquis* as the great day of liberation approached. At the moment we were strictly limited in the number of planes at our disposal, for in the absence of definite results the high-ups were unwilling to believe that SOE was a really effective fighting force.

I was continually badgered by well-intentioned officers who thought that we should be able to provide up to the minute inter-round summaries of each phase of our build-up. I was neither able nor inclined to do so. I knew that the more paperwork one undertook the less attention one could pay to the actual job itself; it was no use having tidy records if our whole organisation was in tatters. People wonder why we never kept proper files and they jump to all sorts of wild and preposterous conclusions; the reason is simply that when you have worked every night till somewhere between three and five in the morning, you feel little desire to tabulate the events of the day in order to earn the gratitude and admiration of some hypothetical historian of the future. I held the future more important than the historian. The Free French specialised, even in the field itself, in the compilation of exhaustive records; at one stage these were captured by the Germans and men who would never have been caught otherwise lost their lives.

Ben Cowburn's men had no difficulty in placing explosive charges where they could do the most damage and on the night of 3 July 1943 the engine sheds at Troyes and their contents went up in smoke. In order to cover the explosion we tried to arrange for a RAF plane to fly over the area so that the Germans might think that bombs had done the damage; we often used this tactic, for though it seldom deceived the Germans, they were willing to lay the blame on the RAF if they could, since it made them look less foolish and was less harmful to civilian morale than the admission that there actually was a Resistance movement. We were prepared to accept this loss of propaganda if it prevented the taking of civilian reprisals.

We now had *Réseaux* (nests) in a fair number of key places, including Nice, Marseilles, Bordeaux, Annecy, Lyons, Le Havre, Rouen, Troyes and Lille. I cannot, of course, give details of the setting up of each of these, and the agents whose personal histories I give are representative of many others whose adventures both resemble and differ from theirs.

Certain men both by reason of our orders and their force of character became responsible for several groups in these early days, supervising recruiting and maintaining morale; it was only too easy for agents and French recruits to feel neglected and become dispirited. Men like Peter Churchill (Raoul) in the south, Major Suttill (Prosper) in Paris and Richard Heslop (Xavier) in the east were tremendously valuable, and their dynamism and that of others like them held the organisation together.

From the beginning of 1942 these men were the lynch-pins. They instilled that *esprit de corps* which enabled the talents of the other agents to emerge. Their flair was of tremendous help in the field, both in the selection of French recruits and in the allocation to them of suitable tasks. Apart from the railwaymen, most of our best section heads were drawn from the ranks of professional men – doctors, dentists, lawyers and school-teachers – while what one might call the yeoman class (gamekeepers, small farmers and so on) provided the most reliable rank and file.

By the terms of the agreement we had made with de Gaulle I was forbidden to recruit any Frenchmen into the London end of our organisation and this was a rule to which we adhered rigidly, though we were often able to avoid its apparent rigours by the employment of technical exceptions – dual nationals, Mauritians and French Canadians. I always tried to have as little as possible to do with the politics of the Resistance both in England where I found them distasteful and in France where we were bound, by the terms of our mission, to avoid all interference in internal matters. Our job was, at all times, strictly military.

IV

Doctor Lévy hid Denis Rake in his cellar for six days while the *Milice* conducted one of the most thorough checks which they had ever had in Antibes. Denis and Clément were to go to Lyons by train and it was upon the railway station that the *Milice* were keeping their most vigilant watch. It was not until the second week in March that the *miliciens* switched their attentions to another area and our two men were able to board the train.

'Frankly, I think we could have risked it earlier, old boy,' was Clément's view as they settled themselves in their second class compartment. 'I'm not in favour of hanging about when there's a job to be done.'

'I don't think we'd have ever got through,' Denis replied.

'Nonsense. Of course we'd have got through. These Vichy boys are no use at all.'

All the same, Denis thought, they could recognise a wireless set when they saw one. The battered suitcase which contained Denis's was on the rack above his head.

They reached Lyons without incident and there were able to meet their contact in a tiny café on the Quai Perrache. She was a tall, fair-haired woman of striking handsomeness whom they called Renée.[†] She was in fact an SOE agent, one of the first women to work in France for us. Denis was quartered in a small and grubby hotel near a railway bridge. The patron was extremely surly and extremely sleepy and hardly paid any attention to the *fiche* which Denis was obliged to

---

† Virginia Hall, US citizen. Renée was one of her field names. Her code name was HECKLER.

fill in, storing it away in a drawer which Denis was pleased to observe contained a large number of used *fiches* which had plainly never been surrendered to the authorities; Frenchmen are not always over-punctilious in their efforts to pay their taxes and to conceal *fiches* was a fairly elementary move in this evasion. Denis's room smelt abominably from the faulty drainage of the hotel (there was only the most primitive sanitation) and a large dog quite as surly as his master completed the picture. The dog was not such a bad thing in fact for it deterred inquisitive visitors by growling in the most offensive manner.

That night Denis went to the cinema with Clément. It was the first real moment of relaxation since he landed. The film was absorbing and as the lights went up in the interval, Denis observed: 'How marvellous this is!' Unfortunately he said it in English. He and Clément left the cinema quickly.

It was not always wise to relax too much.

Soon Denis was operating his wireless from the various safe houses which Renée was able to arrange through local contacts. One day, after he had been working for nearly a month, the *patron* stopped him.

'I am afraid I shall need your room from Monday,' he said.

Denis, knowing that the hotel was almost empty, replied: 'But why, monsieur? I pay my rent.'

'I shall require the room,' the man insisted. 'It's booked.'

'Well, perhaps I can move to another.'

'I shall need all the rooms.'

Denis realised that he would have to go and the sooner the better. He talked to Renée about it.

'We should have found you somewhere else before,' she

said. 'I don't much like the idea of you living in a hotel anyway.'

'Why not tell the hotel man the position?' Clément suggested. 'He'll probably change his tune if we tell him you're a British officer.'

'Shut up,' Renée said. 'That's just about the most stupid idea I've ever heard.'

'Anyway I've just about had enough of sleeping on the railway line,' Denis said. 'I wake up more exhausted than when I went to sleep.'

Renée met him next day in the Place Lyautey and by this time he was getting very worried for he had seen the *patron* walking with a member of the *Milice* down the embankment on which the hotel stood. Accordingly he paid off his bill – on which he was grossly overcharged – and left. He had long disembarrassed himself of the wireless set which was hidden in a safe house and only collected when needed for skeds by the protection team with whom Denis worked, while the money had been incorporated in the *Réseaux* funds, so he had nothing incriminating on him. Renée had procured him a proper identity card and a *carte de travail* which showed him to be a signal box operator on the SNCF. His name was Gerard Blanc.

'I must have somewhere for tonight,' Denis said.

'It's all right. I've fixed something for you. It isn't very grand, I'm afraid.'

Denis shrugged. The rooms were in an attic in the Rue Violette la Chatte. Denis and Renée were met by a hard-looking woman with a cigarette stuck between red-purple lips.

'What's it all about, love?' she demanded.

'I want a room for my friend,' Renée told her. 'Guillaume told you, didn't he?'

'Well, I see,' she said, staring at Denis. 'Means I've got to move.'

'Yes, of course, we'll compensate you whatever you think is fair. My friend wants to move in today.'

'You're in a hurry, love, aren't you?' she cackled.

At length terms were agreed and Denis moved into the small, perfume-laden flat. The prostitute was very inquisitive and kept demanding who Denis was and why Renée wanted him and whether he was an escaped prisoner; she explained how she loved soldiers, and could hardly be restrained from staying to comfort Denis herself.

Denis was able to continue his job without snags. He reported back to us that the railwaymen in one of their subgroups had perfected a new way of sabotaging trains which was both simple and undetectable; they put grit in the axles. The trains were able to move on from the sidings in which this had been done, only to seize up or burn out miles away, often in open country, so blocking the line until they could be shifted. We at once saw the value of this, for it meant that reprisals could not be taken against anyone as it was impossible to know where the damage had been caused.

The railwaymen became adept at this game and could judge almost to the mile where the eventual seizing up would take place. We were thus able to warn the local groups that such and such a train would be burning out in their area at such and such a date and they could then pilfer arms and other supplies from it while it lay helpless in open country. Ben Cowburn and his men added to the discomfiture of the

Boches by destroying several large railway cranes which were the only things capable of removing obstacles from the line. Our task in London was so to link these operations that they could happen with a bewildering simultaneity which, to the harassed Germans, seemed like black magic.

It was about this time that we started using the BBC extensively in the manner that was to become so famous. It was tiresome for us to have to burden our operators with messages confirming earlier arrangements when these confirmations could be made by another means, for the operator was in great danger all the time he was on the air and at home our object was always to find ways of lessening that time.

We now hit upon the idea of using the BBC's French Service for giving the word to field sections that men were to be dropped to them on such and such a night, that certain operations were to be undertaken, others cancelled and so forth. Innocent messages like *Le cheval est dans l'écurie* would convey to a striking force that they were to blow up wireless masts in a given area. These messages were sent, as most people know, through the *messages personnels* after the news. They were, of course, not code messages in the usual sense, for they conveyed only that a previous instruction was to be acted upon, not the text of the orders themselves. The Germans did not know this, at least until much later, and employed a large staff trying to decode messages which in fact were not in code at all, a somewhat arduous and definitely frustrating endeavour. Many of the messages had no application whatsoever and were merely designed to fill in time, for we nearly always filled up the full time allocated for messages, so that the Germans could not divine from their numbers the amount of activity they could expect at any one time. We kept them permanently jittery. Another objective was being fulfilled. Europe was not yet ablaze, but it was beginning to smoulder.

Chapter 5

Suspicion

'The *Milice* have been asking my landlady questions,' Clément said.

'What questions?' Renée asked.

'When I arrived, what I do, where I spend my evenings.'

'We'd better get you out,' Renée said. 'You'll stay with Gerard tonight and we'll get instructions about what to do with you.'

Denis and Clément left together. 'I'll just pop back to my place and get my things,' Clément said.

'Don't be a fool,' Denis replied. 'If you're suspected you don't want to go back.'

'Look, all my things are at the flat. I won't have anything unless I go back. You wait in that café over there. I won't be a minute.'

Before Denis could protest any further Clément had dashed off. Denis waited in the café and it was not long before Clément returned with a suitcase. 'All clear,' he said.

They set off for the Rue Violette la Chatte. It was getting late now and the streets were almost deserted. That was why Denis noticed the man who was following them.

II

'We've got to get Clément out,' Denis said to Renée. He had had the greatest difficulty in throwing off the man who was following him; by the time the morning came the original follower had called up help. The situation was critical. That afternoon Denis sent a message to us in London in which he explained briefly what had happened.

'I think the best thing is to recall Clément,' I said to Bourne-Paterson. 'I don't think he's fitting with the circuit.'

'What about Rake, then?' Bourne-Paterson asked. 'He seems to be doing a good job out there.'

'Yes, he does, doesn't he?' I observed wryly. 'I don't think we ought to bring him back yet. Wireless operators are much too scarce to bring 'em back after one scare.'

'Why don't we tack him on to Xavier?[†] They can use another W/T boy in Paris.'

'I don't much like hooking people on to new circuits. If he's recognised it means another whole section is suspect. Still, he said he'd shaken off his tail, didn't he? Yes, I think we'll risk it.'

Clément got out of Lyons and came back to England through Spain. Denis got our message to move to Paris. Renée gave him an address in a village just short of Chalons-sur-Saône where a man would help to get him across the demarcation line into occupied France. She also gave him 78,000 francs to take to Xavier, in accord with our instructions from London. On 3 May he set off.

A tiny shop labelled 'Jean Aimé – CHARBONS' was the address given to Denis. He found it easily and presented himself to Monsieur Aimé. The man was not expecting him but nevertheless agreed to talk to him in the back room of the shop.

'What can I do for you?' Monsieur Aimé demanded, somewhat suspicious.

[†] Field name of Richard Heslop, organiser of the MARKSMAN Circuit.

'I rather want to get across into the occupied zone,' Denis explained.

'That can be arranged easily enough,' said the *charbonnier*. 'Be at the farm at the far end of the village at six-thirty tomorrow morning. It has a red gate; you can't miss it. That will be 2,000 francs.'

The arrangement was brisk and businesslike and there was clearly a frequent service across the frontier. Denis stayed overnight in an auberge near the farm. After dinner he got into conversation with a young girl who, he found, was also making the crossing the next morning. They arranged to wake each other and Denis felt emboldened to ask her to do him a favour: 'If we are stopped—'

'Ah, that will not happen, Monsieur—'

'No, but if it does, will you tell them that you know that I came south from Paris and am now returning?'

'How could I know that?'

'You could say that we travelled south together.'

'We won't be stopped,' the girl said again. 'But if we are, I'll do what I can.'

There were nine people in the charcoal van in which Denis was to make the crossing. It was drawn by two horses. Most of the travellers looked rather shady and it was clear from the bundles which they carried that the majority of them were black marketeers returning to the occupied zone with loads of contraband food.

The cart creaked off down the road towards Chalons and then turned off down a rutted track towards some woods. Denis was sitting next to the girl whom he had met the previous evening and he asked her, in a whisper, whether she knew where the demarcation line was. She said she didn't, but that she thought it was on the far side of the woods. The cart entered the woods which were in the pale green leaf of late spring, and creaked onwards towards the frontier. Most of the travellers seemed to be old friends of Monsieur Aimé and they chatted and joked with him quite unconcernedly. Denis and the girl were at the back of the cart and felt rather out of things.

The cart came round a corner of the track and they could see open country. The cart rolled ponderously on. With a dramatic suddenness three German soldiers, under a sergeant, stepped out from behind the cover of the trees and grabbed at the reins of the horses. As they were plodding forward with the greatest reluctance this seemed an unnecessary precaution.

'What's going on here?'

'I'm giving some friends a lift,' Monsieur Aimé replied with a wink that suggested earlier complicity.

'You know this is strictly forbidden,' said the sergeant.

Aimé shrugged. He reached inside his pocket and drew out two bars of chocolate and some money. He handed them down to the sergeant who stood irresolute. Monsieur Aimé added a packet of cigarettes and folded his arms.

The sergeant tucked them away in his pocket and Monsieur Aimé made to move on. The sergeant grabbed the reins again, however, and said 'Not so fast.'

'But sergeant – surely—'

'My officer is getting suspicious,' the sergeant said, 'at the fact that we haven't brought anyone in lately. He's getting questions from the CO. I'm afraid I shall have to ask you for a couple of your passengers again.'

To Denis's horror, the driver did not protest. Plainly, this had happened before. 'You can take the two at the back,' Monsieur Aimé jerked his thumb at Denis and the girl who were at the back. There was no time to move and to run would be fatal. The sergeant and a private came round and undid the flap of the cart. 'Come on, you two,' the sergeant said. The girl and Denis were forced to jump to the ground.

The cart creaked forward.

There were five German officers in the interrogation room at the Controle Central in Chalons-s-Saône and they questioned Denis with great persistence.

'I tell you I came south to see my aunt in Lyons who is sick. I am on my way back to Paris.'

'It is quite true, Messieurs,' said the girl who had been brought in with Denis.

'How can you explain all this money you have with you? How much was it – 78,000 francs? This aunt of yours, is she very rich as well as ill?' They all laughed. 'Is she perhaps also a leading light in the black market as well as being rich and ill?' Again they laughed and Denis saw that it was best to humour them; he smiled ruefully as if to suggest that they were too clever for him. This seemed to be successful in averting further examination either of himself or his papers, and he was put in the cells overnight. The next morning he went in front of the magistrate together with another bunch of supposed black marketeers.

'Three weeks,' said the magistrate, 'and 15,000 francs.'

Denis spent his three weeks in constant fear that someone might decide to pass the time by examining the validity of his papers, but they did not do so and at the end of the time he was released, along with those sentenced at the same time as himself and was at liberty to proceed – northwards.

He went straight to Auteuil where Renée had told him his wireless set would be waiting for him in the house of a certain Princess Wilma. The princess's house was a large one set behind a screen of tall trees and approached along a broad sweep of drive; cupolas stood at each end of the front elevation of the house. A maid opened the door. 'The princess is not at home,' she announced. 'Go away,' she added quickly. 'Go away. Hurry.'

Gathering that something was very wrong, Denis hurried out of the drive and went back into the centre of Paris. There he treated himself to a large dinner at the Boeuf sur le Toit. As he was having his coffee, a new waiter came on duty. No sooner did he see Denis than he came straight over to his table. 'Why, Monsieur Rake! What a long time it has been!' Denis regretted that his nostalgia had brought him back to a restaurant where he was known, nevertheless he turned the meeting to good account, for through the friendly waiter he was able to ask if there was anywhere safe for him to stay the night. The waiter told him to wait on the stairs for a moment while he spoke to the *patron*. After a minute, the waiter rejoined him. 'This way, sir.' He took Denis upstairs, asking questions in a loud voice about where Denis had been and what he was doing in Paris. 'I think this gentleman will help you,' the waiter said at last, opening the door of one of the private dining rooms. Denis walked in and the waiter closed the door behind him. Sitting alone at the table in the window was an SS officer.

Denis spun round, but the door was already shut. The waiter smiled. 'It's all right,' he said reassuringly. Denis looked back at the SS man. The latter put down his napkin and smiled.

'Come and have something to drink.' Denis knew that

whatever was going on he would have to play it out, so he sat down and soon he and the SS man were talking amiably. Apparently he was a very wretched man, sensitive and artistic, who had found himself, owing to his family connections, recruited into the SS, in spite of his detestation of Hitler. He often came to the Boeuf sur le Toit to get away from things. He said that Denis could stay the night in his flat in the Rue Tilsit.

In spite of the SS man's melancholy bonhomie, Denis was glad to get away from him the next morning and set out to give the slip to anyone who might be following him. He took the métro and he climbed up to the Sacré Coeur, doubling back through the narrow back streets of Montmartre. At length he was convinced that there was no one after him, so he set out for the Café Napoléon near the Folies Bergère.

His contact was to be a tall thick-set man with a Roman nose. He was supposed to be there every alternate hour from ten o'clock onwards. But he did not turn up the first four times that Denis went. Denis seemed to be spending all his time at the café and was growing very self-conscious about it. He resolved to try once more and then give it up. Although he knew the times at which his man would be there, Denis had no orders about how to contact him. He could think of nothing better to do than drop his wallet containing a picture of a man called Wilkinson, another agent whom he knew to be in the Paris Circuit, at the feet of his contact.

With any luck he would recognise it and know who Denis was. He put this plan into operation when, on his fifth visit to the Café Napoléon, a man answering the description Renée had given him entered. Denis dropped his wallet at his feet. The man bent down and picked up the wallet which lay open.

He saw the picture and looked for a fraction of a second at Denis and blinked to show he had recognised it. Denis rose and followed the man out of the café, having already paid his bill; this last was an important hint given in training – it enabled our men to follow their contacts without wasting time and drawing attention by calling for the bill.

Denis's contact turned out to be Xavier himself. Denis explained to him the difficulty in which he stood and told him that he was ready to do whatever Xavier thought best. 'My wireless set should have gone through to the princess's at Auteuil, but I've got a feeling that something's gone wrong there. They were going to put it in a consignment of vegetables and my guess is that the Boches have discovered it.'

'I'll send a man to find out,' Xavier said.

The man never returned. They waited for him in a safe flat and finally Xavier said: 'He must have had it. I think the best thing would be for you to go back to Lyons and see what's happened. If necessary you can pick up another set and come back. Report back to me when you get there.'

'Where will you be?'

The agent whose real name was Edward Wilkinson and whose code name was Alexandre was also present, and he suggested that they should all proceed at once to Limoges, separately. There they could rendezvous in the unoccupied zone and could operate with greater ease. This plan was adopted and they agreed to meet at the Hotel des Faisans in two days' time. Denis still had no papers with which to cross the demarcation line, so he was forced to use his ingenuity. Again he used the method favoured by black marketeers. At a railwaymen's café he managed to get put in touch with the driver of the night train to the south. For 5,000 francs the latter agreed to smuggle him over the line hidden in the train's fuse-box. This was a roomy compartment and immune from the attentions of the border police. Denis arrived safely in Limoges. He went straight to the Hotel des Faisans which stood in a small side street in a poorish quarter. He walked past it to make sure that there were no *miliciens* about and then entered. The landlady was a white-haired woman, small and sullen, whose face lit up with a rather artificial smile when Denis said that he would be staying for several nights. He was given room number thirteen.

That night and the morning of the next day passed without Xavier and Alexandre arriving. Denis was forced to stay in his room, waiting for them. The landlady came in with her pass-key to find him still there at three in the afternoon. 'Are you ill, monsieur?'

'I'm waiting for some friends of mine whom I met on the train,' Denis replied. 'I have some business to conclude.'

At that moment there was an imperious ringing at the bell downstairs. Madame hurried away. A few minutes later there were heavy footsteps on the stairs. They halted outside the door of number thirteen. Denis heard Madame say something and then she opened the door with her pass-key. It was the *Milice*.

'Come on,' said the officer in charge.

'What is all this?' Denis demanded.

'He has some friends coming for him,' the landlady sang out with gleeful subservience.

'To have a drink,' Denis said. 'I demand an explanation. What is all this about?'

'Wait here with him,' said the officer to two of his men. 'You two come with me. We'll wait downstairs for the others.'

Denis was powerless. The officer and his men went downstairs with the landlady to catch Xavier and Alexandre. Half an hour later there was the sound of a brief struggle in the hall and then again the footsteps on the stairs. Xavier and Alexandre were shoved into the room. Denis looked at them and shrugged. To his surprise, they both shot him looks of the greatest hatred. With horror he realised what had happened: they thought that he had betrayed them.

He could do nothing to disabuse them of this misconception, for they were put in separate cells to wait for interrogation.

'Who are these two men you arranged to meet?' was the first question that Denis's interrogator, an Alsatian by the name of Morel, put to him.

'I met them on the train. I arranged that we should have a drink together as I thought they might be useful to me in my business.'

'Why do you have all this money with you?'

'One needs it these days,' Denis replied lamely. Again he was hoping to be taken for a black marketeer.

'70,000 francs in 10,000 notes,' the Alsatian said.

'Is it that much?'

The interrogator looked up suddenly straight into Denis's eyes. 'Tell me,' he said, 'why are you working for the Germans?'

Denis blinked: 'I beg your pardon?'

'Why are you working for the Germans? It's quite obvious, you know. These notes are unpinned. If they had come from a French bank they would certainly have been pinned together at some date. But these,' he held them up to the light, 'have never been pinned. And they say that we paid too much attention to details!'

'I am not working for the Germans.'

'My dear fellow, you cannot trick me. Not that I know of any reason why you should want to. After all, I come from Alsace, you have no need to check up on me.'

Denis detected something in the man's voice which suggested otherwise, and he decided to take a chance.

'I don't work for the Boches—' he began, and was relieved that the man did not react to his use of the word. 'I work for the British.'

'The British! That explains another source from which unpinned notes might come.'

Denis went on. 'Look, I and my friends need your help. I can see you are not very fond of the Boches. Will you help us?' Denis's hunch proved correct, for the man agreed to do what he could. The next day he had Denis taken to his flat for further interrogation and when the *Milice* escort had left he introduced Denis to his French wife and their son and daughter.

'I will certainly do what I can to get your friends out of jail,' he told Denis. 'I've also got a plan to get you away. I'll tell you the exact details tomorrow.'

The next day Morel told Denis that he had some bad news for him: Xavier and Alexandre had both been transferred to a prison farther south. There was no way of getting them out. Denis's escape was all set, however, and at once they left the flat for the prison hospital. Here Denis was put into a white gown and shown into a room where a number of out-patients were waiting for X-rays. A door led out to the street. Morel had warned him that he could not allow much time between letting Denis into the waiting room and giving the alarm. He feared for his wife and children if he were suspected. Denis edged his way towards the door and walked boldly out into the street – straight into the arms of two *miliciens*. He was promptly returned to the jail.

The next day a Corsican thug, a member of the *Milice*, came into the cell in which Denis had been locked and told him that he was moving. 'Like this,' he added, snapping a handcuff on to Denis's wrist.

'Here's the prisoner,' said the governor. 'As escorting officer you'd better sign for him.'

The escorting officer was Morel. Plainly he had not been suspected of engineering Denis's amateurish escape and now they set off, together with the Corsican, to the station.

'Where are they going?' Denis asked as their car pulled away from the curb.

'Lyons,' was the reply.

As soon as they were on the train Morel explained to the Corsican that Denis was a British Officer. Denis looked anxiously to see what the reaction would be. It seemed reasonably favourable, for the Corsican at once produced a bottle of wine and they all drunk happily to Britain as the train rolled east.

At Lyons they drove straight to the central prison. Denis was taken away from Morel and the mellowed Corsican, and led along a row of cells. At last a door was unlocked and he was pushed inside. There were two men in the cell already: Xavier and Alexandre.

III

For four days they refused to have anything to do with him. They behaved as if he were not there. Again and again Denis went through the story of what had happened, of how powerless he had been to warn them both. It was futile. By neither word nor gesture did they acknowledge that they had heard or believed him. They talked to each other, but never to him; they played card games which they did not even allow Denis to watch. Convinced that he had betrayed them, they were furious not only at being caught but also at having all their plans disrupted and their circuit left leaderless. None of them felt in danger of death, unless they were extradited to the Germans. The Vichy men were not vindictive and allowed them cards and books. Neither Xavier nor Alexandre shared either of these with Denis. Again and again he tried to explain his innocence. Nothing convinced them.

On the fourth day, a Red Cross parcel addressed to Xavier was thrown into the cell. Somehow the others had managed to contact some friends outside prison, presumably before Denis joined them. By now Denis was sunk in the depths of depression, for to be suspected of treachery was the final straw. Xavier and Alexandre enjoyed the contents of the parcel with the greatest relish, chocolate, tinned meat, cigarettes, condensed milk, dried fruit and so on. Their consciences were picked by Denis's reproachful expression and derisively they allowed him a teaspoonful of condensed milk, for he had only the roughest food. They continued to keep him in Coventry.

Meanwhile, Alexandre had managed to get on friendly terms, with the aid of the Red Cross cigarettes, with one of the guards who promised to bring a file in a piece of bread. This old-fashioned deception was discovered by the guard's superior officer and Alexandre was hauled off to solitary confinement in the next cell to his erstwhile guard.

Xavier, even on his own, continued the unremitting silence, though it must have got him down as badly as it did Denis.

A week passed and then both Xavier and Denis were transferred to another prison, still Lyons. Here they were shackled by the feet and left in a dark cell. Denis feared that their treatment would worsen, even that they would be returned to Paris and the Gestapo, but suddenly they were taken up to the Commandant's office and asked to sign a declaration saying they had been well treated. Denis looked at Xavier, wondering whether to sign. Xavier read the piece of paper and then glanced at Denis and nodded contemptuously. Both men signed. A change of attitude now occurred in their captors and both men were treated as escaping British officers. They were given a lavish meal to which Alexandre was brought, released from solitary. Still the other men refused to speak to Denis. It was a sad celebration. For another month they were kept in the same quarters and still the other men refused to pay even the smallest attention to Denis's presence. In the last days of October they were taken to the Commandant's office.

'We have decided to let you go,' he said in a tired voice, that of a man who had had many conflicting orders and could not guess what would happen next. Denis could scarcely believe what was being said. By now he was almost too depressed to care. 'Get out of France as quickly as you can,' were the Commandant's last words.

The three Britons were given a small amount of money and railway warrants to take them south. On 1 November 1942, the prison gates shut behind them. They were free. Xavier turned to Denis and said the first words he had addressed to him for the four months they had been together: 'Push off.'

Denis stared at him, tears in his eyes. By now he hated them for their cruelty as much as they loathed him for his supposed treachery.

'Go on,' Alexandre added. 'Get out.'

Denis turned from them and walked away without a word.

IV

He made for Perpignan. There he stayed in a brothel near the station. I may say that this was not from inclination but because if you stayed in brothels you were not, naturally, expected to fill in a *fiche*. This is the reason for the frequency with which they were used. Denis was anxious to shake off the Vichy police lest they change their minds and re-arrest him. Already there were rumours that the Boches were going to occupy the whole of France and he knew he must get out before that happened. He had no contact in Perpignan and therefore gambled on the fact that most of the gendarmerie were ready to help the Resistance whenever possible (the gendarmerie were quite distinct from the *Milice* and in fact despised them); he approached a gendarme officer in a café and asked for his help.

He struck lucky: the Commandant Fette was a man of firm patriotism. He took him back to his flat where two men on the run were already hiding, sharing the limited accommodation with the Commandant's wife and their nine children. He was cheerfully greeted by the other two fugitives (a happy change from his treatment at the hands of Xavier and Alexandre) and soon they were all enjoying a huge meal, procured at great expense by the Commandant. There was no room for Denis to sleep at the Commandant's, so that evening the latter said in a jovial tone, 'You'd better come along with me.' He took Denis to the Police Station. Here he was introduced as the cousin of the Commandant and given a comfortable cell. Each morning he went back to the flat and remained there all day, eating the massive meals which the Commandant insisted on providing. Apart from forming a refuge for escapers, this flat was also an arsenal; the Commandant's daughters had a chicken coop on the roof which was packed with contraband arms brought across from Spain at the end of the civil war.

After a week's stay with the Commandant and his family, Denis and his two companions moved down the coast towards the Spanish border. For safety's sake, the Commandant arranged for them to travel in a Black Maria.

On the night of 10 November they crawled across the bleak frontier near Portbou. The next morning, as they walked through the town of Figueras, they were arrested by the Spanish police. Tedious weeks of internment followed during which fate played Denis another strange trick: his hut-mate in the concentration camp at Miranda was a man named George Wilkinson; he turned out to be Alexandre's brother. He and Denis became firm friends. Denis was still very depressed at what he considered the failure of his mission. He had an attack of dysentery which further weakened him and he was a very sick man by the time our embassy in Madrid was able to get him released. He was told, when he reached Madrid, that the Ambassador would see him.

'I should like to thank you, sir, for all you've done,' Denis said. 'I really do appreciate it more than I can say.'

Sir Samuel Hoare regarded the sad figure before him with dapper disdain. 'Really,' he observed, 'I sometimes think you people are more trouble than you're worth.'

Chapter 6

First Flames

The Bordeaux area was one especially suited to our purposes. Just inside the occupied zone, a group operating from there could have ready access both to the north and to the unoccupied zone. We landed Claude de Baissac there late in July 1942. By the middle of 1943 Claude had recruited a small and efficient organisation including a Frenchman named Fragonard who was the leader of his subsection within the group. His code name was Le Chef. He had already canvassed likely resisters in the district and he was therefore a valuable aid to Claude in the early days.

Claude was soon anxious to establish permanent contact with us in London and we decided to drop him a wireless operator. After our successes in destroying the engine sheds at Troyes the RAF listened to our requests for help with more readiness and it was agreed that they would drop Harry Peulevé to the Bordeaux group during the next suitable moon period.

Harry was another of those who came to us very much on their own initiative. Having heard that French-speaking Britons were at a premium, he phoned the War Office and asked to be put in touch with us. He was a sergeant in the BEF at the beginning of the war, having acquired British citizenship by some legalistic fluke, although his father was a French consular official in North Africa. He was told by our selection board that his French was not really good enough, but his name went forward and he was trained as a wireless operator.

He was very keen to get to the field and when Claude's need for a wireless operator became acute we agreed that he should go. De Guélis and I went with him to the airfield from which he was due to take off. Although the moon was right, it did not seem a very pleasant night, for the wind was gusty and the RAF seriously considered scrapping the whole thing. 'I hope they don't, that's all,' was Harry's comment, 'this is the bit I want to get over.' The jumping was never a thing that our agents particularly relished, less because they feared the actual drop (they would never have got this far had that been the case) than because, dangling on the end of a parachute, you never knew what to expect when you hit the ground and there was the risk of being picked up even before you got your harness off.

The routine of the drop was more or less invariable. The plane flew low over the dropping area, at about 600 feet, and the agent hung ready over the aperture. At the dispatcher's shout of 'GO' he let himself fall; the static lines snatched at and opened his parachute and within about fifteen seconds he was on the ground.

'GO.'

Harry let himself go. He fell and then the webbing of his chute caught him up like a netted fish. Yet he seemed to be falling much too fast. He yanked frantically at the lines of his chute, realising that somehow it was twisted and had not opened properly. He had only a few seconds to straighten it out. Now he seemed to be falling less fast but still the rigging lines were tangled. He knew he would hit the ground with a tremendous crack. Branches snapped and then the ground smashed into him. He rolled over with a groan and groped for his pistol. Silence. He banged the release mechanism of his chute and the harness fell away from him. He tried to pull himself to his feet and the pain cut him like a knife. He fell again. Still there was silence in the wooded field into which he had dropped. He put the pistol on the ground beside him and reached for his Thermos flask; there was tea in it, well laced with rum, and he took a long gulp. He knew he had broken his leg. He dared not feel it with his hands.

He looked around. Silhouetted against the skyline in the middle distance was a farmhouse. He started to crawl towards it, dragging himself forward inch by inch over the stony ground, with the undergrowth pulling at his fractured leg, leaning back again and again to disentangle it from brambles and hawthorn. Inch by inch, forcing himself with gritted teeth, he advanced on the farmhouse, his forearms raw with the effort of pulling him forward.

He reached the farmyard and dragged himself across the caked mud of it. A dog howled in the back somewhere. Harry thumped feebly on the door of the house. There was a long silence, so with a piece of stick he tapped again. An old lady answered the door.

'Help me, madame,' Harry said. The pain was coming now, growing and growing, faster and faster.

'What is happening? Who are you?' She bent down and whispered to him. 'Are you – a Gaullist?'

'That's right,' he replied, 'a Gaullist.'

'So am I.'

'Hide me,' was all Harry could groan.

The old lady went and fetched her son, a strong and bronzed

farmer. Harry at once saw that he had struck lucky. The farmer said that he would hide Harry in a disused part of the house where no one ever went. He hurried off to get a wheelbarrow. Harry fainted with the agony as they tried to lift him into it. They forced some brandy down his throat and gave up the attempt. At length they improvised a stretcher on which they carried him into a cobweb-filled annexe. They lit a candle and examined his leg. When he saw the extent of the injury he passed out again. The bone was sticking through the torn flesh like a knitting needle through wool.

They gave him a bottle of brandy to drink and said they would send for a doctor next morning. Obviously the people at the farm must have had a pretty shrewd suspicion who Harry was, but they did not bother him with questions though they did ignore his delirious demand that no doctor should be called.

'How did this happen?' was the doctor's first question.

'I fell out of a tree,' was the reply. 'A fig tree.'

The doctor looked at the farmer and shrugged and said sorrowfully, 'But there are no figs at this time of year, monsieur.'

Harry had to go to hospital. He fought the suggestion fiercely when it was first made, but the doctor said in a meaningful voice that he would take care of the staff. If he did not go to hospital gangrene was almost certain. He would die.

Harry gave the farmer a message to take to a certain address in Bordeaux in order that Claude might know what had happened. The wireless set which had been dropped with him had to be located with the greatest speed. Claude would see to it. Harry half hoped that Claude would come and see him in hospital, for that loneliness which so afflicted agents in the field was already affecting him. He knew that the farmer could be trusted, for if he had not betrayed him yet it was unlikely that he would do so in the future.

The fact that Harry was able to go to hospital and not be given away either by the doctor who operated on his leg, the nuns who nursed him, or the barber who came to shave him, is a sufficient indication of the solidarity, if I may use that term, of the Resistance spirit. That our men were able to move about with a fair immunity may be demonstrated by the fact that Claude arranged for Harry to have visitors and for a wireless to be installed in his room so that he could listen to the BBC news. One of Harry's visitors was Peter Churchill, who came specially from Antibes to see him. I am not sure that I would have been very pleased had I known of this gross breach of security, but it is evidence both of Churchill's wonderful sense of team spirit and the confidence he had in himself, a confidence he was able to transmit to others.

Nothing could be further from the truth in any attempt to analyse the personality of our organisation than the notion that we were constituted out of a number of brilliant and volatile individualists; men like Churchill worked exclusively with a team and knew that they were useless without it. They seldom attempted anything on their own except when it took the burden off someone else. Most of our agents were ordinary men and women and it was their ability to maintain that appearance of ordinariness while performing extraordinary actions which most distinguished them.

Harry was terrified of the operation which was due to be performed on him, for he thought that he might talk under the influence of the chloroform with consequences disastrous to himself and his colleagues. In the event, all passed off without incident, though he never knew whether this was because he did not say anything or because what he said was ignored by those present.

Claude de Baissac was anxious to get Harry out of the convent hospital as soon as possible. The staff were magnificent, but you could not tell when the Gestapo might decide to make a swoop and then the staff would be powerless; Harry's cover story was hazy and would not stand investigation. For him to remain in hospital might endanger his and his nurses' lives.

In late August, when Harry had been in hospital for two and a half months, the doctor said he could be moved. He had had a desperate time. The bones in his leg had failed to knit and a further operation had become necessary to pin them together. Claude ordered Raymond, a Spanish anarchist refugee, to look after Harry during his convalescence.

Raymond was a burly Basque, ruthless and without fear; somewhere over forty years old, he preserved a youthful physique and a contempt for danger which made him a trying as well as a trusted companion. Claude had fixed for them to rest up in a safe farm some miles out of Bordeaux while arrangements were made for getting Harry out of the country once his leg could stand the trip. They travelled to the farm in an ambulance whose bell Raymond clanged delightedly, clearing German soldiers out of the road with reckless authority.

Harry discovered that the farmhouse was one commonly used by escaping prisoners of war making their way south and the farmer and his wife were hardened resisters. The farm lay in rolling country, far from any big town and was seldom visited by anyone. Harry and Raymond were made very comfortable there and Raymond helped the farmer with his work. Harry rested in the house while his leg slowly healed. Raymond proved an excellent companion, full of stories and indignation over the way the Allies had treated the Spanish Government. 'If they'd only helped us when we asked them we wouldn't all be in this mess today,' he would shout, and the blood would pulse in the hole a piece of shrapnel had made in his head during the defence of Barcelona.

One day when the farmer and Raymond were out in the fields (it was near harvest and there was much to do) Harry was sitting in the orchard behind the house reading a book when he heard a stranger talking to Madame Anjou, the farmer's wife. Harry took his pistol from his pocket and slid it under the blanket which covered his knees.

'Here's a visitor for you,' said Madame Anjou, leading the stranger up to the chair in which Harry was sitting. The stranger was a man of about twenty-five, fair-haired and blue-eyed, who walked with an agreeable looseness which made it no surprise when Madame Anjou informed Harry that he was an RAF officer.

'Sit down,' Harry said, 'I can do with some company. My pal's out helping the farmer. How did you get here?'

'Came from Paris,' the man replied in English. 'Is it all right to talk English? My French is jolly rotten.'

'Escaped from a POW camp?' Harry asked.

'That's the ticket.'

'When were you captured?'

'I was shot down, old boy, over Holland. About a month ago.'

'What were you flying?'

'Spitfire. Tell me, how long have you been here?'

'A while,' Harry replied. Something about the man's manner made him uneasy. 'Where were you stationed in England?'

'Near Cambridge,' was the reply.

The stillness of the summer day gave the scene a deadly innocence.

'Really?' Harry said. 'Do you know that little pub near St Peter's College? The – what's it called?'

The man scratched his head. 'I can't remember.'

'The College Arms,' Harry said, as if suddenly remembering.

'Of course,' said the other.

An insect rasped in the high grass. There is no St Peter's College at Cambridge, nor is there a 'College Arms'. Harry tightened his grip on his revolver. The sound of voices came over the hedge. The men were returning from the fields for their lunch.

'Tell me,' went on the RAF officer, 'how are you going to get across the frontier from here?'

'I don't know,' Harry said. 'And if I did I wouldn't tell you.'

'I say, what do you mean?'

Harry undramatically uncovered the revolver. 'Just sit there and don't move.'

'Now look here – are you a Jerry or something?'

'Just sit.'

'Henri, Henri, where's this visitor Madame Anjou—'

Raymond stopped in the gateway to the orchard, seeing in the bright sunshine the dull metal of the revolver pointing at the stranger. 'What's going on?'

'We have a new friend,' Harry said grimly, 'come to question us.'

At once the RAF man burst out into voluble French: 'I assure you, Monsieur, I don't know what this chap's talking about—'

'Your French has suddenly improved,' observed Harry drily.

Raymond turned the RAF man around with a cruel grin. 'So you came to ask us questions.'

Quickly, Harry explained how he had trapped the man with the name of the fake pub and college. Raymond grinned. 'Wait there,' he said.

In a moment he was back, carrying a box which he put down on the grass floor of the orchard.

'Look, you're making a bloody silly mistake.'

'Who are you?' smiled Raymond. 'Who are you, please?'

'I am an escaped RAF officer.'

Still grinning, Raymond hit the man in the face. 'No,' he said, 'the truth.'

Madame Anjou came and said: 'Lunch is ready.'

'We're busy, Madame,' Raymond said. 'We will be in any minute. But just now we are busy.' He bowed and Madame withdrew. He turned back to the RAF man and said: 'Please don't keep us from our lunch.' His expression changed with terrifying swiftness. 'Now who are you?'

'I don't understand what this is all about. You must believe—'

A small sapling grew under the orchard wall. Raymond picked up the box he had brought from the house and walked over to the sapling. 'Watch me,' he said. 'Carefully.' Raymond attached a detonator to the sapling and then turned to the others and grinned again. 'Are you watching carefully?' He lit the fuse and stepped back. The explosion twisted the slim tree to green pulp. Raymond came back to where the others were sitting in the sunshine. He took a length of rope from the box and another detonator. 'If you would be so good,' he said to the stranger, pointing to a tree, thick and gnarled in the middle of the orchard.

'What are you going to do?'

'Ask a few questions.' Raymond grabbed at the other's arm and dragged him to the tree, his grip like steel. In a moment the man was lashed to the tree. Harry watched as if he were in a dream. Raymond fastened the detonator to the tree between the man's legs. Casually he uncoiled the fuse and fretted it between his fingers, shortening it. 'No sense in dragging these things out,' he observed amiably.

The stranger watched him with cold terror. Raymond gave Harry a wink and lit a match, allowing it to burn round until there was a good flame. 'I should hate to have it go out and spoil everything.'

'What do you want to know?' the man said, in a low voice.

Raymond looked surprised, as if he had forgotten the man's presence. 'Who are you? Who sent you here? What do you know and how much have you told? That sort of thing,' he explained.

'I am a German officer.'

'Ah. He is a German officer,' Raymond said, untying the man and leading him gently by the arm back to where Harry was sitting.

The man knew that the game was up and he told them everything. He had been educated in England and had been sent to try to blow the escape line south from Paris. So far he had not made a report.

With the man's confession, the tension had gone out of the scene. It was almost with regret that Harry said: 'You know what we must do, don't you?'

The man nodded. 'The fortune of war,' he said stiffly. 'It might have been you.'

Raymond put his hands on his hips and said: 'We may as well get it over. I want my lunch. Give me the gun.'

Harry said: 'Wait.' He turned to the German. 'Have you a last letter to your family you want me to send?'

'No thank you.'

'Are you a Catholic? Would you like to see a priest?'

'What is this—?' Raymond began.

'I'm in charge here,' Harry said.

'I would like to see a priest.'

Harry said: 'Raymond, go into the village and get a priest.' Raymond hesitated. 'Do as I say, Raymond.'

The Basque rose and left the orchard. Harry sat there with the sun coming over his shoulder into the fresh face of the man opposite him. Neither of them spoke. The revolver pointed at the man's heart. There was nothing to do but wait.

'The funny thing is,' the man said after a long while, 'I know Cambridge quite well. I went up there for the Greek play once.'

'I hardly know it at all,' Harry said. 'Don't think that was the only thing which gave you away. I had guessed before I asked the question that something was wrong about you.'

'What?'

'I don't know. Your hair is too short.'

The farmer's wife came again to the gate of the orchard, stood for a moment and then went away.

'Are you hungry? Would you like something to eat?' The man shook his head.

Raymond came back with an aged priest, bustling the old man impatiently. The priest seemed frightened, as if he himself were to die. The two of them, the priest and the German, turned their backs to the others and the priest whispered and whispered in the still of the orchard and the German nodded from time to time as if he, too, were impatient. Harry held the gun in the man's back.

At last both men crossed themselves and the priest with a last look at the three men walked from the orchard out into the lane. Harry pulled the trigger. The man fell. Raymond took the revolver and put it to the man's temple and fired again.

'Just for luck,' he said.

Shortly after this, Claude de Baissac came to the farm and told Harry that arrangements had been made for him to be passed on down the escape line into Spain. His leg was in a bad way and it was plainly senseless to keep him in France any longer. He was still able to walk only with the aid of two sticks.

It was with great regret that he said farewell to Raymond who had been so loyal a friend. Raymond's sense of humour was on the robust side and he had insisted on parcelling up the body of the German officer they had shot in a foil-lined packing case which he had sent off by rail to Gestapo headquarters in the Avenue Foch, Paris. Inside was a note which read, 'With the compliments of British Intelligence.'

Harry went back with Claude into Bordeaux where the escape route could most easily be picked up.

'The place is alive with escapers,' Claude said as they rode into the town. 'The other day there was a great horde of British sailors down by the harbour, pretending to be Portuguese. They were talking English so loudly you couldn't miss it – but the Boches managed to!'

Harry's first link was at Roquefort, between Bordeaux and Pau. Here Le Chef, Claude's French link, had told him to get in touch with a Monsieur Carre, an architect. He was forced to sit in the man's waiting room, which was full of people, while his name was taken in. He felt very conspicuous: an obvious resister. However, no one seemed to worry about him and Monsieur Carre offered to put him up in a flat in his own building. This Harry refused and accommodation was found for him above the shop of a hairdresser who was a Communist. He paid highly for the room.

The escape line ahead of him was surfeited with customers and he had to wait several weeks before Monsieur Carre gave the word that he could move on; in Pau he was to contact a certain Abbé Theophile who would be in a church in the Rue St Jacques at eleven the next morning. Harry went by bus to Pau. The weeks in Roquefort had allowed his leg to improve somewhat, but he still suffered considerable pain if he tried to walk more than a few hundred yards.

'Abbé Theophile?'

'That's me,' said the burly figure by the altar steps.

'I am sent by Dumas.'

'Follow me, old chap.' The Abbé led Harry through a dark corridor into a tiny room where vestments were hanging. He shut the door and bolted it behind him. 'We shan't be disturbed here,' he said, removing his cassock to reveal a chest full of medals.

'You've been in the service?' asked Harry.

'Sergeant, in the Foreign Legion,' was the unlikely reply. 'But I took up the ministry afterwards. One needs security.' He glanced upwards for a minute to acknowledge the eternal nature of his security. 'They told me you were coming. So I fixed up for you to meet some people I think you'll find helpful. We've got about an hour. I'll show you round the church.'

The Abbé showed Harry the stained-glass windows and the carved pulpit of which he was quite as proud as he was of the hand grenades stored under the porch and the cache of pistols in the organ loft.

An hour later Harry had met one of the Pyrenean guides whose job it was to be to guide the party over the mountains.

'Will there be much walking?' Harry asked.

'A bit,' was the reply.

Till nightfall, Harry wandered about the streets of Pau, staying in cafés for as long as he decently could. At one of them some frontier guides were resting, their great Pyrenean Mountain Dogs lying docilely at their feet.

That night Harry went up to the foot of the mountains together with three other escapers and a band of saccharine smugglers. They lay up all the next day at a hut in the deserted approaches to the Col du Pourtalet. The next night they were told to be ready to move as soon as it was dark. At nine o'clock the march began.

Before they left the path to climb through the mountains the guide turned to the party and said: 'Keep up, whatever you do; anyone who drops behind will have to be left. We must be over the border by daybreak.'

By midnight Harry was in agony from his leg. But not until nine the next morning, after zigzagging back and forth across the snow did they reach Spain. He had climbed through the mountains for twelve hours on a leg which could barely support him when he walked down the street. When he returned to England he came up to see me in the flat in Orchard Court.

'Sorry I made a mess of it,' he said. 'When can I go back and try again?'

Chapter 7

Cradle of the Resistance

Both Denis Rake and Harry Peulevé were the victims of unfortunate flukes and it said a great deal for both of them that they were able to weather this spell of bad luck and eventually return to France and complete missions of equal danger to those in which, through no fault of their own, they had failed the first time. I shall recount these in due time. On the whole, in spite of misfortunes of this kind, our position at the end of 1942 was considerably healthier than we might have expected at the beginning of it. In the absence of German interference until the very end of the year, the *Réseaux* in the south of France were in the healthiest condition. This was due, in large part, to the magnificent work of Hilaire,[†] one of our very first recruits, who built up an intricate network of groups before the Germans occupied the whole of France and maintained it superbly afterwards.

Hilaire started off the war as a batman, having been a mining technician before it; as a result he had been employed in the Belgian mines and this fact accounted for his mastery of French; although he always spoke with a telltale Belgian accent this passed unremarked as there were many Belgians in France during the war years. Hilaire's simple ambition was to take out to dinner after the war the officer whose batman he had been at the beginning

---

[†] George Starr, organiser of the WHEELWRIGHT Circuit.

of it. This was achieved after the liberation; at that time Hilaire was a Colonel and his erstwhile master a Major; for three years in constant danger of death, this was a modest reward. Hilaire typifies the sort of person who was best suited to our work. He appeared on the surface a man of the most unassuming character and you would certainly pass him without a second glance; this was something we were not unwilling to have the Germans do to our men. Underneath he was a person of great patience and determination. Both were vital qualities. Hilaire built up his series of *Réseaux* with the patience of a genuine strategist, never bothering about any fireworks, reserving his best and final effect for the days when it would best serve the cause to which we were all devoted – the extirpation of the German forces in France.

His patient strategy may be demonstrated by the fact that no one of his many *Réseaux* from the Landes through Lot-et-Garonne, part of the Dordogne, Lot proper, Gers Tarn, Aude down as far as the Hautes Pyrenees on the Spanish border, knew of the existence of any other. When you consider that this area was as large as Yorkshire you may have some idea of the extent of ground which Hilaire and his lieutenants covered. When the call came for action in the days immediately before and after D-Day, Hilaire's *Réseaux* were so perfectly organised that each was able, in spite of knowing nothing of its neighbours, to be perfectly co-ordinated with them by ourselves in London; Hilaire's network totally dislocated, contained and destroyed the German troops stationed in the south-west of France.

Apart from creating this vast offensive organisation, Hilaire was also responsible for the setting up of the escape lines which assisted in the escape of both Harry Peulevé and Denis Rake. He is one of the great names; too modest to tell his own story and too wise to let others know it, his activities can only be guessed at by the scope of his final achievement.

A large number of the men who did brilliant work for SOE started in the ranks. Few of them were of distinguished origin or came from famous regiments, yet all possessed a quality which I can only describe as that most likely to make an officer – initiative. We had no use for those who could not think for themselves and we placed a premium on those whose common sense could be relied upon. Inflexibility was the most dangerous drawback to a man's selection; a man had to make his own appraisal of a situation, obeying where obedience was necessary, acting on his own authority where he found good cause to vary the judgement of superior officers.

It was no use trying to do things by the book. There was no book. It may be thought that we encouraged eccentricity. This is not so: our officers, when in uniform, were among the smartest in London; their *esprit de corps* forbade them to be otherwise. Ours was a strictly military set-up; there was nothing irregular about it. (When the time came it was integrated with supreme Allied strategy and when the Americans were fully in the war it took on a properly Anglo-American character and I had an American number two, Major Huot.) As opposed to spying in the full sense, our men were engaged on offensive work, not predominantly on sending information. Starting with the destruction of the engine sheds at Troyes we gradually extended our scope, by planning new targets in London (in consultation with the Ministry of Economic Warfare) and by approving those suggested by men actually in the field.

Every officer was trained in demolitions (with the exception of Denis Rake) and we instructed them in the most effective way of interrupting railway traffic by derailments. The most important thing was to derail trains in cuttings and not on embankments; the reason was simple: a train derailed in a cutting would block the line until hauled away, while one derailed from an embankment could be rolled down into the fields adjacent to it, so allowing traffic to continue as before. On the other hand you might deliberately choose an embankment for derailing a troop train since the crash over the side of the line and the fires which might result could cause greater loss of life than a cutting derailment where the damage to the actual train and its contents would be slight. You had to use your head. When a train was carrying French civilians the idea was to keep casualties down; we did not want the Resistance to get a bad name. Our men became so skilled that they were able to derail a train without even tipping it over; the charges exploded as the leading coaches came over them and the train simply ran off the line and parked itself in the cutting.

There was a great art in sabotage and always our ideal was to harm the Germans as much and the French as little as possible. It was our claim which we were later to substantiate again and again that we were more accurate and less destructive than bombing; when we managed to convince the RAF of this fact they became much more willing to provide us with aircraft for transport and supply; earlier they had been both suspicious and parsimonious. The notion that we were all amateurs died hard among the high-ups. To scotch it we arranged meetings between our officers and high-ranking officers of the other arms of the service; our officers' smartness, intelligence and obvious knowledge of their job served to convince them of our seriousness.

We also instituted joint training schemes for our men and the airmen who were to transport them – Lysander pilots would thus get to know our men so well that there would be a personal bond between them so strong that if they heard one of our men was trapped and had to be got out in a hurry they would feel that they had to get Harry or George or whoever it was before the Boches did. This was another instance of the sense of individuality we tried to instil in all who worked with us. Our men were lonely in the field, that was inevitable; we had to make them feel that we – and all at home – cared for them personally and were prepared to take risks for them. I think we succeeded.

II

'Last night's drop to Hilaire seems to have gone all right,' Bourne-Paterson said. 'I've got the crew's reports and so far as I can see it all went swimmingly.'

'Good stuff,' I said. 'I only wish we could get supplies dropped to the north as easily as we seem to manage it in the south. I've had a message from Conrade in Paris that the Resistance around Lille is crying out for arms and explosives.'

'The flak's so thick we haven't got a chance in the Lille area,' Bourne-Paterson said.

'I'm not unaware of that,' I remarked. It had been one of our biggest headaches since the very beginning – the Germans had so protected the north of France with antiaircraft guns that the parachute drops which we were able to engineer with comparative immunity in the sparsely garrisoned south were impossible in the industrial north. Furthermore, the density of population made 'parachutage' less practical than in open country; it was no use dropping supplies into a gasworks or a smelting-kiln. This was especially annoying since Lille was one of the very first of the Resistance areas; it claims the proud title of 'Cradle of the Resistance'. Yet though there were many willing and tough resisters in the organisation, they remained virtually without arms. The problem seemed insoluble. We knew how anxious they were to take action and by now, towards the beginning of 1943, we were as keen as they to step up sabotage, for already we were staging the softening up which was preparatory to D-Day.

Lille has always been a place where the British are very popular; our troops were there in 1940 as well as from 1914–18, and our stock remained so high, even after Dunkirk, that Lille never really acknowledged the armistice at all, remaining truculent and unyielding. Nonetheless, the people had to live and the only way in which a living could be earned was in the factories. Whether they liked it or not, the Lillois had to work for the Boches; unless the factories could be put out of action. That was the objective of the local Resistance who were clamouring for our help. They had already performed several acts of sabotage and had killed a number of Boches; but they needed co-ordination and arms.

We sent them Michael Trotobas, who had lived in northern France before the war and had been stationed in Lille before the German breakthrough. He was the ideal man. We dropped him in the Yonne area with orders to make his way to Lille as quickly as he could.

In Lille he began to co-ordinate the Lille *Réseau* with the rest of the organisation. The first step was to maintain wireless communication with London. So strict were the controls and so rigid the curfew in the Lille area that I had taken the view that it would be suicidal to send a wireless operator to it; he would have little chance of survival. I had discussed all this with Michael before he went and he promised to try to find a way out of the difficulty. He and the leader of the Lille Resistance travelled together to St Quentin.

At a shop which sold hardware they had a rendezvous with Yolande.† This rendezvous would not have been approved by us in London, had we known of it, for it involved contact between two *Réseaux,* but it bore fruit. Yolande, an SOE girl, was operating in St Quentin for Guy who was in charge of the *Réseau* there. She was a girl of great initiative and when Michael put the position to her, she promptly suggested that she should help. 'I've got a French operator, a first-rate chap called Max Leroux,' she told him. 'He's been cleared with London and I've already issued him with a full set of codes. He's ready to go to work as soon as you need him.'

'It'll mean removing him from your circuit altogether,' Michael warned the girl.

'We are all here to help each other,' was the reply.

Max Leroux was a burly and opinionated man whom Michael found very likeable. 'I won't work for de Gaulle,' was his first remark. 'Are you anything to do with him?'

'I am a British officer,' Michael said.

'Mm, well, what do you want me to do?'

'We want you to maintain contact for us with London. Exactly the same sort of thing you were to do for Yolande.'

'This really is a British set-up too, isn't it?'

'That's right.'

'I'll do as you say,' Max snarled, as if he had refused. 'Let's have something to drink.'

Michael sent his first message through Max the next evening at a sked time agreed before Michael's departure. He asked for

---

† Yolande Beekman. Field name Mariette. Code name PALMIST. Wireless operator for the MUSICIAN Circuit. Killed in Dachau on 13 September 1944.

arms, but could not give us any idea of how to get them to him; we were not much further forward. The two men had to get back to Lille which lay in the most restricted of all the zones of occupied France, ringed with guards and continuously subject to all kinds of checks and hazards; to enter it, a special card was needed and the Boches kept the closest scrutiny on all traffic. The C had procured a pass for Michael stamped with the German eagle and proclaiming him to be a special consultant to a glass works; there was not too much difficulty in getting back, but Michael realised what a tremendous task it would be to get arms through the controls, yet to drop them within them was equally impossible. What solution could there be? Michael and the Resistance leader travelled the last part of their journey to Lille on local buses; there was less likely to be a thorough check of passengers on them than on the trains from Paris.

'There seems to be a hell of a lot of traffic on this road,' Michael observed, as they rolled through the black industrial landscape.

'It's the *routiers*,' the Resistance leader told him. 'They still use this road all the time, bringing supplies to and from the factories.'

Michael said: 'My friend, I have had an idea.' When they had safely returned to Lille, Michael told his friend the plan: 'We'll use road transport to bring the supplies in. London can arrange for them to be ready to be picked up in Paris and the *routiers* can bring them in.'

The next few days Michael alerted the organisation in Lille to recruit as many really trustworthy *routiers* as they could find. A way had been found of bringing arms to Lille; no further incentive was needed: the Resistance started recruiting long-distance drivers.

III

'We can make the first drop near Meaux,' I said.

'Do you think this plan will really work?' demanded Vera Atkins, now my personal assistant and an invaluable member of headquarters staff.

'It has to,' I said. 'The Air Ministry want the locomotive shops at Fives-Lille to go up. If we can't do it, they're going to. There are workmen's houses all round that area – it'll mean hundreds of civilian casualties.'

'Fives-Lille! That's a tremendous job.'

'That's why we've got to get busy. Now then, Armand[†] can receive the arms on Monday night. The reception committee is all set to go, we know that. We'll send a message to him tonight that he must lay on transport for Monday night – I want all the stuff cleared out of the Meaux area by the next morning. Alert Max in Paris that he must get Michael to be ready to take over the lorry when it comes in from Armand's area. Michel himself will do the first run in with their best long-distance man on Tuesday morning and I want a report on how it's all gone from Max the following morning after that.'

Vera looked up. 'They'll need a lot more than one lorry load to blow up a locomotive repair shop,' she said. 'How long have we got?'

'A month,' I said.

IV

Three long flashes. Two short ones. Three long ones. The throb of the plane grew closer and closer. On the ground Armand and the

---

[†] René Dumont-Guillemet. Field name Armand. Code name SPIRITUALIST.

reception team stood in the shadows of the hedgerow and waited. All were armed with Sten guns except for the ground-to-air wireless operator and the men with the lights.

'Is that C for Charlie, is that C for Charlie?' came the voice of the aircraft's captain.

'This is C for Charlie, this is C for Charlie,' Armand replied. 'What have you got for us?'

'Eight sacks of toys,' was the reply. 'No bods.' 'Bods' was the RAF term for agents. Probably the plane that was bringing supplies to Armand's group was also taking an agent or two to another group in a different area. We often combined two operations in this way to save the RAF conducting two dangerous missions where one would suffice. It was a highly risky business, this solitary low flying, and it required the greatest coolness on the aircrew's part. Often the ground-to-air communication (if any) was poor and the guiding lights dim. Occasionally the RAF boys would be new to the job and did not appreciate the difficulties of the people on the ground. One captain was rash enough to comment, 'Look at those bloody awful lights.'

The man on the ground heard this over the intercom and cracked back in a broad Lancashire accent: 'Ay, and your lights'd be bloody awful if you had the Gestapo on your tail!'

The plane turned and came back over the reception area. 'This is it,' Armand whispered to his team. 'Collect the stuff as quick as you can and report back here.'

Four containers dropped from the plane and for a moment their parachutes plumed out before they smashed into the ground. These packages were very heavy and they fell a good deal faster than a man could dare to. They were usually lagged with layers of sorbo rubber to protect them against the jolt of landing. The plane turned and came back again. The lights still pointed to the sky to guide it. The sten gunners patrolled along the hedges. There was silence. Four more packages thudded to the ground.

'Out lights,' snapped Armand. Already men were racing across the field to collect the packages, two men to carry, two pairs searching for, each package. Down a small lane off the side road which connected the dropping zone to the main road a lorry was parked, camouflaged even in the darkness under layers of branches.

Within four minutes each group leader had reported that one or other of his pairs of men had collected a package, and that all were regrouped. 'Sten-men number,' Armand whispered. The sten gunners numbered off; the radio man reported himself present and Armand knew that there was no risk of anyone being left behind – always a danger in the darkness and one which it was important to eliminate, since the Germans might be on the scene in a very short while and would pick up any stray men who had not heard the order to reform and make off. A Sten gunner leading, the team made off towards the lorry. There was no alarm and the branches were removed and the stuff loaded up. The driver was already in the cab and within a quarter of an hour of the plane's coming over he had driven off, amid whispered calls of 'good luck' towards Meaux, Paris and the north.

'Well done, everyone,' Armand said. 'Disperse as quickly as possible.'

Another typical night's work was over. In many departments of France similar reception committees waited on suitable moonlit nights for the supplies which were to give France new life. As the weeks went by France, little by little, rearmed.

Westwards from Meaux towards Paris, its back laden with

the contraband arms, drove the truck with the words 'Audubon-Charbons, Melun' written on its dirty flap-board. Just short of the village of Moret the driver swung it off the road into a small yard. It was now after midnight. The truck drove straight into a small barn where three men were waiting.

Je viens de la part de Churchill,' said the driver hurriedly leaping out of the cab. 'Let's get it done. I want some sleep. I've got to be on the move early.'

The three men nodded and at once a chain was formed along which sacks of slate and coal were passed. The sacks were emptied all over the bundles of arms and soon the latter were completely obscured. One of the men passed the driver a bottle of wine. He took a long swig and wiped his lips. 'Now for some sleep,' he said.

By five he was on the move again, joining the carts and trucks moving along the N7 towards Paris. He had two hours in which to make his rendezvous in a small private garage in Montmartre. There Michael and Jules, a *routier* well known to the German controls along the Route N17 which led to Lille, were waiting. Jules was confident.

'They all know me,' he said. 'There'll be no trouble.'

Michael looked at his watch. It was half-past six. Their man was due at seven. Michael said: 'Have you got your papers?' He did not want anything to go wrong through carelessness.

'I have my driving licence,' Jules said. 'What else do you want me to have – my birth certificate?'

Michael looked again at his watch. Boots crunched up to and past the locked gate of the garage yard.

Suddenly there was a hiss of brakes and an imperious hoot. Michael and Jules swung the gates open. Monsieur Audubon de Charbonnier, Melun drove into the yard. It was seven o'clock.

Quickly the lorry was driven into the garage and the portcullis shutters were clamped down behind it. The three men now removed the arms from under the charbonnier's coal and loaded them into a lorry which, according to the slogan on its side, belonged to Hubert et Fils, Lille. A further slogan stamped over it read: *'Au service de l'Allemagne.'* Eight large drums of gas-oil were piled on top of the load and the engine started up.

'Au revoir et bonne chance,' called Monsieur Audubon. The two lorries drove out of the garage. Monsieur Audubon, his job done, turned south to Melun. Michael and Jules, their job just beginning, turned north towards the N17 and Lille.

V

The lorry hummed easily along the N17. Michael sat beside Jules and watched the landscape slip past. Jules sat confidently at the wheel, a cigarette barely held between his half-parted lips. He looked across at Michael. 'We're coming up to the control proper,' he warned. 'Got your papers?'

'I've got them,' Michael smiled.

The control barrier resembled that which usually guards a frontier. There was a large command post and a barrier across the road. Ahead of them, Michael could see a row of halted lorries. German soldiers were searching the contents of some of them while the drivers went into the command post to have their papers examined. Jules drew the lorry into the side of the road and hopped out. 'Come on,' he said. Michael realised that they would have to leave the lorry unattended and trust to luck that the Boches did not go through the contents too thoroughly. Regretfully, Michael got out of the cab and followed Jules into the command post.

A crowd of *routiers* stood around the harassed clerk behind the desk. They clamoured so loudly and cursed so effectively that the clerk barely had time to stamp one set of passes before the next man slapped his papers on the desk. Jules and Michael took their places, Jules first. He handed over his driving licence when the time came. The clerk looked up and sighed. He frowned at Jules. 'Won't you ever learn?' he asked. Jules shrugged and took the licence and the stamped pass.

Michael put his papers on the desk. The clerk took them in his hand and was about to stamp the pass when he stopped. There was a sudden silence. Michael's papers were made in London. He looked at Jules whose ruddy face had gone quite pale. The clerk turned the papers over, thumbed through the complicated pages of forged stamps and endorsements and sighed again.

'Francois Gelin,' he read out.

'That's right,' Michael said.

'Gentlemen,' said the clerk, looking round the circle of *routiers* who crowded the room. 'Look at these papers. Have you ever seen such papers?' he went on scornfully.

I've had it, Michael thought.

'Why can't you all have papers like these?' the clerk snapped. 'Why can't you learn a lesson from Monsieur Gelin here and keep your papers in proper order?'

The *routiers* mumbled among themselves. Michael smiled shyly. 'It's nothing,' he said.

The clerk handed back his papers. 'Thank you, Monsieur.'

Michael and Jules walked out of the command post.

'Why can't you have lovely papers like mine?' he taunted Jules.

'When I have to go to England to get them?'

They walked past the parked lorries back towards their own. Michael stopped. A knot of German soldiers were clustered around their lorry. They've found the stuff, Michael thought.

'What shall we do?' he whispered.

'Keep going.' Jules walked boldly up to the lorry. '*Bon jour, les gars*,' he said in a comradely, yet somehow contemptuous tone. 'Yes, I've got something for you.' He reached into his pocket and drew out a battered set of photographs. The Germans smiled when they saw him and clustered round him. 'Only twenty-five francs each,' Jules said. 'And they're – magnificent.' He kissed his fingers and rolled his eyes suggestively. The Germans pressed forward. Michael realised what was going on. The Germans had not been searching the lorry at all. They were waiting for Jules. He was bringing them their quota of pornographic pictures. 'I do it every trip,' Jules said when they had safely drawn away from the control. 'It stops them asking awkward questions. They never bother me. They like what I bring them too much for that. I get them in the Boulevard Montmartre before every trip.'

'You must let me know the tricks of the trade one day,' Michael observed. 'It will prevent me having heart failure every time you use them.'

Jules rolled his cigarette along his lip with his tongue in a comic gesture. 'What is life without surprises?' he asked.

Through Cambrai and Douai they drove, one grubby lorry, indistinguishable from the other trucks rolling along N17 *au service de l'Allemagne.*

By nightfall they had safely parked the lorry in a lock-up garage and the arms had been unloaded and stored away in the attic of someone's house.

That night they sent a telegram to Max in Paris: 'mother and child both well send more toys'. The next morning Max transmitted the message to us. The plan had worked. Lille could be armed.

VI

It was only the beginning. We had to ship in a lot more stuff if we were to blow up the locomotive sheds in the time which the RAF had 'allowed' us. We told Michael to get together as many lorries as he could. We would begin mass shipments, or shipments as massive as we could manage. The next lot would go to Armand on Thursday night.

Michael worked with reckless speed. Two lorries were stolen from a German dump and new number plates attached to them. Small vans and huge long-distance lorries were taken at tremendous risk and added to the Resistance transport pool. At Meaux, Armand and his men arranged for extra transport to make the vital trip to Montmartre where Michael and the others waited for the stuff.

The Germans did not interfere with transport as much as one might imagine. At this time there was no private traffic of any kind, either lorries or cars. Everything was in the service of Germany. Now the Germans, knowing that this was the law, could not believe that anyone would dare to break it; they are a literal-minded people and it seemed inconceivable to them that the French would do anything so flagrant as to use a road and transport which was totally reserved for Germans.

Sometimes our big munition loads were broken up before the lorries reached Lille, for purely local traffic was less likely to be subject to checks. This was where the small vans came in useful. They could draw up in front of the places where Michael cached the stuff without exciting too much comment in the neighbourhood. One of Michael's most trusted van drivers was a girl called Brigitte. One day she was driving along the road from Douai in a small charcoal burning vehicle laden with plastic explosives and detonators and other equipment when, going up a small hill, she began to hear most unpromising noises from the engine. The van topped the rise, sighed, and gave up. It was useless to try and find a garage, because all the French garages were forbidden to give service; theoretically there was no French transport to service. There was only one thing to do. At the bottom of the hill was a German depot. Brigitte started to push the van. A couple of German mechanics, on their way back to the depot, came out of a café. She smiled at them. They smiled back. Within a few seconds both were pushing the van. Brigitte sat in it and steered.

'Where are we going?' they asked.

'To the depot.'

She turned the van in through the front gate.

'It's all right, Hans,' one of her helpers called to the sentry.

'You're very kind,' she said to the two men. 'Now could you take a look at the engine and see what's wrong with it? I'd be so grateful.'

Willingly (she was an attractive girl) they set to and repaired the vehicle. 'I'm in a hurry to get it to the hospital, you see. They need the supplies so badly.' Soon she had nearly all the mechanics in the place seeing what they could do to help. At the slightest sign of friendship on the part of the French, the Boches were quite likely to be bowled over. A lot of men got out of tight spots by affecting a love of the Germans which the latter could hardly fail to approve and enjoy. Brigitte sat in the van and dimpled prettily and the Boches could not do enough for her. 'Haven't you finished yet?' she taunted them.

At last the repairs were completed. 'I shall write and thank your commanding officer,' she told them.

As she drove off one of the NCOs said: 'Now mind you don't

go and pick up any of this terrorist equipment they say they're shipping into Lille, will you?'

Everyone roared with laughter, none louder than Brigitte. 'What would you do if I did?' she demanded roguishly.

'We know you wouldn't do such a thing,' grinned the NCO.

'Don't you be too sure,' she cried, wagging a naughty finger.

They all rocked. The van drove out of the depot.

'Be careful how you drive all that dynamite,' was the last laughter-laden advice she heard. Luckily, of course, the plastic explosive with which the van was loaded needed a detonator to set it off. But you could hardly expect the Germans to know that!

VII

It was obvious that we would have to postpone the blowing up of the sheds at Fives-Lille. Although things were going ahead well, there simply would not be enough explosives and arms there in time for the men to know how to use them. An operation of this kind required very careful planning, for there could be no rehearsal and Michael had to go over the plan again and again with his gang of railwaymen whose job it would be to lay the stuff.

I rang the Wing Commander at Bomber Command and told him of the necessity for delaying the operation a week or two.

'The old man won't like it,' was his comment.

'I don't like it,' I said. 'But that's the way it's got to be.'

'I'll let you know what the old man says.'

'All right,' I said. I was tired of internal politics. I seemed to spend too much time busying myself with policy. I was keener on maintaining contact with our men than on deciding theoretical priorities and keeping up appearances. All the same, this delay at Lille was trying. I hoped Michael would do a good job when the time came. By now it was January 1943 and all over France our chaps were organising sabotage in a way that at one time seemed impossible. Yet more was always being asked of us. I restrained myself: of course it was quite right that more should be asked of us. We were equal to it.

***

Information about France was still very important to us and we could never have enough of it. Things were changing there all the time, particularly since the Germans had taken control of the whole of it, and we had to be up to date. Our briefing officers had to know everything there was to know about the areas to which our men were to be sent. They had to know which days you could have meat in a restaurant, which days and at what times the cinemas were open; the natives would know these things and our men had to be natives, not only in the eyes of the Germans, but also in their own eyes: they had to have the confidence which only thorough briefing could give them.

They were going in greater numbers now and it was inevitable that some of them were heading for areas where the conditions were unknown to us and these men justifiably felt inadequately briefed; they arrived to find things very different from the way they had thought they would be. I am afraid that nothing could be done about that. We collected every scrap of information we could, but that was all that was possible.

To some extent we were hampered by the uncommunicativeness of other arms of the Intelligence and Secret Service. Each little organisation treasured its special nuggets of information with the zeal of prefects hanging on to their privileges. We could get nothing out of them. Sometimes they might know that a certain circuit was blown, yet because they wanted to protect their own men, they would keep the secret to themselves, fearing that to reveal it would lead to arrests among their own chaps. They preferred others to be caught. One could see the reasons for this; no one likes to think that he is responsible for the death of men whom he has sent out, but at times one could not but resent the secrecy which almost amounted to suspicion of the loyalty of others. On the whole I was able, through personal contacts, to get at most of the Secret Service information which was relevant to SOE, but at times it was a struggle. Of course, all secret organisations suffer from this security phobia; they think that the fewer people know the safer they are. This may be true, but liaison among allies should be willingly offered rather than grudgingly conceded.

The German counter-espionage services were at loggerheads with each other in a way which made any departmental squabbles or rivalries which might distress us at home look very trivial indeed. The Abwehr, the military counter-espionage, was constantly at odds with the Gestapo. This rivalry came to a head with the arrest by the Gestapo of the Abwehr commander, Admiral Canaris, in August 1944, after the Hitler bomb plot. Whether or not Canaris was actively implicated, it was an ideal opportunity for the Gestapo to exert their authority over the Abwehr. Before then, however, the Abwehr had shown itself a wily enemy to our cause, as we shall shortly see.

The Wing Commander phoned me again later that week from Bomber Command. 'The old man's pretty sceptical about the ability of your chaps to do this engine-shed job at all,' he reported cheerfully. 'Just thought you would like to know. Are you sure you wouldn't rather we took the whole operation off your hands?'

'I said we'd do it. We'll do it.'

In Lille, Michael had arranged for the railwaymen to take small quantities of explosives in their lunch baskets into the locomotive sheds. The German guards detected nothing and at the price of the railwaymen eating slightly less than usual for lunch Michael was able to begin salting away explosives within the perimeter of the German sentries. The explosives were hidden in the lockers where the men kept their tools and overalls and each day the quantities grew. By the beginning of March Michael was ready to put his final plan into operation. The scheme would take place on a night when there was no moon. He and three men would enter the marshalling yards, all wearing engine-drivers' overalls liberally daubed with oil-dark paint to make them merge with the background. Michael and the men all had revolvers in their pockets, but he had given orders that they were not to be used unless the danger was desperate. Two other sets of men, under the local Resistance leader, had been detailed to be in the marshalling yards adjacent to the locomotive sheds. If they heard any fighting they were to come to the help of Michael and the others, if not they were to keep off. The fewer men about, the less the chance of discovery.

The night of the second of March was dark and it was raining slightly. Michael's courier alerted his men and they assembled in the soot-stained house of Paul, a foreman in the locomotive sheds, at one o'clock in the morning. The Resistance fighters were scheduled to be in their places at one-fifteen. The fuses would be ten-minute ones and they would withdraw as soon as they saw Michael and his men come out of the sheds. The blow-up was timed for two o'clock.

'Come on,' Michael said, after they had darkened their faces with the grease Paul had provided. 'No talking, keep together and do exactly as I say without question. Understood?'

The men all nodded. Paul led the way out of the tiny house and down an alley leading to the yards. The lines glistened like fresh paint in the rain. Far off an engine hooted and the flare of its cab shone in the darkness. A lantern bobbed somewhere down towards the shunting yards. Paul, Michael and the others stepped over the lines carefully – some were electric – and tried to stay as much as possible in the shadow of the parked rolling stock. They filed down between two rows of goods vans, taking care not to make a noise as they trod on the ballast between the lines. The rasp of a match sounded ahead of them. They froze. The silhouette of a sentry at the far end of the row flared in the darkness and then went out: only the glow of his cigarette remained. Paul drew them into the gap between two trucks, led them over the couplings and across the empty lines towards the sheds. Michael was ready to deal with sentries if he had to (all our men were skilled in unarmed and silent killing) but naturally preferred not to risk raising an alarm. They approached the sheds. Suddenly they stopped. Michael went forward. Two men were standing at the corner of the shed. He could just see them. One of the men left the other and made off across the yards. Rain glistened on his hair. Michael went quickly forward and got in behind an electric fuse-box. He could see the man as a dark smudge against the wall of the shed. The man walked forward and came towards the fuse-box. Michael stood on the balls of his feet, ready to spring. The man walked past the fuse-box and then turned. Michael started forward and then stopped. It was the local Resistance leader.

'What the hell?' he whispered.

'Michael? There are two sentries at the far end of the sheds. You must go in this end. My men are keeping a watch on the sentries. If they make any move to enter the building we will follow them. If they come round to this end we will keep with them and kill them if necessary to secure your retreat.'

Michael clasped the Resistance leader's hand. 'Excellent.' He was shaking with shock at the closeness he had come to killing his friend. He signalled to Paul and the others to come forward. Silently, the Resistance leader withdrew. Michael and the others reached the door of the locomotive sheds and Paul opened the padlock with his foreman's pass-key. The four men slipped into the black interior of the shed and shut the door behind them. They placed a bucket against the inside of the door. If anyone came in he would involuntarily make enough clatter to warn them of his presence.

Paul led the way straight to the locker room. A pale pencil of light from Michael's torch was their only guide. Within a few minutes the lockers had been emptied of explosive and each man went to his task with silent certainty.

Outside, the Resistance fighters lay in the dark shadows of the marshalling yards, one party keeping watch on either end of the engine sheds. A quarter of an hour passed. Twenty minutes. It was a quarter to two. The slightest gleam of light shone out from the door of the shed and went out. Four figures came silently, barely visible, through the door of the shed. The torch shone wanly for a fraction of a second in the direction of the Resistance leader: the signal that all was completed.

'Scatter,' he said. 'Pass the word. Mission completed.'

'Scatter,' Michael said to Paul and the others. 'Well done. Get going.' They turned away from him and each man ran across the gleaming lines of the yard, anxious to get as far away as possible before the bang – and the Germans – came. Michael watched them go and smiled. He walked slowly away, his eyes still on the sheds, as dark, as massive and as silent as before. Five minutes to go. Michael climbed over the low fence at the edge of the yard and turned to watch the explosion. Promptly at two a dull orange bubble of flame burst at the far end of the sheds and a muffled crump followed almost at once – and almost at once the sheds were shattered with an uncontrollable series of explosions, here there and everywhere gouts of flame were spewed out into the night. Running footsteps and cries of pain and alarm. In the glare of the burning sheds, Michael could see guards and railwaymen running towards the explosions. A German was blown clean off the ground by a new explosion. The far end of the huge sheds crumpled slowly down, like an animal driven to its knees, and the flames stuttered and caught at the fallen wreckage. By twenty past two the sheds were an inferno. Michael turned away and ran down the alley towards Paul's, where he was going to spend the night. Behind him the fires grew steadily and the wail of sirens filled the night.

The next day I was in my Baker Street office when I had a phone call from the Wing Commander at Bomber Command.
'Well?' he demanded.

'I haven't heard anything yet,' I replied.

'The old man—'

'I know all about the old man,' I said. 'And I'll let you know as soon as I hear any news.'

'Very well.'

Not till five o'clock that afternoon did I receive a decoded message from Max in Paris. It read: 'MISSION COMPLETED WHAT NEXT.'

I phoned my man at Bomber Command.

'They've done it,' I said.

'Have they though? How do you know?'

'I've had the news from our man on the spot.'

'How much damage have they done?'

'Look, they completed the mission. What do you want – photographs?'

'Might be an idea, old boy.'

'I'll see what I can do.'

VIII

Michael looked at the message which had arrived from Max. 'What the hell does this mean?' he asked. '"WELL DONE SEND PHOTOGRAPHS." What the hell—?'

The fires had not been extinguished in the locomotive shops till nearly noon of the next day. By that time the whole enormous works were gutted skeletons. The engines inside the shops had been badly damaged by the explosions and further incapacitated by the firemen's foam with which they had been deluged. The lines were blocked by the twisted wreckage and the Germans were in a frenzy of anger and frustration. The captain of the guard was under close arrest and all his men were in detention cells. The whole yard was swarming with Gestapo men and officials.

'Send photographs,' Michael said bitterly. 'There's headquarters for you!'

The yards were closely guarded now and the well-dressed businessman with the camera slung round his neck had to go through a control before he could gain access to them.

'What do you want in the yards?' snapped the Gestapo man at the barrier.

'I represent the *Societé Nationale d'Assurance Maritime et Industrielle*. There is a claim against my company for part of the damage in this dreadful affair. I must make a report, you understand,' the man finished.

They inspected his papers and allowed him to pass. He walked sadly towards the scene of destruction. It was obvious his company had taken a bad knock. He took out his camera and sorrowfully began to photograph the mess. There were tears in his eyes behind the thick glasses as he snapped the twisted girders, the ruined machinery and the smashed engines. After an hour of steady photography, the little man seemed more mournful then ever. He came back to the barrier through which he had passed earlier and his whole attitude was one of complete dejection. He was shaking his head and as he passed between the guards he could be heard mumbling 'Dreadful, dreadful'. The guards felt quite sorry for him. In this way the Resistance leader managed to get photos of the wreckage sufficient to convince even Bomber Command. A week later the pictures arrived on my desk, '*Avec les compliments de la Résistance.*' I passed them on to the Wing Commander with the acknowledgements unchanged. His reply came by return: 'Compliments of Bomber Command to our friends of the Resistance.'

I passed on the message from Bomber Command to Michael and his men. This appeal for photographic evidence that we had completed the sabotage which we said we had was the culmination of a long wrangle, at times verging on the acrimonious, between myself and the heads of other services. This attack on the locomotive shops at Fives-Lille did the trick and from now on the RAF were ready to believe that in certain cases we could carry out demolitions with greater accuracy and less loss of civilian life than they. Henceforth we were to get many requests for acts of sabotage which required a finesse impossible to achieve by bombing: often there would be one vital component of a factory which had to be destroyed or all other damage was pointless – sometimes a single well-placed stick of dynamite or plastic explosive could succeed where tons of HE had failed.

By now the guard on factories was well maintained and some of our best men, even Peter Churchill and Ben Cowburn, were forced to abandon plans for the destruction of certain buildings because to approach them was suicide. After the war we were to be grateful that at least some of the power stations and other installations escaped the attentions of our men.

From now on Michael extended his organisation in Lille with great rapidity. After the success with the locomotive shops, morale was high and recruits could be selected from large numbers of willing young men. He planned numerous acts of sabotage. Germans were shot and their bodies floated down the canals. At Tourcoing, on the outskirts of Lille, rolling stock was blown up and piled across the line. In Armentiéres a factory manufacturing breech blocks had its machinery so mangled that it could not resume production for months. All over the Lille area the Germans were on tenterhooks as each night some new sector exploded in twisted steel and smashed machinery. Michael was everywhere, planning and leading the sorties of resisters which made it dangerous for any German to go out alone. The Gestapo did everything it could to infiltrate the organisation. Two double agents were caught and shot and their bodies dumped outside Gestapo headquarters.

One day Michael himself was driving a truck full of small arms ammunition from Cambrai into Lille when he was ordered to stop by a *milicien*. He slowed up and stopped. 'Your papers.'

He handed them over. The policeman looked at them and handed them back. Michael started up the engine again then the policeman said: 'What have you got in the back?' 'Hospital material,' Michael replied. 'Bandages and things like that.'

'I'll take a look. Come on. Open it up.'

Michael put a hand on the *milicien*'s arm. 'Come now, officer, we all have to live—'

'What's this?'

Michael took out his wallet. 'We all have to make a little on the side,' he said with a wink. 'Selling a few eggs and things like that, you know how it is.'

The *milicien* drew his pistol. 'Open it up,' he said.

Michael got out of the cab of the truck and walked round resignedly with the *milicien* to the back. As they rounded the corner Michael turned and his arm flashed up, knocking aside the gun; the other hand slashed across the man's windpipe. As the *milicien* gasped with shock and pain, Michael brought his knee up into the man's groin. A punch to his belly finished him and he dropped limply into the road. Michael leapt back into the truck. A whistle blew. He slammed the gear into position and accelerated. Another *milicien* ran out into the middle of the road, his arms spread wide. Michael accelerated into him and he went sprawling into the gutter. Michael turned the van into a side lane by a sawmill and pulled up behind a pile of wood. He jumped out. Two *miliciens* on bicycles appeared at the far end of the road. One saw him, clutched the other's arm and fired a shot. Michael ducked through the sawmill yard where wood was stacked, and heard, beyond it, the whine of a police siren. He had to warn Thomas Franck, a butcher whose van he was using, before the Gestapo got to him. In a moment they would find the van, trace it and all would be up. Michael ran up some wooden steps to where the yard-foreman's office was. There was no one in the office. A phone stood under the window overlooking the yard. He snatched it up.

'Yes, Monsieur Eustache?'

'Get me Tourcoing 23-97. Hurry.' The pause was agonising. At last he heard Thomas's voice saying 'Hullo?'

'Thomas.' He could see two *miliciens* now in the yard. 'Get out, get your family out and warn the others. Hurry, hurry.'

'What is this—?'

'This is Michael. Do as I say.'

'There he is,' called one of the *miliciens,* pointing up to the office. He fired a shot at Michael that smashed the glass of the window.

'That is an order,' Michael shouted. 'Do you understand?'

'I understand,' Thomas said.

The foreman came into the yard and was stopped by the *miliciens*. Michael threw open the door of the office and shouted: 'Stand clear.' The foreman jumped aside and Michael fired at the *miliciens* as he came running down the steps back into the yard. One of them clutched at his elbow and the other ran out of the yard. The foreman looked astonished, not committing himself to either side.

With a scream of sirens a German van drew up at the gate of the yard. Michael had five clips of ammunition. He called to the foreman: 'Tell them I went that way.' The man nodded, still apparently dazed by the suddenness of this invasion. Michael ran between two high stacks of sawn wood towards the canal. There were five Gestapo men at the far end of the lane. Michael turned. Two *miliciens* fired at him. He fired back and one dropped. The men at either end began advancing. Michael was trapped. He started to try to climb up the steep sides of the woodpile, firing as he went. A *milicien* knelt and shielded his eyes against the setting sun. Michael

Left: Maurice Buckmaster, Head of F Section.

Below left: Vera Atkins, initially Buckmaster's PA but swiftly promoted to intelligence officer.

Below: Pierre de Vomécourt, the leader of F Section's first circuit, Autogyro. He was captured in April 1942 and spent the rest of the war in Colditz.

Virginia Hall, the American who led the Heckler Circuit.

Richard Heslop, head of the Marksman Circuit.

Michael Trotobas, head of the Farmer Circuit.

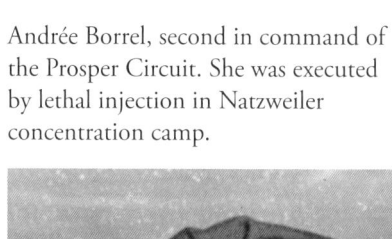

Andrée Borrel, second in command of the Prosper Circuit. She was executed by lethal injection in Natzweiler concentration camp.

Left: Peter Churchill was the head of the Spindle Circuit around Cannes. Odette Sansom was his courier. They were captured and sent to separate concentration camps but survived to marry in 1947.

Below: Peter Churchill's fake identity card.

Noor Inayat Khan, wireless operator for the blown Prosper Circuit and then the Cinema-Phono Circuit. She was captured, tortured and executed in Dachau in September 1944.

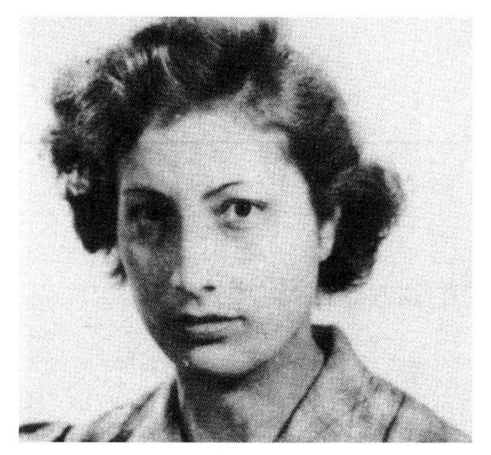

Yolande Beekman, wireless operator for the Musician Circuit. She was captured and taken to Dachau with Noor Inayat Khan and two others and executed there in September 1944 (pictured at her 1943 wedding).

Violette Szabo, who parachuted twice into occupied France. She was captured shortly after D-Day and taken to Ravensbrück concentration camp, where she was executed aged twenty-three in February 1945.

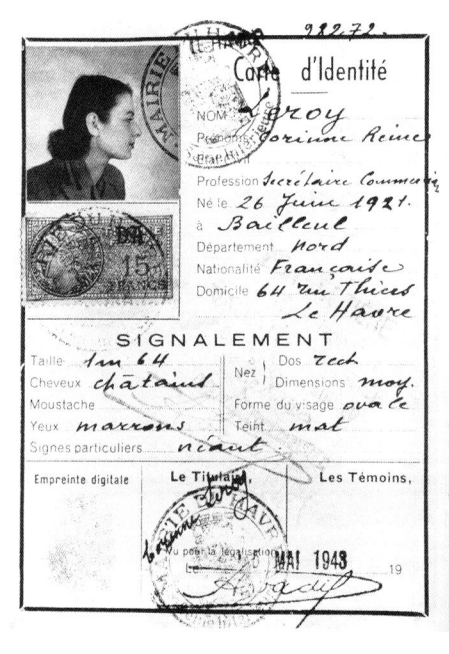

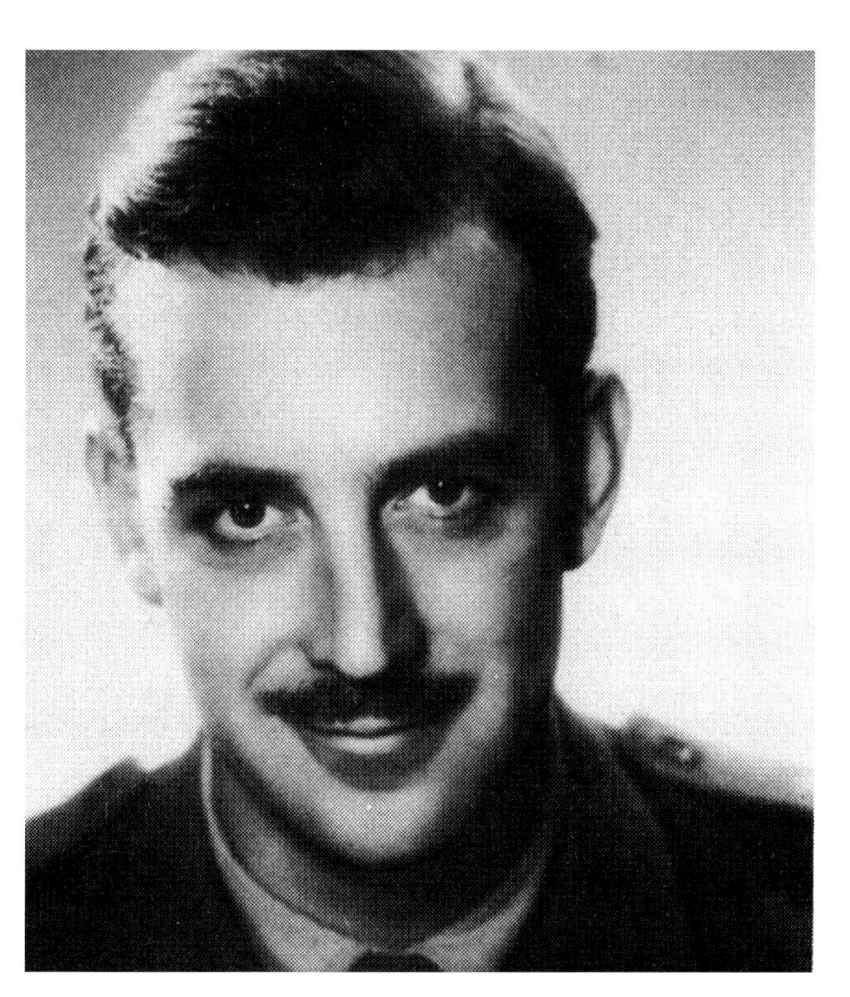

Top: Francis Cammaerts, head of the Jockey Circuit.

Right: Christine Granville, the Polish courier who bribed and cajoled Cammaerts and his SOE colleague Xan Fielding out of jail.

Top left: Pearl Witherington, head of the Wrestler Circuit.

Top right: Jacqueline Nearne, courier for the Stationer Circuit.

Right: Tony Brooks's Playfair card.

Bottom: Tony Brooks, head of the Pimento Circuit.

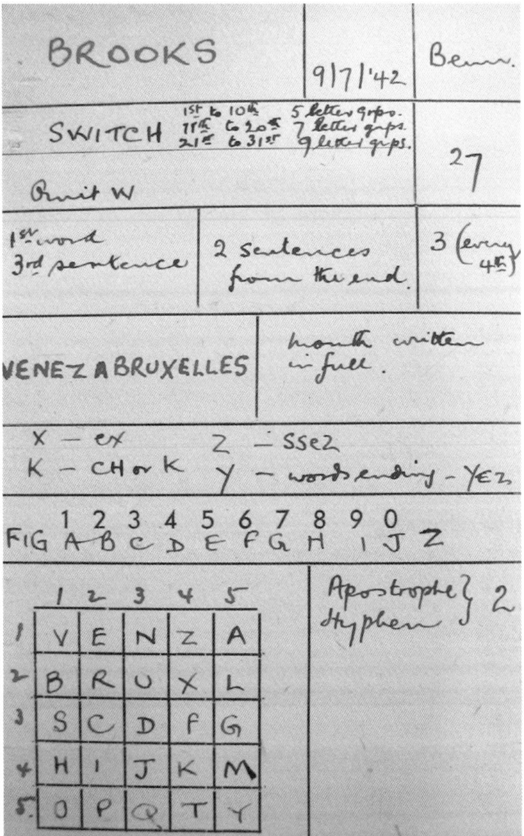

Roger Landes, head of the Scientist Circuit and then the Actor Circuit.

The FANY memorial at St Paul's Church, Wilton Place, Knightsbridge.

The SOE memorial at Valençay to the ninety-one men and thirteen women from the SOE and the FANY who died to free France.

fired off one clip of ammunition and paused to reload. The *milicien* fired and Michael fell, clutching at the side of the stacked wood. The Gestapo men advanced firing their submachine guns. Michael lay there, firing back. He dropped another one of them and then collapsed. So died Michael, one of the bravest and most effective of our men.

By the time of his death Michael had so organised the Lille patriots that they could continue with undiminished efficiency after the loss of their leader. Under their original leader, they dealt the enemy many more devastating blows before the liberation for which they had all worked ended their dangers and revealed their glory. Michael was not forgotten, for when I myself visited Lille in October 1944, I noticed a huge banner suspended over the Avenue de la Liberte with the initials OFACM printed on it in enormous letters. I asked one of the men what they stood for.

'They are the initials of our organisation,' he replied.

'OFACM?'

'*Organisation Française des Amis du Capitaine Michel*,' he explained. 'One does not forget a man like Michael.'

Chapter 8

Blackmail

By late 1943, RAF raids on Germany and on enemy-held Europe had been greatly stepped up. This fact enabled us to put into general operation a plan submitted to us by Harry Rée, our *Réseau* leader in the Franche-Comté. Harry was a very tough and very daring man and his idea required a good deal of nerve on the part of an agent, for he was required to get in touch with the owner of a factory and ask his permission to destroy it! Harry first put it into operation with a Peugeot factory which was manufacturing tank turrets for the Germans.

He rang up Robert Peugeot himself and after a number of secretarial intermediaries was able to speak to him.

'Monsieur Peugeot, I am ringing you about a rather special piece of business I would like to conclude with you. I wonder if it would be possible for us to meet?'

'Who are you?'

'Shall we say my name is Léon? I want very much to speak to you. Could I come to your home tonight?'

'You've got a certain nerve, my friend,' Peugeot said. 'What is this about?'

'I'm sorry—'

'All right. Come to the house at eight. I will see you.'

The Peugeots lived in considerable luxury, for the factory was doing well in the service of the Boches. It cannot be concealed that a large number of French industrialists were finding it very rewarding to co-operate with the Germans; in Robert Peugeot's case, however, it was with the greatest reluctance. For a long time he had resisted strong pressure to turn his factory over to war production and had only given in when threatened with expropriation and the removal to Germany of his trained technicians. Harry Rée was very direct with him.

'We want to blow up your factory,' he said.

'You what?'

'Some friends and myself – we want to blow up your factory.'

'Blow up … are you mad?'

'I am a British officer, Monsieur Peugeot; I am not mad.'

'A British officer? Really? Really? And how can you prove this? Why should I believe such a fantastic story?'

'Does it make any difference whether I am a British officer or not?'

'Of course it does. I don't want to be – well, I don't want to agree to anything—'

'I understand.' Rée saw that Peugeot was afraid that he might be a German provocateur trying to lure the industrialist into saying something incriminating. 'Do you ever listen to the BBC?' he went on.

'Not as a rule, no.'

'I will arrange for them to repeat any message you like to give me now before the seven o'clock news the evening after next. Would that convince you?'

'You can arrange this?' Peugeot asked. Harry nodded. 'Well, prove it. Have them say "*La guerre de Troie n'aura pas lieu.*"'

'I will call on you at the same time the evening after next,' Harry said. 'If the message is sent. Otherwise I will not come again. I can tell you on Thursday what my plan is—'

'I don't guarantee to allow this,' Peugeot said. 'I don't guarantee it at all.'

Harry had his wireless operator send us an urgent message on his next sked. Peugeot's message had to be sent on the very night which he had named or the plan might not go through. I got on to the Personal Messages section of the BBC French Service and told them the message. They promised to send it. I was very keen for Harry's plan to work, for if it did I wanted to put it into general operation. We were now using the *messages personnels* extensively in order to confirm the identity of our men to Frenchmen with whom they got into contact. No more certain proof of an agent's link with London could be provided than the transmission from the BBC of a message personally selected by his contact. There could be no deception, since positively any short phrase could be chosen by the Frenchman and the agent could not possibly have had prior knowledge of it or of what the BBC were going to broadcast.

This means of confirmation was used in another way. At the beginning we dropped a lot of money with our men. This was both dangerous and wasteful, for a man carrying a large sum of money would undoubtedly be detained for questioning if it were discovered on him, while if he were captured the money – and the amounts were not inconsiderable – would be a write-off. We therefore decided to allow our men to borrow cash from patriotic Frenchmen on the promise of reimbursement after the war. Nothing at all was given to the lender as receipt for the loan. Naturally, however, the contact was not going to part with thousands of francs without being convinced that the agent was what he said he was. He had to show that he did come from London. How could this be proved? Only by a BBC message confirming the claim. The Frenchman chose, quite at random, a phrase for repetition by the BBC's French Service. Our agent transmitted the request to us. We had the BBC repeat it and the Frenchman was convinced, as if by magic. The money was handed over without a qualm, the contact being confident of post-war reimbursement. It was my job, in 1944, to go round and repay the money – in every case the Treasury met the claims without question – and the total sum involved was considerable.

Harry Rée relied on us to transmit Peugeot's chosen phrase. The BBC did not fail him or us: *'Quelques messages personnels,'* came the announcer's measured voice. *'Charles est très malade … Marcel aime Marceline … Il n'y a pas de bananes … La guerre de Troie n'aura pas lieu … Yvette a dix doigts…'* As soon as Harry heard the announcer repeat Peugeot's message, he rushed out of his digs and hurried round to the industrialist's house.

'Monsieur—?' the maid inquired.

'Léon,' Harry said.

'Wait here please.' The maid went away. She seemed to stay away a long time and Harry grew rather apprehensive. Then she returned. 'Will you wait in here please?' She opened the door to a small sitting room, expensively furnished and hung with tapestries. Harry went in and the door was shut behind him. He was alone. He went to the window and looked out. It gave on to an interior courtyard: he could not get out that way. Suddenly there was the sound of voices – German voices. Harry went to the door and he could hear them even more clearly. He ran to the window and heaved it up. There was a shout of laughter from outside and then he heard shouts of 'Bon soir, Monsieur Peugeot,' in rough French accents, the accents of Germans speaking French. There was the sound of the front door shutting. Harry's heart stopped pounding and he shut the window. The door of the room opened and Robert Peugeot came in. When he saw Harry he smiled. 'Were you about to make your escape?' he asked.

'What were the Boches doing here?'

'They were members of some trade commission. They came to ask if they could see over the factory tomorrow. Now, come into the sitting room and we can talk.'

'Did you hear the message?' Harry asked anxiously. 'The trade commission—'

'We all heard it,' Peugeot laughed. 'I insisted that we all listened to the ridiculous things that the BBC broadcast. The Germans laughed like pigs at the silly messages.' Harry smiled.

'I'm glad you're convinced,' he said.

'I am. But what is your plan?'

'I will tell you quite frankly what the position is. The people in London want the Peugeot factory put out of action. They will bomb you, they say, unless production can be stopped within a short time. Now if they bomb you there will be much loss of life among your workers. They live very close to the factory, a lot of them, and there would certainly be heavy casualties. Now if you were to let a few of my men get into the factory one dark night…'

'I am to destroy my own factory? My dear man…'

'One way or another it will be destroyed. If we do it there will be few casualties and furthermore we can put the explosive where it will do the greatest harm to production and the least to the fabric of the factory. If the RAF bomb you the whole place will be smashed to smithereens. The cause of the Allies will be better served if you let us do it and in the long run you will suffer less.'

'You are very persuasive,' Peugeot said. 'Very persuasive.'

II

Harry Rée and his men were put in touch with two foremen in charge of the production line. Both were eager resisters and their job was to lead Harry and the others to the part of the factory where Harry knew by his training in England that the explosive would do the greatest damage. Certain machines were virtually irreplaceable under about six months – it was upon these that the dynamiters would concentrate. Peugeot himself knew nothing further of the operation, but he gave them every co-operation, though he was kept out of the inner workings of the plan. Obviously security could not be relaxed in his favour and he had to be treated like any other outsider. He knew neither how nor when his factory would be knocked out, only that it would be.

Harry and two of his gang were signed on as hands and thus were able to get in and out of the factory without exciting comment. They became thoroughly conversant with the machinery which they were to sabotage and on the pretence of explaining its workings the foremen were able to learn from Harry the vulnerable spots where explosive would do the most damage; Harry remembered with the utmost clarity the many hours he had spent in a Hertfordshire 'school' studying the weak spots of presses and lathes.

On the night of 14 May 1943, three operatives remained in the factory after the other workers had left. Soon after knocking-off time, two foremen let themselves in with their pass-keys and returned to the shop floor which they had only just left.

They liberated the three men who were shut in a cleaner's cupboard on the executive floor and took from it several large boxes labelled 'cleaning materials.' The contents of these boxes were tubular containers of scouring powder. The tops of these containers were unscrewed and several long sticks of explosive were revealed. Some flat tins contained plastic explosive which could be fastened to machinery rather like sticking plaster. The five men made their way downstairs to the night-watchman's room. This was no longer used. The Germans set their own guard on the place. The men could hear them forming up outside. The five ate their sandwiches and settled themselves to wait for the darkness.

At eleven o'clock they moved to their pre-arranged stations in various sections of the factory. Harry and one of the foremen set their explosives in place, working with quiet detachment. The other men, under the other foreman, were engaged similarly in another sector of the shop floor. By midnight – the agreed time – all the explosive was in place. The ten-minute fuses were set and the five men hurried down to a disused side door of which one of the foremen knew. They came out into a deserted yard at the back of the factory. Another door was unlocked by the foreman's pass-key and they were out of the factory in a side alley. They all shook hands and hurried away: they had to get home as quickly as they could, for curfew had started and there would be a terrific turn-out of police and military as soon as the factory went up.

At about ten minutes past midnight the shop floor of the Peugeot factory was rent by several violent explosions. Fires were started and equipment so ruined that production was suspended indefinitely. There was nothing the Germans could do to incriminate Robert Peugeot or any of the staff of whom five were missing. The two foremen had decided to join the Rée group rather than risk arrest by resuming their work. It was upon Harry and the others that the full fury of the authorities was directed. An intensive search was began.

If it should be thought that Robert Peugeot himself is not entitled to as much credit as those more directly concerned in the affair I think it only right to point out that he voluntarily incurred the risk of associating with Rée and further he actually connived at the destruction of a factory which his family had built up over the years into one of the finest in France. If one imagines one's own feeling at seeing one's house or shop or car or business being systematically destroyed, one may get some idea of the feelings that must have possessed Robert Peugeot on that May evening in 1943. I think he did rightly; let no one imagine that it was an easy decision. There were some who were not so public-spirited.

After the explosion the Germans were naturally determined to get the factory into full production again as soon as possible. They therefore set about replacing the presses for tank bodies which had been wrecked by the sabotage. They managed to get a fresh press sent in from Fallersleben. For transport they proposed to use a barge on the Canal du Doubs.

Harry and his men were now able to devote their full time to foiling the Germans' plan, for they no longer had to report each day for work at the plant. Accordingly, the gang made their way down the canal bank, having been tipped off about the imminence of the press's arrival. The canal ran through deserted yards and behind disused sheds and shabby allotments. Harry and his men hid themselves in a large gardening shed and waited.

Shortly afterwards the barge came into sight. It was manned by a French crew and there was a guard of a few Germans on it. As it came up to them, Harry and his men opened up a murderous fire with automatic weapons and soon the barge came to a halt, swinging across the placid canal as the crew left the controls and jumped for the shore. The Germans fired back, but they were soon overpowered and the barge was in the hands of the Resistance. Harry's men boarded her, taped explosive below the waterline, on the new press and in the engine-room and quickly left before anyone could give the alarm. Within a few minutes the exploding barge herself gave the alarm. By then it was too late. The new press and the barge were useless. So was the canal, a fact which further infuriated the Germans, for it was one of their favourite ways of passing midget submarines from the Loire to the Mediterranean. Harry and his men pulled back to wait for the next move.

Weeks passed, in which the Gestapo worked feverishly, but to no effect. Then the Resistance farther up the line warned Harry and his men that the Germans had managed to find another press which they were sending under heavy guard to the factory.

'What are we going to do?' one of the gang demanded.

'We'll meet them when they arrive,' was the decisive answer. 'Send the word round that everyone's to be ready to go into hiding as soon as the shooting is over. We'll go to Claude's. Tell him to expect us. Things are likely to be pretty hot.' Claude's was a safe house where they should be able to hide-out.

On the day when the press was due at the Peugeot factory, Harry and his men were in position in a small tabac opposite the factory entrance. Three more men with submachine guns were hidden in a yard next to the gate. The idea was that when the convoy pulled up at the gate waiting for the keeper to open up, the resisters would strike. At midday police and military motorcyclists cordoned off the adjacent streets. Ten minutes later the tank-body press arrived on a huge truck. The whole area in front of the gate was filled with Germans, police and transport. Harry gave the signal – a grenade lobbed on to the carrier truck – and from two sides a murderous fire was unleashed on the massed Germans.

A free fight ensued. The Germans were enraged and confused and opened up indiscriminately on anything they saw. Harry and his men dodged from shop to shop, through back doors, and hammered the security forces. Bombs were lobbed from a roof on to the lorry and a small fire was started. Everyone was rushing about loosing off machine-pistols and small arms and motorcyclists were ordered to cut off the resisters. Harry gave the order to pull out. He and his men made their getaway before the Germans became sufficiently organised to seal them off. Nevertheless they sent in hundreds of police and Gestapo agents from Besançon to the area around the factory. They arrested large numbers of workers and forced from them descriptions of the men who had absconded – of the two foremen and the three auxiliary workers who had been in the factory for the weeks before the sabotage. Pictures of the foremen were posted in the streets. Drawings of the other three were alongside them. The time had come to move off. Harry delegated control of the *Réseau* (not all the members were involved in the affair) and with his four wanted companions made for the Swiss border. There was little snow on the mountains but it was fairly chilly on the higher slopes and it was not easy going. Just before nightfall on the evening of 18 May, Harry and his men were lying up in a hut situated just short of the Swiss border in the vicinity of the Sainte Croix.

'There's a stream about five miles due east of here,' Harry told them. 'Once you're across that stream you're in Switzerland. They may keep shooting – if they've spotted us – but I don't think they'll dare come and get us. Marcel, you will lead with Denis and Frédéric; I will follow half an hour later with René.'

The first three made off at the agreed hour and Harry and René waited in the hut. Harry paced up and down, consulting his watch frequently. 'They should be at the stream by now,' he said. 'If we hear any shooting we'd better move away from here.' There were no shots. The half hour passed. Harry and René left. There was no one about. They walked in silence. Soon they came to a small cluster of shuttered houses. They passed them. They crossed a wooden bridge. It was getting chilly. 'Another half hour,' Harry said.

They came to a wood and passed through it to a series of barren fields strewn with boulders. They were very close to the frontier. They squatted down in the shelter of a large rock and Harry went forward to see what lay ahead. All seemed quiet, so he came back and gave René details about the crossing of the stream into Switzerland. 'You go ahead first,' Harry said. 'I will follow when you are safely across.'

The two men crawled forward now, fearing frontier guards, across the rough ground which sloped down to the banks of the stream. They lay down in some rushes and Harry said, 'Go when you're ready.'

René lay there for a few seconds and then moved from the cover of the rushes, crouching, and slipped down to the water. He strode silently into it and soon he was swimming towards the far shore. Suddenly, unbelievably, two shots rang out. Then more. They came from a curve in the river some few hundred yards farther up. 'Halt,' someone shouted. Harry thought quickly. There was only one thing to do. The police would be on the spot in no time. He had to follow René. He scrambled along the bank away from the direction of the shots and then flung himself into the river and started to swim for the far shore. He saw René scramble ashore and collapse on the bank. The shooting continued. But now it was directed at him. 'Halt.' He plunged on through the freezing water. The flashes of the guards' rifles were like stabs of pain. The impact of the bullets which hit him were dull hammer blows that seemed incapable of stopping him, though he was hit in the back and in the shoulder. Perhaps the chill of the water anaesthetised the wounds. He swam on. The river seemed as wide as a sea. The shots pursued him and the angry shouting seemed to grow into a roar like that of a crowd. He suddenly knew he could go no farther. He was exhausted. His lungs were solid with effort. He dropped his legs and prepared to be swept away; the water was only about three feet deep. He was safe. He crawled out of the water on to the shore. René was lying where he had collapsed a little farther up. The Germans continued firing. He crawled over to René who moaned and spat water.

'Are you all right?'

'Oui, mon Capitaine.'

'Come on then.' Together they drew themselves away from the river and lay out of range of the Boches in a culvert. They were saved. They were found in the morning by Swiss border police and Harry suffered an internment sufficiently indulgent to allow him to continue to direct the *Réseau* at Besançon from Switzerland. His other men had crossed the border without incident. On D-Day plus one they crossed back into France and joined a *Maquis* group originally formed by Peter Churchill.

III

Harry Rée's 'blackmail' plan seemed to have been very successful in the case of the Peugeot factory and I decided to give details of it to those *Réseaux* where I thought it might effectively be used. In October 1943, I had a call from the Ministry of Economic Warfare suggesting that it would be a good idea if we could attack German rubber resources. The big Michelin factory at Clermont-Ferrand was particularly in the minds of the high-ups. Could I arrange something?

I decided that *Réseau* Hector[†] which centred on Châteauroux, some distance north of Clermont-Ferrand, was the one most suited to the mission. I asked Vera Atkins to get a message ready for transmission to Amédée Maingard, Hector's wireless operator, giving details of the scheme.

This *Réseau* was a first-rate one. Hector himself, more commonly known on the continent as Maurice or Philippe, was (and is) a man of the greatest devotion and application: he stuck to his job without any thought for his own safety or welfare. He worked long hours – sometimes as many as twenty a day – and he inspired the fiercest enthusiasm in all who worked with him. He was lucky in his colleagues as they were in him. Amédée was a first-rate man; a young Mauritian, he carried out the highly dangerous role of wireless operator with skill and calm. Hector's courier was Jacqueline Nearne, an agent of the most perfect kind, full of flair and yet steady as a rock; never shirking a risk, she never recklessly incurred one. I had some difficulty in getting her accepted for SOE; although of Scottish origin, she seemed French through and through and had trouble in

---

[†] Maurice Southgate, organiser of the STATIONER Circuit.

accustoming herself to British military life and though tremendously popular, her sense of routine, discipline and training method was sketchy. I persisted with her, for I guessed that she would be excellent in the field itself. So it was: she never put a foot wrong.

She took the message from Amédée to Hector at Châteauroux. 'They want us to tackle the Michelin factory, do they? I'll say one thing for HQ, they don't ask much!'

'They seem to be in a hurry for results,' Jacqueline said.

'I don't fancy our chances of getting any co-operation from the management,' Hector said. 'They seem to be very happy in their work. Very happy.'

'Do we have to approach them?' Jacqueline asked. 'It seems to me we're going a long way about it.'

'I doubt if we could ever get into the factory to set the charges unless we can get in with someone on the executive level. I think we must do as Buck suggests.'

'Right you are,' Jacqueline said.

Hector made devious inquiries and found that things were much as he feared. The management of the Michelin factory were not particularly well disposed towards the Resistance. Most of the staff were of like mind. But orders were orders. Hector made an appointment with a Monsieur Legros, one of the managing directors, on the pretext of having some invention to show to him.

The magnate was sitting in a luxuriously furnished room, a cigar in the ashtray at his elbow, a glass of brandy on the coffee table. 'What can I do for you, Monsieur—?'

'Maurice,' Hector said. 'I would like to put to you a little proposition which I have.'

'My secretary said something about an invention—'

'She must have misunderstood. No, I have a rather different purpose from peddling inventions. I want you to let me blow up your factory.'

Monsieur Legros reached for his brandy and took a long sip. He leaned back in his chair and said: 'You want what?'

'It is very simple, Monsieur. I have to tell you that the RAF have decided to bomb your factory unless you let me destroy it first—'

Monsieur Legros rose to his feet, pale and shaking. 'You are raving. J-Jacques, Jacques, come here—'

Hector pointed his revolver at Monsieur Legros. 'Don't be foolish,' he said.

Jacques, the manservant, came into the room, looking apprehensive.

'A cognac, please,' Hector said. 'Now listen, Monsieur. We cannot destroy your factory from the air without doing much damage but if you were to permit—'

The interview took much the same course as the one which Harry Rée had had with Robert Peugeot, but with a difference: Monsieur Legros refused point-blank to have anything to do with the scheme. 'I do not believe that you can put this absurd threat of air raids into effect. I don't believe you're a British officer. I don't believe that you are anything but a crank – or possibly worse. The British have never bombed Clermont-Ferrand and I see no reason to believe that they ever will. I give you five minutes, Monsieur, to be out of my house or I shall call the police.'

Hector smiled in a friendly way. 'If you call the police,' he said, 'you will not live the week out. Good night.'

'Monsieur Maurice—'

'I will give you till tomorrow night to make up your mind

whether or not you wish to save the lives of your workers and the fabric of your factory, Monsieur Legros.'

'You're bluffing. I know you're bluffing.'

'We shall see. I will phone you tomorrow night at eight o'clock. You will tell me your decision then. Whether you care for yourself or for France. Good night, Monsieur. Oh, remember what I said about the police, won't you?'

Hector left. The next night he phoned Monsieur Legros: 'Well, have you decided what you are going to do?'

'I have nothing further to say to you,' the managing director said. 'Nothing. I call your bluff. If you try to get in touch with me again—'

'I wouldn't say that if I were you,' Hector interrupted.

Hector saw Jacqueline that night.

'I really don't think it's going to work,' he said. 'Legros won't help us. We'd better get Amédée to tell London what's happened and see if they can get the RAF to show Monsieur Legros and those like him that our threat is no bluff.'

I got the message the next morning. It seemed desperately short time in which to try to arrange a raid on the Michelin factory. One couldn't lay on an air raid as if one were calling a taxi. I rang Bomber Command and asked them if there was anything they could do. My friend, the Wing Commander, said he would see what could be done. 'But frankly, old boy, I'm not very hopeful.' It was obvious that if the raid were to achieve anything it had to take place within the next few days, and the sooner the better; only then would a real causal connection be set up in Legros' mind. Once it was, he would be sure to pass the message on to his fellow industrialists. The blackmail plan would explode altogether if he told them it was all bluff.

The whole scheme hinged on getting the RAF to bomb the Michelin factory at Clermont-Ferrand. At midday I phoned an Air Vice-Marshal I happened to know in the Air Ministry. I put the case to him as forcefully as I could. SOE had recently been incorporated on the COSSAC (Chiefs of Staff for the invasion of Europe) organisation, and this new official status greatly aided my negotiations with other branches of the service; nevertheless, the Air Vice-Marshal was gloomy. He thought there was little chance of the target lists being changed at short notice.

At a briefing in the south of England, the Squadron Leader was just finishing giving details of the night's targets when he was called to the phone…

In Clermont-Ferrand, Hector had Amédée send another urgent message to us. We must hit the Michelin factory or the Resistance would lose face, possibly irrevocably, and its attacks on French factories in German use would be desperately hampered.

The meteorological office forecast that the weather would be fine that evening. Bombers should be able to make their primary objectives without interference from adverse weather.

The Squadron Leader in charge of briefing returned to say that he had a message for the squadron from the Air House. If the bombers could not get through to Turin, their secondary target was, as they knew, dock installations at Marseille; failing that, their third target was marshalling yards at Lyons.

'We know all this,' a pilot muttered irritably.

'Now here's the new bit,' the Squadron Leader went on.

'If you can't get through to any of these three targets—'

There was some laughter. 'Listen to this, carefully; if the weather closes in and you can't get through, your fourth target will be the Michelin factory at Clermont-Ferrand. Now here are the details. Look at this map, please…'

The weather, towards evening, was perfect. 'It'll be a clear run to Turin,' was the verdict in the mess.

I was powerless to pull any further strings at the Air Ministry. We could only wait. Night fell. The sky was as clear as water.

In Clermont-Ferrand, Hector and Jacqueline sat morosely in a café. At nine o'clock Amédée joined them. He had two messages from us. Neither promised the raid. Both concerned a derailing which we wanted done the next week. The three agents were deeply depressed. Hector had tried once again to get in touch with Monsieur Legros to see if he had changed his mind. The man would not speak to him.

At ten o'clock the bomber squadron took off for Turin. The night was still fine. I rang the met. people and asked them what the forecast was. 'They should hit the primary objective, Colonel Buckmaster,' was the smug reply. I sat glumly in my office as the night ticked away.

In Clermont-Ferrand, the three agents said good night to each other and went home. The bombers crossed the French coast and headed south-east for Turin. When they were over Tours, the leader said to his co-pilot: 'Hullo, it's closing in.'

'Looks like it,' agreed the other.

Visibility closed down like a shutter. Ahead of them the sky was rent by electrical storms. The planes started to be thrown around like dice in a box. With each second things worsened.

'What's our position?'

'A hundred miles north-west of Clermont-Ferrand.'

'I don't much fancy this lot over the Alps. It'll be murder.' The lightning filled the cockpit with its bright flashes and the rain rattled like bullets on the hulls of the planes. 'I don't think we can make Marseille even.' All around them the conditions grew suddenly more ominous, thicker and more electric.

'If I had my way we'd turn back now,' the Squadron Leader's co-pilot grinned.

'Squadron Leader to all Captains. Change of plan. Change of plan. Abandon objective Turin…'

The heavy bombers turned in the silent sky and one after another came in on their bombing run. Within a quarter of an hour of the raid's beginning, the Michelin factory at Clermont-Ferrand was a gutted ruin. Hardly a pane of glass was broken in the surrounding houses; even if the weather closed in, even if Michelin was only a fourth alternative target, the bomber pilots took trouble to carry out their missions with deadly accuracy.

Chapter 9

Check

Roger Landes – or Aristide as we called him – was dropped to the Bordeaux Circuit in October 1942. He, like so many of the others, was a British subject of French origin (he had an English father, but was born in France) and in fact his French was better than his English. He was a lean man of medium height, who had applied to join us in 1941, though he was not ready for the field till the following year, largely owing to the long time which it took to train a wireless operator from scratch. By late 1942, he was ready to go and Claude de Baissac who had been in training with him and was now in charge of our Bordeaux *Réseau* applied for his services. Roger was the sort of person that anyone would want in his circuit. He radiated determination, coolness and courage.

There were two agents to be dropped that night: Aristide to the Bordeaux Circuit, Archambaud[†] to the Paris Circuit run by Prosper. There was a lot of cloud about as the plane crossed the French coast.

'I think we ought to turn back,' the pilot said. 'What do you blokes want? Shall we risk it or would you rather go back and try again another night?'

[†] Gilbert Norman. He was arrested in June 1943 and died in Mauthausen on 6 September 1944.

This kind of disappointment was not infrequent and there was nothing our men hated more than getting themselves keyed up for the drop and then finding that the weather was too bad to permit the completion of the mission. It was subconsciously humiliating to say goodbye to all of us in London and then, a few hours later, to return; agents were always deeply depressed on these occasions and I often spent the evening with them trying to take their minds off a kind of failure for which they could not even remotely be blamed. The risk lay in the fear that they would somehow come to think of themselves as unlucky. There was not a great deal of superstition among our agents (most of them were too level-headed for that) but the feeling of being 'unlucky' was a subtle, and could become a pervasive, one.

Roger had had no less than six shots at getting into France and each had been in vain. He was determined to drop this time, no matter what happened.

'I'd sooner try it this time,' Aristide said casually. 'What do you think?'

'I'm with you,' Archambaud said.

'I'll drop you if we can see the reception committee all right. Otherwise not. OK?' the pilot inquired.

'It'll have to be,' Roger replied.

The plane droned on. Soon they passed over Le Mans.

'Approaching the dropping area. Stand by,' came the words of the Captain.

The cloud was very thick as they came up to the dropping zone. The plane lost height steadily as the pilot sought to drop below the clouds. Not till they were only 250 feet above the ground could he get into the clear.

'Can you see anything?' he asked. Roger and Archambaud could hear his voice over the intercom. Archambaud was to drop first and then, seconds later, Roger would follow. The atmosphere was very tense.

'There they are,' the co-pilot called suddenly.

Soon the plane turned in to make its run. 'Stand by.' The dispatchers stood waiting to give Archambaud the word 'Go.'

'GO!' Archambaud dropped through the bottom of the plane and Roger jumped into his place. The plane turned and came back again. Even at this height there were wisps of cloud tearing on the wings.

'Go,' called the pilot.

'GO!' Roger let go and the slipstream tore him away from the aircraft. His parachute jerked him and checked his fall. The ground rushed up. Within ten seconds of leaving the plane he had hit earth. He rolled over and knocked the release mechanism of his chute. He bundled the chute into a ball and stood up. There was no one about. Not a sound disturbed the midnight silence.

Roger walked to the hedge and covered the parachute with the trailing branches of a bramble bush and then he looked around. The reception committee should have found him, should indeed have been waiting for him. He dare not make any noise, for he could not be sure that the Germans had not disturbed the committee. He caught his breath and considered what to do. He decided to wait. It was an hour before a dark figure broke through the hedge on the far side of the field and came across towards him. Roger was in the shadow of the woods which bordered the field. The other man seemed quite alone and was definitely looking for something or someone. As he came almost as far as Roger, the latter stepped out of the wood and gripped his arm. The stranger jumped with shock and astonishment.

'We thought you were dead,' he stammered, never doubting that Roger was the other parachutist. 'We'd given up looking for you. I was trying to find your body—'

'Thanks, my friend,' Roger said.

'Come, I'll take you to Paul.'

It was raining quite hard by the time the reception committee was ready to move off from the dropping area. They were between Tours and Blois, near a place called Mer. Paul, the leader, took them to a small hut which belonged to a gamekeeper and here they were given something to drink and some sandwiches. 'Now I'm afraid we shall have to turn you out,' Paul said. 'I don't know where you are heading for and I don't want to know. Good luck to both of you. Vive la France. Vive l'Angleterre.'

After this speech both the agents were politely shown the door and, having shaken hands with their hosts, went out into the darkness. It was still pouring with rain. Roger turned to his colleague. 'Good luck, my friend.' They shook each other's hands. They were never to meet again. One would die and one would survive.

'Good luck, Roger,' Archambaud said.

II

The docks at Bordeaux were empty of the invasion barges which had been ranged there when the first of our men were dropped into France during the summer of 1941, but there was still a certain amount of shipping in them and there was an air of sufficient bustle to cover the comings and goings of Claude de Baissac and his subordinates. Roger Landes was to meet his leader in a café called La Coquille down by the waterfront. He had reached Bordeaux without too much trouble, surprised, as many of our men were, by the fewness of the Germans; an agent often expected to see the place infested with the Boches and it was an agreeable shock to see that except in the larger towns and at the railway stations there were many less than he had been led to believe.

'I'm glad you got here safely,' Claude said when Roger had given him the password that confirmed Claude's own recognition of his training companion. It was not always wise to rely on personal recollections; you might be deceived into greeting someone who was not the person you thought. The result could be fatal.

'Glad to be here.'

'The first thing is to find somewhere for you to live and somewhere for you to transmit from. You've got the set?'

Roger nodded and pointed to the suitcase under the table. Claude looked tired; he had been in the field for over a year now and the strain was telling on him, particularly as the Germans had questioned him recently and, though they had let him go, he was conscious of being under continued suspicion. We knew of this suspicion in Baker Street and our instructions were for Claude to initiate Roger in the set-up of the *Réseau* as quickly as he could. After that we would move him to another circuit where he was not so well known. He would take on another identity and resume his work. We would always do our best to remove agents from areas where the danger was becoming too great, but we could only do this if we were told of their fears and if they were prepared instantly to do as we told them. This last remark is not supposed to suggest that there was indiscipline in the organisation; people took tremendous risks to obey orders, but there was always the factor that we were in London and the agents were in the field: they knew the atmosphere better than we and sometimes they backed their judgement against ours. They were picked to show initiative and they would always do what they thought best. But sometimes their judgement was faulty or their appraisal unlucky, and they only knew their own particular sector, while London had a more general view. There was little margin for error. Sometimes tragedy resulted from the view taken of a situation. But individual catastrophes could not deflect us from our purposes.

Our men and our women were volunteers: they knew all the dangers and they faced them open-eyed; if a mistake was made – and there were not as many as some people would think – we at home felt the loss as a personal one, but it is hardly fair to suggest, as certain books and individuals have done, that it was our fault. Our organisation was human, so were its judgements, its failures, its achievements. The heroism was all the agents', but the faults were not all ours.

Claude de Baissac lived in the room above the café in which he and Roger met. He did not go out more than he could help and it was this fact which caused him to arrange meetings in his own lodgings, a practice which, in general, our men avoided. Roger Landes was found a room on the Quai des Chartrons, above a tabac where his comings and goings would pass unremarked. He set up his wireless in an empty house at Quatre Pavilions, close to the German headquarters. This was not a piece of deliberate bravado – Claude and he took the view that the Germans would not look for an operator on their own doorstep. Quatre Pavilions was on a hill and transmission was excellent except for the fact that the German HQ sets and Roger's occasionally clashed and interfered with each other. Both put up with the inconvenience. Roger was able to start his skeds within a week of arriving in Bordeaux and they continued steadily. He found the house on the hill admirable for his purposes and he was never challenged by any of the military who infested the HQ nearby.

The Bordeaux *Réseau* was a model one, as Roger soon came to realise. The whole thing was arranged in the manner which was supposed to be standard practice: there were a large number of separate knots of resisters who knew, of course, of the existence of others, but knew nothing either of names, identities or areas. Only Claude – and later Roger – had the full picture. Each subsection had its couriers for liaison with the others and its own operator to receive orders from London, but a single section could, theoretically, become infiltrated by German counter-espionage without the others automatically becoming contaminated. Claude had done his job in an exemplary manner.

'Now then, I think you should have the picture pretty well sorted out,' Claude said at the last meeting. 'Are there any other questions you want to ask me?'

'How much do the Germans know about us? They know we exist – that's quite certain.'

'They know that, yes. The men whom I have already pointed out to you are the only German agents whom I could definitely pick out. There are probably others. Things are deceptively quiet and frankly I imagine you may have a sudden flurry of arrests as soon as I have left. They'll notice I've gone and they may suspect that someone else has taken over, in which case they may try and give you a hot time to start with. Now Le Chef, that's Fragonard I told you about, he's done a lot of fine work and he'll probably have tabs on a lot of Boches. You can get one of his boys to let you know what he feels about things.'

'He doesn't know who I am of course, does he?' Roger said.

'No one does except Jean, who'll act as your courier.'

'The longer we can keep it that way the better.'

'I quite agree; it's fatal to have too many people know you,' Claude smiled. 'Not that I doubt the loyalty of our people, but you can never tell when the Boches will catch someone and force him to talk. You know how. One has to try and minimise the risk. I'm sure you'll manage all right, Roger. Everyone is ready to work under you and they've got confidence in you. That's half the battle.'

Claude took his leave with this encouraging message and Roger Landes – alias Aristide – took over the command of the Bordeaux *Réseau*. It was a large and complex one and there were many ramifications. Two first-class men were needed, and we decided in London that Harry Peulevé should be sent to the area. He had been desperately unlucky to break a leg on that first drop of his, and he continually begged us to give him another chance. Now he was to have it. In the autumn of 1943 he again dropped into the Bordeaux area and later he teamed up once more with Raymond, the Spanish republican.

Raymond was, if anything, more reckless than ever, and Roger sent a message to Harry to keep away from too close an association. Wireless operators were precious. Raymond was very much of a lone wolf and he had now established himself in a deserted chateau with a store of arms and explosives. So daring had he become that he had three flagpoles on the keep of this chateau from which he flew the French, British and American flags. The chateau was sufficiently remote to attract little attention, but this show of bravado caused some alarm in the more staid elements of the Bordeaux Resistance. Raymond was undeterred. He ran his own version of the 'blackmail' plan. He not only threatened the factory owners with the RAF: he was not above suggesting that they themselves might be roughly treated – all by mistake, of course – if they refused him permission for 'a little explosion'. Few could resist the charming menace of the grinning Spaniard.

Harry gave orders that a certain factory, Malin et Fils, should be blown up and Raymond was deputed to see Monsieur Malin. The man was especially truculent.

'I think you would be foolish to refuse us, Monsieur,' Raymond told him. 'I would hate to see you shot down on your own doorstep…'

'Are you threatening me? I am a loyal Frenchman—'

'Then you must prove your loyalty.'

'Well, if the explosion were only a small one,' the man said, 'I might consider allowing it, as a special favour, you understand—'

'You cannot do your own country a favour, Monsieur.'

'If you will promise that it will only be a small explosion,' persisted the other.

'It won't be as big as some,' promised Raymond, with a broad grin.

'Well, all right. But I won't take responsibility if anything goes wrong.' The man turned away from Raymond. The latter gripped his arm and turned him round again. 'You will, you know,' the Spaniard said.

Raymond left the man and went straight to tell his dynamiters that they were to do the job that night, in case the man changed his mind and informed the Germans. He had given Raymond the key to the side gate and a plan of the factory. The whole thing should be fairly simple.

'We mustn't use quite as much explosive as usual,' Raymond told his men, 'is that clear?'

Most of them had been in the Spanish Civil War with Raymond and they were tough and remorseless. They nodded gravely. At two in the morning the men met, each one carrying a large crate of explosive. By the time they had finished laying the charges the factory was unlikely to work for the Germans again. At four in the morning a colossal explosion wrecked the place. Turbines were flung hundreds of yards by the force of the blast. The entire shop floor was destroyed. There had never been a bigger explosion in the area.

The owner was absolutely livid. He did not know to whom he should protest; it would scarcely do to tell the Germans that he had never agreed to so large a bang, while the Resistance was not prepared to accept liability. He stored his rancour, however, throughout the war and after the liberation he refused, I fear directly because of Raymond's little joke, to allow his factory to manufacture sacks for the British Army. 'They said a small explosion,' he protested, 'and my factory is out of action for over a year. That is not British justice!'

Raymond was undeterred. There was no action which he would not undertake and Harry used him for a number of highly dangerous missions. Messages to Raymond were generally taken by a courier called Rex. One day in January 1944, Harry suggested to Raymond, through the medium of Rex, that he should devote a little time to the disruption of a jam factory (working for the Germans, of course,) situated near the small town of Belin. Raymond was delighted. He collected some of his gang and they set out from the chateau where the three Allied flags flew at the mastheads, in a 'commandeered' lorry. It was late and even if their business had been harmless it would have been illegal since all French traffic was forbidden on the roads and curfew was in force. Raymond bargained on the well-known German inability to believe that anyone would do anything which he knew was against regulations; brazenness often paid off. They reached the factory without incident and soon they had laid their charges. During the course of the operation they found themselves in the sugar store. 'Be a shame to burn all this lot,' was Raymond's view. 'We'll come and collect it before we leave. There's no point in going home with an empty truck.'

They laid their charges with their long fuses and then returned to the sugar store. They formed a human chain and soon the lorry was loaded with sugar. The men jumped in and soon they were back at the chateau. Early the next morning the citizens of one of the Bordeaux suburbs were on their way to work and to market when a lorry honked its way through their midst. The driver halted it in the middle of the market square and got out of the cab. A fair crowd surrounded it and they watched with curiosity as the driver ran round to the back and opened the flap of the tailboard. A great notice-board was attached to it, upon which was printed in enormous letters: 'Housewives! Free Sugar Today – By Courtesy of the *Maquis*!' By the time they looked round the driver had disappeared. Very shortly afterwards so had the sugar.

Gestures of this kind had an electric effect on civilian morale; once people were really aware of the Resistance and of the activities of our agents they were encouraged to help us in every possible way and to hamper the Germans whenever they were able. By the beginning of 1944 we were able to arm the *Maquis* on a scale that had never been thought of before. More and more young men, fleeing the clutches of the Todt labour organisation, were taking to the hills and the remoter areas of the countryside, and they demanded arms to enable them to take an active part in the war against the Germans. It was Peter Churchill, to the best of my recollection, who first saw the possibilities of organising these young men into really efficient fighting forces. To begin with the supply of arms was very limited, but by 1944 the flow was considerable. There were arms dumps stocked and ready for D-Day in many of the *Réseau* areas and we dropped weapon training experts to instruct the French. The presence of these dumps and the numbers of the new recruits greatly added to the hazards of our men, for they were less able to check up on the new members of their organisations and the chance of double-agents infiltrating them was commensurately greater. Equally, the detection of an arms dump was much more easy than, for instance, rooting out a wireless operator. Arms dumps are bulky affairs and cannot be concealed in old suitcases. The dangers grew with the expansion of our power.

Meanwhile Aristide had not been idle. He had established what he believed to be a fool-proof liaison through Jean and Rex with Harry's group, and thus with Raymond. He told Rex, the courier, that Raymond could be used to do arms drill with a new batch of recruits who had recently joined the *Réseau.* Rex went and told Raymond and Raymond told him to notify the group to rendezvous in a farmhouse not far from the chateau where Raymond had based himself.

The group that Raymond was to instruct was a mixed one – some of them had been recruited by Le Chef, others by Roger and others by Jean, the other courier – and they were all to form a separate group under Raymond once their training was completed.

Raymond left the chateau to meet his men early on a Sunday morning. It was a fine winter morning with frost sparkling on the ground. Raymond walked along the lane towards the farmhouse and met a group of men going in the same direction. He recognised one of them and they all walked on together. In the woods approaching the farm there were a number of other men. The farmhouse itself was deserted. Raymond opened the door and led the men inside. There was a large quantity of arms there, but little ammunition. The arms training lesson was completed according to plan and the group sauntered out of the farmyard.

A machine-gun opened up at point-blank range.

'Put your hands up, you are surrounded.' A German officer was standing beside the machine-gun on the edge of the wood. Raymond pulled his men back into the shelter of the farmhouse. The machine-gun fired again.

'Try the back,' Raymond said. The men took what arms they could find and dashed to the back of the farm. No sooner had they opened the door than a murderous fire opened up. They were trapped.

'Right,' Raymond said. 'I want volunteers to come up on the roof and give covering fire.' Several men said they would come. 'We'll have to have the ammunition,' Raymond said.

'Come out of there, you terrorist swine.'

'You'll have to run,' Raymond went on. 'Run as fast as you can and get out of the wood. We'll keep you covered just as long as we've got ammunition. Right?'

'Right.'

'Come on,' Raymond cried. He led them into the loft of the farmhouse and pushed open the flap which gave on to the roof. The Germans did not notice them. Raymond worked his way to the back of the roof where it overlooked the Boches. 'Now,' he shouted. He and his men opened a sporadic fire on the German machine-gun. They dare not fire rapid for fear of exhausting their ammunition too quickly. Raymond shot the German officer commanding the post at the back and the door of the farm burst open. The unarmed patriots ran out and through the yard towards the safety of the woods. The machine-gun swivelled on them.

'Rapid,' Raymond said. The men on the roof concentrated their fire on the machine-gun. The Germans at the front of the farm now hurried round to help their comrades. The machine-gun turned on the roof to return Raymond's fire. The unarmed men were able, for the most part, to get through the cordon, leaving perhaps a third of their number dead or wounded. Raymond and his men were now isolated on the roof.

Another burst of firing from farther off suggested that the men who had escaped had run into further trouble. Raymond and his six companions now crawled round to the front of the farm. The machine-gunners from there appeared to have gone in pursuit of the escapers and Raymond and his men flung themselves down in the yard and ran to the gate. Still no one challenged them. A burst of fire suddenly came from the right and they saw that a section of men were coming back to cut off their retreat. Raymond grabbed the arm of the nearest man. 'Stay with me,' he said. 'You others run for it when we open fire. That is an order.' Raymond and his companion threw themselves on the ground in the open and engaged the section, taking what shelter they could behind the gateposts. The other five men ran for it. Two dropped at once. Raymond jumped up and ran shouting towards the Germans. His companion joined him. They ran, firing from the hip, straight at the Boches. The other three men escaped. Raymond and the other man almost reached the Germans, before they dropped, still firing, on the edge of the wood.

The remains of the weapon training class returned with the sad news to Bordeaux. Out of an original twenty, only eight survived. None of them is ever likely to forget Raymond and his brave friends.

Harry and Roger were deeply disturbed not only by the fact but also by the manner of Raymond's death. Roger sent both Rex and Jean to get as much information about the circumstances as they could. It was not easy to find out very much: those who had escaped really remembered very little of significance about the incident. It had all happened very quickly. Nobody could remember seeing anyone whom they knew directing the Germans and though Roger was suspicious of treachery, there was no definite clue upon which he could build his theory. He resolved to take the greatest care in allowing outsiders to join the Resistance.

Harry Peulevé was especially upset at the death of Raymond and those with him, for he had worked with Raymond since his return to the field. He came to see Roger in a trusted friend's house and told him of the serious gap which the loss of Raymond had made in the *Réseau* up towards Périgueux. In order to make the organisation really comprehensive some recruiting would have to be done.

'I rather think we ought to cut down on recruiting just now,' was Roger's view.

'You know what I think?'

'Go ahead.'

'Well, we know that our chaps must be on their way pretty soon. I'm going to round up as many people as I can get hold of. When the big day comes we shall need as many as we can muster.'

'I'm uneasy about things,' Roger said. 'I rather want to lie doggo for a bit and see what the Boches do next. They obviously have some sort of penetration into one of our groups and I'd like to wait till they show themselves again.'

'Le Chef tells me that he's got a group which is all ready to join us, under a Colonel called Jouas. He says they're absolutely 100 per cent safe, but they haven't got either arms or instructors.'

'Le Chef told you about this man?'

'That's right. He hangs out in Bergerac.'

'Could you contact him?' Roger asked. 'It ought to be all right.'

'If Le Chef says it's all right, it's all right.'

'Now listen, if I have any news and I can't contact you with it I shall send a message on the *messages personnels*. Can you listen every evening? If you hear the message "*Jean est très malade*", drop everything and clear out. OK?' The other nodded.

Harry left Roger and went back to his own group. Five men were to accompany him to Bergerac where they would stay for a few days under the pretext of being a syndicate interested in the purchase of some property. Harry had as his second-in-command a man called Poirier to whom he explained the need for caution.

'Le Chef has vouched for this Colonel Jouas,' he said to Poirier as they drove in their car towards Bergerac.

Harry had a presentiment that things were not going to be as easy as he had thought. Was it simply Roger's fears that gave him this feeling? It certainly seemed that there was nothing to worry about as they entered the small town. There were few Germans about and the whole place was apparently quite untouched by the war.

Harry made some enquiries about Colonel Jouas and found that there was indeed such a person. He lived at the far end of the town, on the Avenue Pasteur. Harry went himself to see the man.

'I hear that you have recruited a large number of men,' Harry said when he had shaken hands with the white-moustached Colonel.

'Well, I have a nucleus, shall we say?' the Colonel said. 'I have my organisation mapped out.'

'What is its substance?' Harry insisted.

'I have recruited almost entirely from the Socialist Party – the real Socialists, that is – none of your Communists, thank you. First-rate lot of chaps.'

'How many are there? How effective are they? What have they done?' Harry went on.

'Well – they – they haven't actually... No arms, you know. No arms at all – scandalous!'

'I want to meet these men of yours,' Harry said. 'That's quite essential before we can give you any arms.'

'Where are your dumps? How soon can you let us have some explosives?'

'That will have to wait. Now then, I want to meet your group's commanders tomorrow night. What about it?' 'Yes, that can be arranged. There's a farm called "La Grise" on the Périgueux road. Be there tomorrow night at eight o'clock and we'll have our chaps ready to meet you.'

Harry went back to his men and told them what he had arranged. Poirier said: 'I don't believe the old boy's got any men under him at all.'

'We shall see.'

'What was he like?'

'The old school,' Harry told them.

'Like the Marshal,' commented Poirier gloomily.

'We'll start from here at a quarter to seven. We can spy out the land a bit before we make the contact. We won't be coming back here after we've made the rendezvous, so we'll take all the arms and the wireless in the car with us. Don't leave anything which might give a clue to where we're going. Clear?'

The other men nodded.

The next night the black Citroën drew up outside Harry's digs. The other five were already in it.

'Let's go.'

Gustave Poirier was driving and they set off at a fair pace. When they were some distance along the road, he suddenly yanked the car to a halt outside a small *routiers'* café.

'This is a fine time—' began Harry jokingly.

'The BBC,' Poirier said. 'We ought to listen in case there's a message.'

'Nervy, Michael?' asked one of the others.

'He's right,' Harry said. 'Gustave, you go in and see if you can get them to let you listen to the wireless. We'll stay here in the car. If we drive off you'll know it's because the "flics" have turned up. You'll have to make your own way to the rendezvous. If there's anything suspicious about it, make your own way home.'

Gustave nodded and went into the café. The road was quite dark and little traffic disturbed it. A German army lorry rolled past, but neither slowed nor stopped. The men in the car waited impatiently. 'Looks as though they've got a set,' Harry said.

'Or a daughter,' suggested one of the others.

At length Poirier came out of the café. He walked round the back of the car and then opened the driver's door as Harry slid over to let him in. He put his head down into the car and looked at each of them. *'Jean est très malade,'* he said.

Another German army truck rolled past the parked car outside the café.

'Let's go.'

Poirier started up the car and turned back towards Bergerac. If the Colonel had betrayed them – and that was what it looked like – he would have some explaining to do to his German friends when Harry and his men failed to turn up.

'Turn off here,' Harry ordered when they had gone a little way. 'We're not going back into Bergerac. The trap may be that end for all we know. Cut across country to Sarlat. I've got a safe address there.'

The headlamps of the car, heavily dimmed, barely illuminated the road ahead as Poirier flung it down the country lanes towards the place Harry had named. It was another smallish place and one in which, barring accidents, they should be secure from the Gestapo.

They found the house, which was empty, and went inside. Harry decided to send a message to London as soon as possible telling them that they were safe. This would lessen the risk of anyone being sent to try and contact them and running into a trap. It was a necessary part of the team spirit of our organisation that the safety of others was as important as one's own. On the other hand a kind of ruthlessness was also necessary: if a man was caught it was against orders to attempt his rescue, if it was going to risk the lives of others and the future of the *Réseau*; if a man was wounded our men were forbidden to stay with him if such a stay were likely to lead to their own capture. It was cruel, but so is war.

Harry told Gustave to take the wireless set upstairs and get it ready for transmission as he fortunately had a sked with London at 2130 hours that night. 'We'll leave the arms and things here in the car,' he said. 'There's no sense in taking them into the house. They might be more of an embarrassment than anything else. Anyway, someone's rather interested in our arrival.' Harry had noticed a curtain in a neighbouring house pulled back to reveal an inquisitive face. 'Let's get this over and push on.'

Harry had intended to stay the night in Sarlat, but he now considered it would be safer to push on as soon as they had sent their message. The face at the window worried him.

'Denis, you keep an eye on the road and make sure no one pays too much attention to the car.'

They started to send their message to London. Maurice stood at the window. A beam from a spotlight suddenly lit up the whole room. 'A car is coming,' called Maurice. 'It must be the police with a light like that.' The beam swept across the ceiling and the car passed. 'Keep sending,' Harry ordered. 'The danger's passed.'

'Let's get out of here,' Poirier said.

'Don't be a fool. We stand a much better chance by keeping quiet.'

'Let's get the arms from the car.'

'And if the car comes back with the Gestapo?'

'It won't come—'

Poirier stopped in mid-sentence. The beam of light stabbed through the darkness again and exploded in a vivid white patch on the ceiling. The car was coming back. The six men stood still. Poirier went on with his message. The final morse groups were dispatched. The Gestapo car stopped outside the house. Harry said: 'Send your emergency danger signal to London.' No one else spoke.

There was the thunder of knocking on the door. The six men were powerless. There was no back way out of the house. They were trapped. The front door was kicked in. Boots rang on the stone steps. The door of the room was flung open. Three troopers with machine-guns covered them. A corporal came in. The six men raised their hands.

'Those are the ones,' cried an excited voice. 'Black marketeers, communists, traitors.' A small female figure burst into the room, quivering with fury and righteous indignation. It was the inquisitive woman from next door. She had rung the Germans, thinking she had trapped a nest of black marketeers. She stopped short on seeing the wireless. She looked at the men she had betrayed, their faces impassive with hatred. She looked from them to the Germans and she burst into tears and ran from the room.

'A lucky break for you, corporal,' commented Harry bitterly. 'You should get a promotion for this.'

'Come,' said the corporal.

They were taken to a prison in Clermont-Ferrand. Harry was utterly dispirited. Ill luck had dogged him and now he blamed himself for the capture of the men with him. In fact, he had no call to reproach himself, for their capture had been so unlucky that no man could have been expected to allow for the circumstances which led to it. In Clermont-Ferrand they were all put into different cells. Harry was not badly treated by the authorities, for the prison was guarded by Georgian troops sent all the way from Russia. The Georgians – or some of them at least (Stalin was a Georgian) – were not much in favour of the Allies and a number had been recruited by the Germans for such tasks as the ones at Clermont-Ferrand were engaged upon.

Harry was taken from his cell one night and led to the quarters of an officer of the Georgians. 'Tomorrow,' this man told him, 'you will be taken to a concentration camp in Germany.'

Harry bowed ironically.

'I am going to give you a chance to escape.'

Harry bowed again, surprised but suspicious. He no longer cared very much what happened to him. He had lost confidence to that degree. He knew that this trick of giving you a chance to escape was a common one among those who wanted to shoot you down. They could then report that you had been 'shot while trying to escape.' Some of the Germans made quite a little sport out of it.

'I will give you my revolver,' said the Georgian. 'I know what you are doing here in France and I want to give you a chance to continue.'

Harry stared at the man. He was holding out his revolver, his dark eyes glowing with what looked like a genuine friendliness.

At the same time, the chances of making a successful escape seemed so remote and the faith of the officer so suspect that Harry hesitated. He shook his head. 'I've heard that one before,' he said. The officer smiled sadly and returned the revolver to its holster. Something in that second convinced Harry of the genuineness of the man's offer. But it was too late to act upon it.

The next day Harry and the others were taken to Germany. Harry was in a concentration camp till he was liberated by the Americans in the beginning of 1945. He came home with four other officers from the same camp. I met them at Victoria. All the men were walking scarecrows. Harry straightened himself and saluted.

'I am sorry I failed in my mission, *mon Colonel*,' he said.

Chapter 10

Traitor

Roger Landes was filled with cold fury at the capture of Harry and his friends. It now seemed that no mission could be undertaken with safety. Roger himself spent most of his time indoors, never straying from his digs except where it was absolutely necessary and never coming into contact with any of the other members of the *Réseau*. He had ten men who acted as his special bodyguard if he did have to go about, and these men were immune from the attentions of the police: for they were themselves policemen. The ten men were members of the Gendarmerie and they had been instrumental in getting Roger genuine papers. The man who actually issued these papers became a close friend of Roger and the latter sometimes spent the evening with his family which included a pretty daughter of whom Roger became increasingly fond. The father had also enabled Roger to get a *carte de travail* – an important piece of equipment if one were long to evade the grip of the German labour organisations who were always looking for unemployed men to ship to Germany. Roger had been introduced to a Vichy labour camp chief and claimed that he wanted to do forestry work for him. He asked, however, for a month's leave to settle his personal affairs. The camp chief gave him a letter granting him a month's leave, stating that he was to be unmolested, since he belonged to an accredited labour organisation. The date on the letter was susceptible to change and month by month it was advanced. The camp commander, of course, never saw Roger again.

'Whom did you tell about Harry Peulevé's mission?' Roger questioned Jean, the courier, when he next saw him. 'I did not tell anyone,' protested the other.

'Who did you talk to?' snapped Roger.

'I do not talk.'

'Everyone talks,' Roger said. 'It's got to stop. From now on anyone who does will be shot. Two vital section heads have been lost during the last month and a good many others as well. I want a message to all section heads that they are not to act at all without direct orders from me. They are never to use any house without sending a scout first. They are not to divulge the nature of any mission to anyone without express permission from me – and they won't get that permission. They are to keep an eye open for anyone who could remotely be suspected of traitorous activities. If their suspicions are strong the man must be shot, if not he must be chucked out and all meeting places changed. Now get that out to all section heads before they are all arrested.'

Jean looked bleakly at his leader. 'Do you really believe that I would betray our men, *mon Capitaine*?' he demanded.

'It's happening too often,' Roger said sternly. 'Someone as close to the centre of things as you – or me – is responsible.'

'Surely not, *mon Capitaine*.'

'Someone that close,' Roger said.

Jean left to take the message to *Réseau* heads. One of Roger's bodyguards turned up at the house a few hours later.

'You must leave here at once,' he said. 'They've made a lot more arrests.'

'What the hell is this?' Roger cried. 'What's going on?' 'You know damn well what's going on,' the gendarme replied. 'We've got a traitor in the organisation.'

'Whom have they arrested?'

'They picked up Auguste last night. He had your telegram on him. I saw him when they brought him in. They also arrested the chief of the forestry camp.'

'What? The man who gave me my *carte de travail*?'

'That's the one.'

'What for?'

'Aiding the Resistance.'

Roger threw back his head and laughed – for the first time in many weeks. 'Aiding the Resistance! *Pauvre salaud*! How did they get Auguste?'

'It looked like a routine check – just bad luck. But I fancy they knew where to get him. The Commandant's arrest looks like an informer's work too.'

'I'd better move right away,' Roger decided. 'You can stay and help me, can you?'

'Of course,' replied the other. 'Incidentally,' he went on, as they began to pack up Roger's things, 'there is one piece of good news.'

'Oh, what's that?'

'They've let Fragonard's wife go.'

'Really,' Roger said. 'I never even knew she'd been inside.'

'Oh yes,' the gendarme said, 'she was arrested in Paris; that must have been before your time. They had her on suspicion for a long time but they could never pin anything on her. Now they've let her go. Apparently our traitor whoever he is didn't have any information about Fragonard or his wife.'

'That's rather surprising,' Roger said. 'I thought nearly everyone in Bordeaux knew about Le Chef.'

'Well, apparently they don't.'

'Unless—' Roger began.

'Unless what?'

'Nothing. Nothing.'

Roger and the gendarme moved his belongings to a safe house of which the latter knew. The family said that Roger was their nephew and seemed very happy to have him with them. Roger was much encouraged by the cordiality of his reception and he was confident of the trustworthiness of his hosts. He decided not to tell Jean of his change of address, for in spite of his faith in the man, he could not afford to take the slightest risk. He knew that the way things were it needed only his own capture totally to destroy the effectiveness of the whole Bordeaux *Réseau*. He owed it to us in London and to Claude de Baissac who had built up the *Réseau* to keep it intact.

For several days things were quite quiet. Then, one evening, there was a knock at the door while Roger and the family were sitting in the front room. Monsieur Barjou, Roger's host, went and answered it.

'I believe you have a newcomer in the house, Monsieur Barjou.'

Roger sat transfixed in his chair. There was nothing he could do.

'Ah, Monsieur Herbisse, good evening. Yes, my nephew is staying with us.'

'He is a young man.'

'Yes, he is in a reserved occupation.'

'I wonder if I could speak to him.'

'He – he is out just now.'

'Isn't that him sitting in your front room?'

'Oh, yes, yes, well – Jules, someone wants to talk to you. It's Monsieur Herbisse from next door.'

Roger went out into the passage where the two men were. His host left him alone with Monsieur Herbisse, their neighbour.

'You are a young man, Monsieur. Are you also a patriot?'

'I hope so, Monsieur,' Roger replied, cautiously.

'I am a member of the Resistance,' whispered the other.

'Yes?' said Roger sceptically, uncertain where the conversation was going to lead.

'Germany has lost the war,' said the other.

'It doesn't look like it to me.'

'It is certain. That is why we need your help.'

'If it is certain you do not need my help.'

'To hasten the day. We are very strong and we have arms dropped to us from England—'

'Dropped? How?'

'By parachute.'

'I'm sorry,' Roger said, 'I just can't believe in things like that.'

'You will be sorry, Monsieur.'

'That is possible. Goodnight, Monsieur.'

Roger went back into the front room.

'He wanted me to join the Resistance,' he smiled. 'Have you ever heard of anything so ridiculous?'

II

So far no information from any quarter had come in which might give them a clue about the identity of the traitor. One idea, however, continually recurred in Roger's mind: that the release of Le Chef's wife had some place in the pattern of events. But there was no evidence of how this fact fitted in or of its significance. Roger could only wait.

In the beginning of February four RAF men were arrested in a farm on the outskirts of Facture. Their safekeeping had been in the hands of a man called Pierre Culioli. He was taken to a barn by two of Roger's special bodyguard and questioned for four hours. He was forced to give an account of every move he had made since the moment the four men were given into his care. He accounted for every minute except an hour on the previous day. The men went on and on at him. He tried to cover it with a journey, but their suspicions had been aroused and they refused to believe him. They said they had orders to shoot him if he refused to tell them everything. He refused to talk. They tied him to a beam and said they would shoot him. He said he had been doing nothing wrong.

'Then why won't you tell us?'

'I have been told not to pass on information from one section to another. I cannot break my faith with my leader.'

'Aristide is in command of all the Bordeaux Resistance,' the gendarmes told him. 'There are no orders superior to his. No one has any business to withhold anything from him.'

'I was simply with Le Chef,' the man said. 'What's wrong with that?'

The gendarmes reported back to Roger at once.

'He was with Le Chef,' they told him. 'What's wrong with that?'

'Tell me more about Fragonard,' Roger said.

'He's been with us for years,' they said. 'One of the first – and the best.'

'What's he done?'

'He did that derailing job at Angoulême.'

'How long ago was that?'

'Oh that must be seven months or so by now,' the gendarme said. Then he looked up at Roger. 'My God, you don't think…?'

'I'm not sure,' Roger said. 'Not yet. When can you get a message to René?'

'Not till tomorrow. We have to go on duty soon.'

'I understand. Well, tomorrow I want you to get a message to René. He's to cut all contact with Le Chef and join our circuit. The same thing applies to all our men who are mixed up with Le Chef.'

'You say he is a traitor?'

'We must wait and see. I'm taking no risks. Get a message through to London telling them what I fear and asking them to tell our men to drop all liaison with Le Chef. All arms dumps are to be moved as soon as possible.'

'We'll see to it,' promised the gendarmes.

But they could not, as they said, notify René of the new orders till the next day. That night René's house was surrounded by the Gestapo. The traitor was getting reckless in the amount of information he was giving. The pressure was on him. If he did not give enough information something would happen. What was it? Roger wondered. Could it be that his wife would be re-arrested?

René held off the Gestapo in a gun battle for five hours. Then his ammunition ran out. The Gestapo entered the house. He hid in the attic. They found him. He fought them off with his fists, knocking one of them down the stairs and breaking his shoulder. At length he was overpowered and taken to the

Gestapo headquarters. He was tortured at once. He managed to hold out for twenty-four hours, in which time Roger and the others were able to notify all those who had had contact with him. Later he was shot. René was one of the best men in Roger's *Réseau* and his brave resistance both to capture and to torture was a characteristic if tragic climax to his service.

Roger's suspicions became more and more fixed on the mythical character of Le Chef (whom he had never met) and he resolved to have it out with him. Then something happened to make him change his mind. Le Chef was arrested.

III

Roger had been meeting the daughter of the man who had first issued him with genuine identity papers. This man, by name Charles[†], now told him, when next Roger visited his house, that he had been questioned by the Gestapo. Somehow they knew that he knew Roger. He had promised to work for them as the only way in which to secure his release. Roger at once arranged for the whole family to go into hiding.

At the end of the week, Alphonse, another of Roger's men, was arrested. Commandant Dhose, the Gestapo chief, was either very lucky or he was still getting expert information. Why had Le Chef been arrested? No news of him could be obtained.

Roger had a wireless set in a safe house which was above a garage in a mews. He considered the set much too precious to be abandoned, so he decided to go himself to get it and move it elsewhere. Roger usually went everywhere by bicycle and accordingly he pedalled off, after dusk, to the house where the

---

[†] Charles Corbin, later the organiser of the CARVER Circuit.

set was concealed. The enormous task of reorganisation which the wave of arrests had necessitated had made him somewhat neglect his own personal end of things; being a trained operator he used his own set, but the pressure of other work had led him to leave it where it was for several weeks.

He entered the mews and leaned his bike against the garage door, entering the house by the side entrance. He was met by the daughter of the family who owned it.

'They have arrested *Maman*,' the daughter whispered as she cut him off on the stairs.

'Why? What for?'

'They were looking for the wireless set. They suspect her of concealing it.'

'Did they find it?'

'No, no, they didn't. They're watching the house. They probably saw you come in. If they find the set they'll shoot *Maman*, that's certain.'

'I'll take it with me.'

'But they'll see you.'

Roger pushed past the girl and went upstairs to where he had hidden the set under a bed. It was still there. He took it out and went back down the stairs with it.

Roger got out into the mews with the bulky set and balanced it on the seat of the bicycle and began to wheel it out into the main road. There were two Gestapo men standing at the end of the mews; they had come round from the front of the house. Roger walked slowly on. As he came abreast of the Gestapo men the bicycle bucked suddenly on a protruding cobblestone and the case containing the wireless set tumbled with a crash to the ground. The bicycle slewed and fell and Roger almost fell on top of it. One of the Gestapo men came forward. He bent down and picked up the wireless set and then he looked at Roger closely. 'Let me help you,' he said. Roger righted the bike and smiled. 'Thank you,' he said. The Gestapo man put the wireless back on the saddle of the bike and nodded courteously. Roger walked on out of the mews. Of course, Roger never used the house again and found a new one from which to send his messages to us. There was an interesting fact about the house in the mews which Roger realised only as he wheeled his bike into the shed at the back of the Barjou's house: it had been recommended by Le Chef.

Three days later Le Chef was released.

Two days after that Jean brought a message saying that he had been in contact with Le Chef himself. Roger met him in a field outside the city.

'Has he been badly treated?' Roger asked.

'He says he managed to bluff his way out. He wants to meet you.'

'What did he say exactly?'

'He said that unless he could see you at once there might be a very serious wave of arrests.'

'Might be! We've already lost some of our best men.'

'You think Le Chef is betraying us, *mon Capitaine,* don't you?'

'Since when do you ask questions? I think no such thing,' was Roger's reply. He did not care to take Jean too fully into his confidence. He was not altogether certain of the man, fearing all who had been in contact with Le Chef. 'Tell Le Chef that I will send one of my staff to meet him at la Chèvre tomorrow afternoon at three o'clock.'

'Very well. You will not go yourself?'

'I will not go myself. Now go. And go carefully.' Roger watched Jean as he walked across the field and disappeared behind the hedge. Who was on which side? Roger began to suspect everyone. He had to deal with Le Chef before the whole *Réseau* was smoked out. He would meet him himself at the field called La Chèvre. Desperate measures were in order. Le Chef, if he was the traitor, would think that.

Roger was not Roger, but a messenger. He would therefore probably not have him arrested there and then, but would wait for the big fish, not realising that the man before him was the leader whom the Gestapo sought.

That night two arms dumps were raided by the Gestapo. Both were in places recommended by Le Chef. There was little room left for doubt.

Roger, in blue canvas trousers and a grubby white sweater, left the Barjou house at two o'clock the next afternoon in order to be at La Chèvre well before the agreed time. If Le Chef were bringing any of his German friends with him Roger would have a fair chance of spotting them and getting away. He had his revolver with him and was prepared for the worst. La Chèvre was a meeting place used with some frequency by our men: it was so-called because of a goat which was tethered in the field. There was a wooden shack near the goat's pen and it was this that Roger intended to use for the interview. In general it was against policy to arrive at meeting places early, since one often became conspicuous hanging about and a policeman or German might grow suspicious.

In general, an agent would be given several times (twenty minutes past every hour, for instance) and would go on returning until all hope of making the contact had to be abandoned. But this was a special case. Too many rules had been broken already.

Roger reached the field. There was nothing in it but the goat on the end of his long chain. Roger ambled round the hedge and down the side lanes. No one was about. He dared not stop and search too closely, for then the purpose of his stroll would be too apparent. All the same, he was as sure as he could be that the Gestapo had not surrounded the place, at least not yet.

He went back to the goat. At three o'clock a figure in a black overcoat entered the field and came across towards him. The man was about thirty-five, rather short, with a rim of black moustache across his upper lip. He walked quite jauntily, like a minor official. Roger sat down on a tin barrel and waited.

'I have come on behalf of Monsieur Igor,' the man said.

'Mmm. And I have come on behalf of Churchill,' Roger replied, giving the other half of the password he had agreed with Jean.

'Well, where shall we talk?'

'Have you got a message for Aristide?'

'Not in writing, that would be too risky.'

'For whom?' Roger said.

'Why, for us. No, I must give you the message verbally. You can remember it.'

Roger put his hand into his pocket and closed his fist round his revolver butt. He led the way into the hut.

'Well, what is the message?'

'The Germans know about me.'

'Did you talk?'

'I had to – to tell them certain things.'

'What did you tell them?'

'About the arms dumps and the wireless sets.'

'And what else? About Charles?'

'That was nothing to do with me. I was arrested myself. Charles was caught before I was arrested.'

'I know.'

'What are you suggesting?'

'You have betrayed us,' Roger said. 'Why should you not also have betrayed Charles?' Roger glared with cold hatred at the man in front of him. He would have shot him there and then had he not feared that the Gestapo might be around the hut. If that was the case, were he to shoot Le Chef the Gestapo would close in, knowing that their stool pigeon would draw no further game.

'Who are you?'

'I am a friend of Aristide.'

'You must learn to obey orders, my friend,' Le Chef said. 'You are here to take a message. Take it. This is what I have to say to Aristide. We are all in danger. Somehow the Gestapo have permeated the whole organisation. In that case we must save as many lives as we can. I have had to reveal some of the arms dumps. We will have to reveal them all if we want to stop the Germans shooting hundreds of people.'

'Do you really think this will stop them?'

'Take the message.' Le Chef stopped and looked at Roger. He smiled sadly. 'Yes, I believe it,' he said.

'I know what Aristide will say,' Roger said.

'How can you know? Are you so close to him?'

'No one,' Roger replied, 'is closer to him than I.'

'And what would he say?'

'He would say that as an officer he cannot think for a moment of surrendering quantities of arms and ammunition to the enemy.'

'You must make him understand. It is the only hope. The Germans will shoot him otherwise—'

'They must catch him first.'

'We know who he is and where he lives—'

'Doubtless you know what he looks like?'

'Of course. He is tall and fair—'

So Jean was not in Le Chef's gang. The courier was the only man who could have described Roger to Le Chef and he must deliberately have given a false description to him. That accounted for the fact that the Gestapo had not arrested Roger when he went to the house for the wireless set. They were looking for a man of a different description. Jean was neither a fool nor a knave.

'Obviously you know more than I think,' Roger smiled.

'I have not told what I know, but the Germans can easily re-arrest me. You know how they can make a man talk.'

'Yes, I know,' Roger said, not without sympathy. In spite of the traitorous activities into which he had been drawn, Le Chef had been a loyal leader in the early days and it was clear that a dreadful strain had been put upon him to make him betray his friends. There could be no excuses. Le Chef must pay the penalty, but all the same he was to be pitied. But in this kind of war we could not afford pity.

'You must take my message to Aristide at once,' Le Chef went on. 'The Germans will not wait long before they strike. I have done all I can, but I can't stall them much longer.'

'You must try,' suggested Roger.

'They are not so bad as you think. They – they realise that the Russians are the main menace. They are prepared to make a deal with us. They want us to go over to them and fight the Communists.'

'Charles was a Communist,' Roger said. 'He was one of the bravest and the best.'

Le Chef shrugged. 'Tell your leader what I have said. Unless he makes up his mind soon I can do nothing.'

Roger again felt the temptation to have done with the frightened man. But he decided to wait. 'My leader will contact you soon,' he promised.

It was clear that Le Chef was under constant pressure from the Gestapo for new information. That night another arms dump was raided before Roger could get word through the BBC to its guards. He took the step of notifying us in London that he was severing all connection with Le Chef and he asked us to notify all sections to do the same. Nevertheless, Le Chef had too much information to be left at large. There was an account to be settled.

The next day one of the gendarmes who acted as Roger's bodyguard came and told him that the Gestapo were patrolling the town in an ordinary black Citroën disguised as railway officials. The number of the car was DJ 342951. Roger had the number circulated and went off to send a message to us giving the number for relay to all sections. He had to go to a house in a district considerably removed from the one in which he was living and accordingly he took steps to disguise himself. He put on a black wig and darkened in a small moustache. He also put on thick glasses. Disguises were generally more trouble than they were worth, but Roger knew that Le Chef might have given his description to the Gestapo, never realising who he was, imagining him to be small fry. He walked along one of the main boulevards and then turned off down a side street and so through to the outskirts of the town. Suddenly, walking along a narrow lane, he heard a car coming up behind him. He stepped into a doorway to allow it to pass. As it came up to him he saw the number plate: DJ 342951. At the wheel was a man in a railwayman's uniform. At his side was a familiar figure: Le Chef. The car drove past. A million to one chance confirmed everything.

The next day Le Chef sent a message through Jean: he must meet Aristide at once. He named the place: a small village called Haute Colline. Le Chef said he would be waiting at a farm called Violette. If Aristide came he could give him some vital news. The stage was set for the final drama. Aristide sent a message to Le Chef: he would come.

Le Chef's rendezvous was along the Angoulême road. Three hours before the proposed rendezvous Roger's men were in place in a farm four kilometres from the farm Violette. Roger had delegated the command of this force to a man called Georges. He himself was in a secluded villa back on the edge of Bordeaux itself. An hour and a half before the time of the meeting three black cars full of men went past the farm where Georges and his men were. 'There they go,' Georges said. 'Le Chef's friends.'

An hour later a lookout tipped them off. Le Chef was coming along the road in a cart. His wife was with him and so was a bodyguard. Marc, one of Georges' men, was ready with a large plough which he now began to drive, very slowly, across the road. Le Chef's cart approached. Georges' men lined the farm wall. The plough stopped in the very centre of the road. The cart halted. 'Get that thing out of the way,' Le Chef cried.

Georges and his men silently approached the cart.

'What is this?' began Le Chef.

'Come on,' Georges said.

Le Chef made no resistance. The grimness of the men who surrounded him left him in no doubt of the outcome of a struggle. He and his wife and the bodyguard were all taken in the cart to Roger. The Gestapo were still waiting five kilometres up the road.

He was taken into the room where Roger was waiting. The others were put into the cellar.

'Where's Aristide?' were Le Chef's first words. 'There's been a trap.'

'I am Aristide,' Roger said.

'Don't lie to me.'

'It is you who have told the lies.'

'What's this – there's been treachery – I never—'

'You did,' Roger said. 'You did. What I want to know is how many times and where and why. You'd better talk. You have nothing to fear.'

'I don't understand.'

'I have orders to return you to London, by air. You will go tonight. All three of you.'

'Is this true?'

'Yes. Now tell me why you betrayed us.'

Roger questioned Le Chef systematically for six hours. By the end of that time a pattern had emerged. Le Chef had been a faithful and brave leader until the arrest of his wife. The Germans had threatened to kill her. He loved her. He had agreed to talk. Anyone, he said, would have done the same. The Germans were not satisfied and threatened to re-arrest his wife if he did not tell them more and more. He wanted to save the lives of the Resistance and that was why he had given away the arms dumps. Then they had asked for names. They had promised not to kill. They had broken the promise, but each time they made it again. Each time, because of his love for his wife, he had believed them.

Towards evening, Georges – who had left the house on delivering Le Chef – returned with bad news.

Roger left one of his men to guard Le Chef while he went out to hear what news Georges had brought. 'They guessed we weren't coming to the rendezvous,' he reported, 'so they put up roadblocks on all the roads round the place. Most of us managed to get through, but they picked up Marc.'

'What have they done to him?'

'We found him. He's dead. He'd been tortured. In the farm, apparently. The people heard – noises. It – it's not very nice.'

At that moment Roger was determined that Le Chef should die. His resolution had weakened somewhat during the long afternoon, as he heard Le Chef's excuses and asked himself what he would have done in the same circumstances. But now he knew he must die; in any case there was nowhere he could be imprisoned and it was out of the question to take him back to England, for why should the lives of an aircraft's crew be jeopardised to save a traitor?

Roger went back into the room where Le Chef was.

'We are going to take you to the plane now,' he said. 'My courier came to tell us everything was prepared. We will have to take you through the town in the car. Your wife and the man who was with you will go also. Now I'm sure you realise that we cannot have you crying out or trying to attract attention. If you do so, we shall shoot your wife. Do you understand?'

'Yes,' Le Chef said, his eyes glazed with tiredness.

'Let's go then.'

Georges, Roger and two of the gendarmes on Roger's bodyguard marched the two men and the woman out of the house. It was dark by now. They all got into a large station wagon which one of the members of the *Réseau* who was a butcher had lent them. There were still roadblocks on the main road out of the city and that was why it was necessary to go through the busiest sections to the woods where the affair would be finished. Le Chef sat holding hands with his wife in the back of the car. The other man sat in the front seat with Roger and one of the gendarmes.

'Where is the plane landing?' he asked after they had driven a few hundred yards.

'You'll see,' was the reply.

They entered the town. In the centre, they were forced to stop for a red light. A German field-policeman was standing on the crossing, scarcely ten feet from where Le Chef was sitting. Roger looked at him in the driving mirror. He was sitting quite serenely. He believed the story about the plane. The light changed. The car drove on.

They traversed the town and entered the country. They came to a downhill part of the road which curved through thick woods carpeted with dead leaves. Roger turned the car into a lane felted with leaves and stopped.

'Where can the plane land near here?' Le Chef asked.

'Never mind. Get out.'

They all got out.

'You lead,' Roger said to Georges.

'Come on,' Georges said to the third man.

'You next.'

One of the gendarmes took Le Chef's arm. The man turned to Roger. 'Can't we all go together?'

'No. In case—'

Le Chef nodded. He turned and looked at his wife. He kissed her and then he let the gendarme lead him down the path. Perhaps he knew. Roger followed with Le Chef's wife. They walked briskly into the heart of the wood. Ahead there was a shot. Then another. Roger pressed his pistol into the nape of the woman's neck. She shuddered. He pulled the trigger.

They buried the bodies in the floor of the wood. Nobody felt very proud of the day's work. But it had had to be done.

Now began Roger's really big job: to get the whole Bordeaux Resistance back on a fighting footing after the alarm and disruption which the betrayals had caused. It was now the end of February. A message was sent to us in London telling us of what had happened and asking that we notify all sections. Roger also needed a lot more arms to take the place of those which had been captured on Le Chef's information. Everyone felt and hoped that the day would not be far off when Allied forces would again land in France. They were eager to do everything they could to help hasten the day. We set about rearming Bordeaux.

Roger was tireless in his reorganisation. The Gestapo were furious at the failure of their ambush and did everything they could to arrest him. There were ceaseless snap controls and endless efforts to subvert more members of the Resistance. Thanks to the strictness of the security precautions which Roger took, Commandant Dhose never succeeded in destroying the *Réseau,* though he had come very close to it.

More recruits were now enrolled and those whom Le Chef had led were severed from all connection with the organisation proper. An almost completely new army was raised which, by D-Day, numbered 5,000. In general, of course, now that the war was turning our way, recruiting was much easier. Those who had failed to join us in the really hard days were now keen to do so. This last-minute reversion to the cause of the Allies became something of a joke with the seasoned *Maquisards* and resisters. Those who joined up at the last minute (and it was not yet arrived) were called *napthalinés* by their veteran colleagues, because they smelt of the moth balls from which they had so lately removed their uniforms. Uniforms were, incidentally, available to most of our officers by the time D-Day came and they put them on to lead the final and most vital missions of their men. Many shocks among the French population were caused by the sudden emergence in British uniform of a man whom they had long regarded as one of themselves.

Chapter 11

Kindling

In the middle of 1943 we had had a top secret message telling us that D-Day might be closer than we thought. This message had been tied up with international politics on a level far above our knowledge and we, of course, had acted upon it without question. In the event, it had not come true and, as everyone knows, our friends in France – and the whole world – had to wait another year before the liberation began. Nevertheless it was from the reception of this message that a certain change in our objectives can be dated. From the middle of 1943 we were specialising much more in the planting of arms dumps and the training of a secret army than we had up till then: earlier we had concentrated on sabotage and 'economic warfare' – attacks on key targets in accordance with directives from the Ministry of Economic Warfare.

Now we attempted to serve two masters, the MEW, to whom we were technically responsible, and Supreme Headquarters Allied Expeditionary Force (SHAEF), newly come into existence, with whom we were strategically linked. The pace increased. And this increased pace was, I think it fair to say, to some extent responsible for the flurry of arrests which, in some areas, temporarily dislocated the French section of SOE. It was much easier to indulge in sporadic sabotage and get away with it than it was to organise large clandestine armies without allowing a single weak link to infiltrate a section and betray his comrades.

The first serious wave of arrests took place in Paris in the months of June and July 1943. It was in these that Prosper, one of the most trustworthy, brave and resilient officers that served in SOE, was caught. Francis Suttill was a barrister before the war and the qualities of his mind were those of keenness, coolness and confidence which go to make the successful lawyer; he knew his limitations, and if they were few, he knew well enough never to go beyond them. He was a tireless organiser in the Paris area, to which he was sent in the middle of 1942. Andrée Borrel, a French girl, went with him as his courier, with the special additional responsibility of making sure that he was not forced to speak too much French at first, for, though he was fluent, our experts told us that Francis's accent might be suspect to someone with a really good ear – as most Frenchmen have – for foreign inflections. His cover story accounted for this by saying that he had been educated abroad, I think in Canada, something that was quite plausible and would account for a non-metropolitan accent.

Francis and his helpers organised a number of excellent *Réseaux* and soon they were planning large-scale sabotage. Their exploits included the destruction of a large stock of German aero fuel which was being used to power bombers attacking London and southern England. Paris was, of course, far and away the most dangerous place in which to work: it was swarming with Germans and with security police of every description. Nevertheless, Francis fashioned, in the face of every hazard, a model organisation. It attempted nothing beyond its abilities nor failed at anything within them. When the time came for the changeover from economic warfare to planning for D-Day, the necessary re-thinking was so sweeping that we decided that the best thing would be to bring Prosper over to England for his new briefing. We sent a message asking him whether he would be prepared to return for a few days' well-deserved leave. He replied that he did not like to leave but would come if it was really necessary. A Lysander was sent for him and he was in London within a few hours.

I had lunch with him the day of his return and he looked older, I thought – hardly surprising in the circumstances – but his morale was high and I had no doubt that he would be able to continue to the end the job which he had started with such conspicuous skill. We had many conferences with Allied high-ups and then, a fortnight later, Francis returned to France. I cannot but think that during his absence that vigilance which was so much a part of the character of the man had been relaxed, in spite of the most energetic and careful measures adopted by Archambaud, his W/T operator, and Andrée. Anyway it was evident that enemy agents or time-servers had permeated the *Réseau*. We had already formed a shadow organisation in Paris, totally separate and beyond the knowledge of Prosper, which was intended to take over if anything should happen to Francis. We now started another shadow organisation beyond that, so that we had three whole set-ups acting quite without knowledge of each other.

Francis began to send us messages which suggested that he himself was worried about the recruits which some of the subsections had made and the pressure of work upon him personally was growing steadily; he was under a grave strain. It may be argued that I should have brought him out of France;

that view misunderstands the nature of war: Francis was very capable, a very brilliant officer, and could not be – nor would want to be – withdrawn because the work was tough.

Our men knew what they were in for when they volunteered and my job was to see that they had the tools with which their task might be accomplished and to do everything I could to facilitate that accomplishment; at the same time, however, this was a military operation and while I have emphasised the personal side, I should not have been carrying out my own assignment if I had allowed personal considerations to override tactical ones. Francis was the best man to do what he was doing and he had to stay there. Of all the men whom we sent to France I think I admired and respected him the most and his death came as a cruel blow to me, yet, thinking as I did that D-Day was imminent, I cannot feel now that I was wrong to leave him in Paris, bitterly though I regret that I did not pull him out in that May 1943. For he told us that he was uneasy about the way things were going; yet one cannot pull out a commanding officer when the situation gets hot: we had to consider the operation as a whole, a military whole. All commanding officers are torn between what they would like to do and what they must do. That is the burden they carry, and it never leaves them.

That Prosper's *Réseau* became permeated with enemy agents was probably the work of the notorious Sergeant Hugo Bleicher whose conceit it was to style himself Colonel Henri. He was a German businessman before the war whose talents particularly suited him for the counter-espionage service; he became attached to the Abwehr and busied himself with rooting out the Resistance in the Paris area. By a series of lucky flukes, of which he cleverly took the greatest possible advantage, Bleicher had also netted Peter Churchill and Odette. His men were able to catch Prosper largely because the pressure of work forced Francis to come out into the open and attend '*parachutages*' in person. It was after one such operation that he was arrested. Nor did the arrests stop with the king-fish. Man after man was picked up, the Germans cleverly synchronising their arrests so that no one could give the alarm. Andrée Borrel was also captured and so was Archambaud who had dropped at the same time as Roger Landes. All were put to death.[†] Bleicher was triumphant. 'We have wiped out the Buckmaster organisation,' he boasted. But even in Paris, there were two shadow organisations about which he knew nothing. He imagined that Prosper was the chief of the whole Resistance: he could not conceive of the staff of a distant officer in London being the sole link between all the different *Réseaux* and fancied that they were centrally directed from Paris, as any efficient German set-up would have been. It was this failure of imagination which led him to think that the Resistance was headless. But like the hydra, it grew new heads to replace old ones.

Bleicher's boast, and to this day he is not ungenerous in his own praise, has led people to think that the Resistance was virtually disarmed by Prosper's arrest. The truth is that it was seriously disjointed, in the Paris area, for a time, but that elsewhere it grew steadily, unaffected by the disasters which Bleicher, by a mixture of genuine ability, cunning and good fortune, had brought upon it in the capital. Many arms dumps in the Paris area were betrayed to the Germans as a result of the arrests they

---

[†] Andrée Borrel was killed in Natzweiler concentration camp on 6 July 1944. Gilbert Norman (Archambaud) died in Mauthausen on 6 September 1944.

made and we were, to be quite frank, never again able to restore the Paris *Réseau* to the full standard of efficiency which they reached during Prosper's command.

Bleicher came to believe that there was little which his suave tongue and his ingratiating manner could not achieve and he did in fact have further successes, for instance in the capture of Peter and Odette, who, thank God, survived the ordeal to which they were put. Bleicher's methods were insidious. He subverted tough and loyal men, who would have withstood torture, by pretending that he was anti-Nazi and hated the thought of handing them over to the Gestapo; in this manner he managed to break them down with a sly and malevolent kindness, so bringing them to implicate their companions and introduce him, as a friend, to Resistance circles.

In London, we remained impervious to his doubtful charm and again and again we warned our men to have nothing to do with him. Some thought that they could deal with him; a few managed to do so for a time, others did not. It was a battle of wits, and Bleicher had his about him. He got Prosper and he captured others. There is no doubt that he was a subtle and, on the whole, chivalrous opponent; that I do not dispute, and while I am unable to regard the death of these men and women as merely the luck of the game, I recognise that Bleicher was doing what he thought was his duty. What I am unable to stomach is the pretence which he has adopted since the war, that he was really 'a lover of France' and that it grieved him sorely to hand patriots over to their executioners and the torturers of the Gestapo. He claims that he did not know what the Gestapo did and was powerless to stop them. That is rather like the Irishman who said he did not steal the bucket and that even if he did it had a hole in it.

Unfortunately, the results of the Prosper affair did not stop with the immediate arrests. Naturally, I considered that we must find out what went wrong and try to plug the holes and extirpate the rotten sections of the set-up. While security sought to insulate one section from another, it might be that certain elements would hook themselves on to the new and healthy organisation and bring about its ruin by the same means which had destroyed Prosper. We had to try to find out where the treachery lay. This was never successfully done. The web of suspicion was a broad one and we did in fact bring some people back to England for questioning: no satisfactory picture of the situation was ever completed and eventually we decided to probe no further and we gave the benefit of the doubt to those for whom torture and terror had perhaps, but not certainly, been too much. As I have said, however, before we decided to drop the matter, Antoine,[†] a magnificent officer, and another of our women agents, Noor Inayat Khan (known as Madeleine), were captured and, finally, shot.

Noor, who has been the subject of a charming, though not very factual book, was altogether a remarkable girl. She too was captured, probably through the agency of one of Bleicher's men, and taken to Gestapo Headquarters in the Avenue Foch. She succeeded, together with two men imprisoned there at the same time, in escaping through a skylight and thence on to the roof. At the critical moment, the air raid siren went. The rule of the Germans was that on such occasions everyone went to battle stations. One of these was on the roof. The three escapers made their way on to a

---

[†] Field name of Joseph Antelme, code name BRICKLAYER. He died in Gross Rosen concentration camp in September 1944.

neighbouring building at desperate risk on the sharply gabled roof in pitch darkness. The Germans were patrolling very near them on the adjacent roof of the headquarters. They forced a window and climbed in. All that was necessary was to get out of the flat into which they had broken, down the stairs and into the darkness. The room into which they had broken seemed empty. Then suddenly a light was switched on and a series of screams pierced the air. An old woman was asleep and had woken up to find the intruders in her bedroom. She screamed and screamed. The Gestapo were alerted and the three escapers were recaptured. Upon so thin a thread did the fortunes and the lives of our agents depend. They never got another chance.

Noor behaved throughout with the greatest bravery and went to her death with that serene defiance which typified the gallant women of SOE,[†] women who, like Violette Szabo, dared everything in the defence of a cause in which they believed. Some people have suggested that we should never have sent women on these missions at all. I cannot agree. Women are as brave and as responsible as men; often more so. They are entitled to a share in the defence of their beliefs no less than are men. The war was not restricted to men. From the purely tactical point of view, women were able to move about without exciting so much suspicion as men and were therefore exceedingly useful to us as couriers. I should have been failing in my duty to the war effort if I had refused to employ them, and I should have been unfair to their abilities if I had considered them unequal to the duties which were imposed upon them. For our part, we tried by our briefing – which became more and more precise

---

[†] Noor Inayat Khan was killed in Dachau on 13 September 1944.

and helpful – and by all the other means within our power to protect and help them, but in the final analysis an agent had to rely on himself, or herself, upon skill, upon coolness, upon courage and, most capricious of all, upon fortune.

II

Violette Szabo was first employed by SOE after one of our men called Philippe Liewer and his French colleague, Maloubier, had made Rouen too hot to hold them. She was sent to check on the position there and upon the possibilities of re-establishing the shattered *Réseau*. The circumstances of its shattering are perhaps worth telling.

Philippe and Maloubier had succeeded in recruiting a first-rate crew of saboteurs and resisters and confined themselves, for a time, with drilling them into a force capable of being a real menace to the Germans when D-Day came. They might have remained inactive till that day had it not been for a target so tempting that they could not resist it. The Germans had anchored a number of submarines in the very centre of Rouen, on the River Seine. Perhaps they hoped that the proximity of the cathedral would protect them from aerial assault.

Philippe observed that the guard which was set upon them was liable to be somewhat slack and accordingly they decided to attack. It was not too difficult to get a case of explosives to a house in the area surrounding the moored vessels and here the two waited till nightfall. Then they made their way nonchalantly along the river bank and down to where the submarines were tied up. The guard was not on the ship itself but patrolled the whole of the lower quay. They waited till he had passed the submarine which they had their eye on and then Maloubier went aboard. Philippe, his revolver in his jacket pocket, kept his eye on the sentry. Maloubier left the case in the engine-room, lit the fuse and came back through the hatch. The sentry had done one complete turn in this time and Philippe whistled to give Maloubier the all clear. The two men strolled away from the quay. Five minutes later the submarine was flung into the air.

The operation had gone very smoothly, but the repercussions were anything but smooth. The Germans went mad. They tortured anyone whom they considered able to give them information. Philippe and Maloubier, knowing they would be hunted men as soon as the Germans got wind of them and knew for certain how the submarines had been sabotaged, had already left Rouen by the time the arrests reached their height.

The Germans were ruthless and persistent. By threatening to shoot whole families they persuaded those who knew something to save their friends and relatives. The arrests went on steadily. They even managed to get a picture of Philippe and one of Maloubier drawn by an artist from descriptions given them by frightened and tortured men. These pictures were hung on many street corners. Both were good likenesses, too good for it to be possible for the two men to return to Rouen until things were a lot quieter.

It was of vital importance to us in London to know something of what was going on in Rouen, for it was one of the places where sabotage and resistance might prove extremely important when the big day came, and it was to this day that we were gearing all our efforts. At this stage we decided to send Violette Szabo to spy out the land. There were good reasons for choosing a woman, the main one being simply that she could travel about without exciting so much interest on the part of the security forces and was less likely to be rounded up in snap controls, since in the first instance the Germans concentrated on male suspects.

Violette did an excellent job. She went round all the contact addresses which Philippe and Maloubier had relayed to us. All of them had been blown. There was not one safe house left in Rouen. Worse, she reported that descriptions of the two saboteurs had been widely circulated: it would be madness for them to come back to Rouen.

Regretfully, we came to the conclusion that we would have to give up all idea of restoring the Rouen *Réseau* to its earlier strength.

Violette was ordered to join Philippe in the Dordogne district where there was going to be plenty to do when D-Day came along. For in the district adjacent to the Spanish border was stationed one of the German crack units – the Hermann Goering Division. That division would have to be harried, depleted and, if possible, stopped altogether. It would be the great test of SOE's efficiency and of the fighting power of the forces our men had recruited and trained through the long years of the occupation.

At this stage, immediately prior to D-Day, the dangers grew. Our men had to come out into the open in order to brief their forces and even now there were double agents and Frenchmen who thought their own ends could best be served by betraying their friends. In the north-east two of our best men were trapped by a double agent and both were later shot. Peter Churchill and Odette had both been caught somewhat earlier, but the organisation in which they had been most concerned was still able to continue without them, so well had they done their work. The commander in that section, Francis Cammaerts, known as Colonel Roger, was rapidly rebuilding the *Réseau* and making good its losses.

In the Jura and the Ain *departements*, where Peter had first realised the *Maquis*' tremendous potential value to our cause, was Xavier (Lieutenant-Colonel Richard Heslop, DSO) who had an army 5,500 men under him, all fully equipped with small arms, but, of course, deficient in anything bigger than a PIAT or bazooka. His men were to contain and, if possible, destroy a German armoured division stationed in the south of France which we thought might start to move north at D-Day along the Route Hannibal, a narrow road through the mountains of the Hautes Alpes, a road full of those hairpin bends and deep defiles most suited to the warfare in which the *Maquis* were trained.

By the first months of 1944, Xavier's men were in virtually undisputed control of an area the size of an English county, and even then several brigades of German troops were needed to contain them. They had been blooded in action with these forces already and we had arranged to drop a doctor to them; this was 'Parsifal',[†] a well-known Harley Street specialist, who set up a field hospital on the barren plateaux of the Jura and treated not only the wounded *Maquisards* but also members of the villages in the valleys whose loyalty to a cause in which they suffered heavily gave the *Maquis* advance warning of troop movements.

Denis Rake, who, it may be remembered, had rather an unfortunate time with Xavier when they were both captured

---

† Field name of Dr Geoffrey Parker, code name PASTRYCOOK.

earlier, had also returned to France and he was now with a tough group of *Maquisards* in the Massif Central. He could scarcely keep them from attempting to liberate France on their own. Everywhere the same keenness for the great day manifested itself.

Xavier wirelessed to us for more arms. In maintaining their perimeter against the Germans they had used up nearly all their ammunition. We decided to send a fully loaded transport plane to them. They told us that they could ensure a large enough landing area and accordingly a supply plane was sent, landed on a secluded plateau and unloaded a vast stock of essential supplies, including drugs and other medical equipment for Parsifal's hospital, which now boasted a nurse, locally recruited. In charge of arms instruction in Xavier's zone was Gordon Nornable, MC, who maintained throughout all his varied experiences the uncompromising toughness of his native Yorkshire.

More and more men, aware that D-Day could not now be long delayed, were joining the *Maquis* and we were driven to desperation – and to desperate means – in the effort to supply them with arms.

Meanwhile sabotage reached new heights. The Germans were driven to fury by its persistence and its effectiveness. Railway lines were the most easy targets and our men were so effective in the wrecking of them that some sectors were never repaired at all. The Germans simply abandoned them. They grew tired of having their repair teams ambushed and their equipment added to the wreckage already on the line. Elsewhere, aircraft were destroyed in their hangars and charges attached to the fuselages of planes parked on the tarmac. Nothing was safe from the attentions of our men.

One of the other most vulnerable targets was lock gates. All sorts of ingenious ways were adopted of blowing these up. They were, of course, an essential part of inland transport, and as the railways became increasingly hazardous, the Germans turned to canal traffic as a means of transporting important supplies. River banks and bridges were patrolled and it became more and more difficult to approach lock installations without exciting suspicion. One of our men near St Quentin in the Oise district formed, with some of his colleagues, a fully equipped fishing party. They had rods and picnic baskets and vacuum flasks and they floated, fishing contentedly, down to the gates. There they attached an underwater charge and punted calmly back past the guards, munching their sandwiches. Ten minutes later the lock gates were stove in by a violent explosion.

Unfortunately, the perpetrator of this daring raid was picked up in the furore which was subsequent upon it. He was a man of the greatest devotion to duty and no account of SOE would be complete without a tribute to him. His name was 'Guy'[†] and he had suffered a dislocation of the spine when he landed on a rock-strewn field after parachuting from his plane. He was in the greatest agony all through his time in France, yet he refused to be brought back or to retire to a safe house, and in incessant pain he organised his *Réseau* and took part in its operations helped in everything he did by his devoted wireless operator, Yolande Beekman. This sort of determination was typical of the spirit which infused our agents.

In the south also demolitions of locks and inland waterways

[†] Field name of Gustave Bieler, organiser of the MUSICIAN Circuit. Killed in Flossenbürg on 5 September 1944.

were high on the list of tasks. Here our men managed almost totally to bottle up a number of ships in the Étang de Berre. More and more targets were presenting themselves day by day as the Germans tried to cover every front upon which the Allied attack could be expected. We had to be very firm in order to restrain our people from using up all their supplies before D-Day ever arrived. Of course, we had many more planes at our disposal now, for each fresh success gained us further approval from SHAEF, and thus made it easier for us to achieve new ones.

Our build-up for D-Day went ahead. We had preserved the independence of each *Réseau* and still no one was sure who was in command of his flanking units. This was still absolutely necessary. Nothing could have been more tragic than to let the Germans infiltrate at the last minute and so render impotent a weapon we had worked so hard to build up at so great a cost, both in men and in materials, over so many months.

I was determined to keep security at a maximum until the last possible moment. In those districts where, through impetuosity or treachery, our units were unable to maintain this secrecy, a fearful price was paid. In almost every *département* of France our men waited – waited for the signal that the great day was at hand. There were 306 wirelesses tuned to London each evening, 306 different *messages personnels* would have to be sent. Each evening we sent large numbers, but most of them were, of course, blinds.

We hit upon a small plan to divert the German attention from the Normandy area where the attack was, in fact, to take place and we told our men to put the word about to their unreliable friends and, through them, eventually to the Gestapo itself that any reference to soup was to the Pas de Calais. The Germans, of course, listened in dutifully every night to the *messages personnels* without having any idea of their exact significance, but now they thought they were on to something. Sure enough, we broadcast endless sentences of the order of '*Monsieur Gérard aime lepotage*', '*Caroline demande du bouillon*', and so forth. The Germans moved a division to the Pas de Calais. It sounds foolish, but of course in Intelligence work you are always trying to see through bluffs and double bluffs. The Germans, it seems, chose unluckily, for while they fell for this small deception and the greater one of the Man Who Never Was, they failed to profit by Operation Cicero and paid no attention to the vital information they acquired through it.

On the whole, as I suggested with regard to Bleicher, their intelligence was in many ways excellent, but they were too prone to imagine a complete triumph when they had achieved only a limited success. It cost them dear in 1940 and it led them into false complacency throughout the war. It never occurred to them that their enemies would fight on whatever the odds against success. This contempt for the fighting qualities of their opponents led them to make many errors of judgement; they always made the mistake of judging others by themselves. When you are a German, that is a formidable disadvantage.

The stage was set for the final battles. We awaited only the word to set things going. On the afternoon of 5 June 1944, that word was given. That evening, 306 messages were sent out by the BBC. Those messages were indistinguishable from the dummies which we had been sending, mixed with genuine ones, since we started using the BBC for communicating with our men. But that night, for the very first time, every single message was loaded with meaning. To men huddled in mountain huts, to men in bistros in crowded towns who hid behind drawn blinds and locked shutters from the patrols which scoured the streets, to men in the Landes, in the Haute-Savoie, in the Jura, in Lille, in the Massif Central, in the heart of Paris, in tiny hamlets on the Gironde, the Dordogne and in the Corrèze and in the black factory country of the Nord and the Somme, in the forests of the Ardennes and the barren hills above Grenoble, in Marseille, Bordeaux, Toulon, Dijon, Besançon, in Clermont-Ferrand, Chartres, Le Mans, Orléans and Rennes, every message carried deadly meaning. '*Vilma vous dit oui*' meant 'destroy all German rolling stock on the railway line Angouleme–Bordeaux.' '*Madame dit non*' meant 'bring down all telegraph wires between Caen and Alengon and Caen and Évreux.' All over France similar tasks were started. Arms were brought down from lofts and dug up from beneath cellar flagstones. Uniforms were brought out and buttons polished. France was ready to help in her own liberation. How much would she be able to achieve? D-Day and the days that followed were to tell us.

Chapter 12

Flame

The nervous strain of waiting to be attacked had taken its toll on the Germans. They had troops stationed here, there and everywhere, and on the slightest hint of danger they moved them from one place to another. This sort of jitteriness lent itself to exploitation by the *Maquis*. There were two main objectives for our men: the Hermann Goering Division and the Panzers on the Côte d'Azur. We were watching their every move. On D-Day the *Maquisards* were in position. Soon after the Normandy landings, Hilaire's organisation got notice from one of their scouting parties that the Hermann Goering Division was making ready to move north to the battlefront, in the firm belief that there were no enemy troops between them and it. It was to be the job of Hilaire, Aristide, and all in the south-western districts, to show the Germans how mistaken they were.

Industrial sabotage now reached new heights. Already much had been done in the immediate pre-invasion period. In March 1944, for instance, the Dunlop factory at Montluçon had been virtually immobilised, thanks to the activities of one of our organisers working in close association with the managing director and with the participation of the workers. The explosives for the job were brought into the factory in lorries working for the firm. Similar operations were now stepped up all over France. Indeed, production was so dislocated that though the

Germans were not driven from France for several months, the factories under their control became largely useless to them.

On the Route Hannibal, Roger and Xavier waited for the German armour to begin its perilous journey north. On the day after D-Day they heard that they had packed up and were preparing to start the journey. An army of 5,500 men waited for them in the defiles of the Hautes Alpes, the Jura and the Haute-Savoie.

All over France we gave the OK for previously reconnoitred demolitions. On D-Day plus two the bridge at l'Hôpital-sur-Rhins, over the Rhone, was destroyed. It was a steel girder modern bridge and it took hours to fix the charges in place and a ladder had to be used to get the charges to the spot where they would do the most damage. The mission was completed with signal success and the Germans were denied the use of the road for over two weeks. In that time large numbers of troops had to be diverted to other routes. More and more roads were sealed off; those that were not became more and more crowded.

The railways were under constant surveillance and the employees, most of them resisters themselves, kept our section heads accurately informed about train movements and what they were carrying. Often the engine drivers themselves were tipped off about the time and place of demolitions so that they could get clear. The Germans had guards on some of the trains, however, and sometimes the drivers had to take their chances with their passengers.

In the south our men took control of whole sections of the country and many places were liberated long before Allied troops reached them. Xavier raised the Allied flags in villages of the Jura and the Germans ventured from their garrison towns only at the peril of their lives. The area north of the Loire was less easily controlled by our men, for the nature of the country, densely populated, full of Germans and offering little cover to guerrilla fighters was not suited to the *Maquis*. Lille, of course, was very eager to get into the fight and there Sylvestre had organised a large number of resisters whose activities caused the Germans plenty of trouble and greatly hampered the productive capacity of the factories.

In the area immediately behind the battle zones the *Maquisards* were active in dislocating German transport and communications. All telecommunications between German headquarters were sabotaged in the days subsequent to D-Day. Down came the wires and German liaison was ruined. Dispatch riders were then sent out. They were shot down. Large numbers of troops had then to be deployed to ensure safety of communications. And every man used for this purpose was one man less fighting the invading troops on the beachhead.

II

The Hermann Goering Division entered Hilaire's district. At once roads were blown up, trees fell across alternative routes and shots ripped into marching columns from crumbled and deserted farmhouses. The advantage of guerrilla warfare in France is that the movements of a road-bound enemy are so easily plotted. There are few usable roads and you can tip off a waiting force of the imminence of the enemy's arrival with the greatest confidence. By now all security had been abandoned in those areas actually engaged in fighting. Hilaire and Aristide were in close contact, cutting off stragglers and maiming transport. The Hermann Goering Division had to stand and fight. It lumbered angrily through the endless foothills of the Gironde, harried and stunned by the constant pressure of attacks. It twisted and turned as bridge after bridge crumbled before it and forced it to turn about. Each village concealed its ambush and the crack troops heading for Normandy were tired and exhausted before they had reached halfway to their objective. And they yet had before them the remorseless *Maquisards* of the Dordogne, the Corrèze and the Creuse, who in turn took their toll on the diminishing band.

Now Hilaire's organising genius was seen to its fullest advantage. The disposition of his arms dumps was such that each village knew where it could arm itself and had qualified leaders to control and direct its effort. The Hermann Goering Division ground to a halt and fought, fought an enemy who, when you stood and urged him to come in, would not show himself but who, as soon as you thought the coast was clear, was again on your flanks, carrying a sting whose effectiveness no corps commander could ignore.

It was during this delaying action against the Hermann Goering Division that Violette Szabo was caught. She and Anastasie,[†] a leader in the Dordogne, were on a briefing mission to some patriots in the region of Salon-la-Tour when they ran into a German ambush. They might well have got out, for Violette's quick eye spotted the Germans before they were able to open fire, but as they left their car and scrambled through a hedge into a field Violette twisted her ankle. Anastasie tried to carry her, but she cried to him, 'Get out, run for it, I'll hold out.'

He looked at her and hesitated for a second. It was the kind

[†] Field name of Jacques Dufour, member of the STATIONER Circuit.

of tragic decision agents were sometimes forced to take. He knew what the rules said in such situations: it was an agent's responsibility to save himself rather than sacrifice his life in the vain attempt to save another's. Anastasie ran across the field towards some woods. Violette lay in the field and started to fire at the Germans who came scrambling through the hedge in pursuit of the fleeing agents. She held them off long enough for Anastasie to get clear (otherwise we should not know this story) and then she was captured, her ammunition having run out, and taken away. After a long captivity borne with dignity and great courage, she was taken to Germany. At Ravensbrück concentration camp she was murdered by the Germans. Even her murderers could not restrain their admiration for her. The British Government recognised it too, by the posthumous award to her of the George Cross.

Aristide's men from the Bordeaux area were not slow to join in the fighting against the Hermann Goering Division and the ponderous wriggling of the Germans to escape from the net of torture into which they had blundered began to take on a desperate quality.

Meanwhile, in the Hautes Alpes, Roger and his men were busily blowing up sections of the Route Hannibal. The German panzers were pinned by giant landslides and their transport columns decimated by *Maquisards* who closed in on their rear. The Germans began to scour the mountains, preparing full-scale attacks against positions that were empty when finally they were stormed. Whole platoons blundered about the deserted uplands and were mopped up by bands of relentless and tough *Maquisards* for whom this battle was the opportunity to eradicate the four years of their country's shame. The villages were openly devoted to our cause and the British and French flags flew on the *Mairies* of the more daring and more remote ones. Now we decided to drop more arms, for, farther to the north, Xavier told us that his men were running short of ammunition. On the night of France's national day, 14 July, we sent seventy planes to the Jura, brought to the right place by the radio of Yvonne[†] and the planning of Lucien.[‡] A vast carnival of red, white and blue parachutes descended on the upland plains to make it clear that we in London were also celebrating France's national day. Enormous quantities of supplies were thus dropped and Xavier was able to arm still further bands who now made for the hills, anxious to strike a blow against the Boches from which either fear or complicity or lack of opportunity had earlier prevented them.

A train carrying rations to the stranded Panzer division was derailed in a railway tunnel in the Poligny district. This sabotage was done by a man called Martial Chaperon who had a highly skilled demolitions team working under him. His best coup was achieved later, however, when he and his men engineered a double derailing, two bauxite trains being simultaneously derailed and totally wrecked. Generally trains were travelling slowly through the mountain passes, but on this occasion both were in great haste and both tumbled over a small bridge, became entangled and, besides contributing to their own mutual destruction, entirely blocked and disrupted the main line.

At St Jean de Losne, the lock gates were totally wrecked when it was learned that the Germans were using the waterway to bring supplies to their reserve forces. Here the local *Maquisards*

[†] Yvonne Baseden. Field name Odette. Code name BURSAR.
[‡] Field name of Marie Joseph Gonzagues de St Genies, organiser of the SCHOLAR Circuit.

had to mop up a detachment of Germans before the demolitions could be successfully concluded. The locks were out of action from June till November, by which time our troops were in control of the area. Meanwhile, on the other side of France, a Ruffec dentist, Gaston Denivelle, had brought the number of his railway demolitions to 243 separate actions, a record I believe. In this work he was assisted by Colonel Henry de Gua, whose valour had already been proved in the First World War.

***

In the Massif Central, the district in which Hubert[†] and Nancy Wake were operating, things were not going as easily as had been hoped. Many of the German garrison troops were, at this stage, elderly men and puny boys. It was against opposition of this calibre that Hubert, Nancy and Denis Rake had been expecting to fight. They were at first disconcerted to find that the Germans had fielded forces of quite a different standard. They had recruited tough Mongol warriors who came from the German-held parts of Russia (or from those parts which the Germans had once held) and these Mongols were ruthless and courageous fighters who cared for little but battle and its rewards. Against these men our forces had only light arms and no armoured vehicles of any kind. The conflict was long and fierce, often hand to hand, and the Mongols hung on so grimly that it was almost impossible to disengage and attack from another quarter, a tactic which was usually successful against more slow-moving and heavily mechanised forces.

Denis Rake, during this protracted battle, showed all the

---

† Field name of John Farmer, organiser of the FREELANCE Circuit.

qualities which I had believed he possessed in the far off days when I fought to have him accepted in the organisation. He was resourceful and calm and he carried out his job with conspicuous acumen and courage. The reports of his exploits were to earn him the MC.

I think it only right to mention at this stage that, though many of SOE's officers earned decorations, we and certainly they did not necessarily think more highly of them than of those who fought and received no reward, or of those who died in agony to protect a trivial secret or conceal information already known to the enemy. In no other department of war did so much courage pass unnoticed. In no other department of war were men and women called upon to die alone, to withstand agony of mind and of body in utter solitude, to face death, often ignominious and pain-racked, uncertain whether they might not have saved themselves by the revelation of petty secrets. In no other department of war were civilians asked to risk everything in order to conceal a man whom they had never seen before and might never see again.

Some it may be have read a great deal about the French being too easily vanquished and too ready to collaborate. For my part, I think it would be fitter to remember the tortures which they faced (tortures which so few in any country could stomach reading about, let alone suffering) and the risks they took in the face of a cruel, vindictive and sadistic invader. Let no one in England criticise the ordinary men and women of France till he has examined his own conscience and found himself blameless of compromise with forces and opinions which he secretly detests. Some Frenchmen, perhaps many, compromised with the invader. Many more, in the face of death, stood true to their country and to her allies.

III

Xavier now had his greatest success. One of his bands was detailed to attack a German formation sealed off in one of the road sections south of Besançon. They attacked and set on fire a number of German vehicles, but at the height of the attack the Germans were reinforced by a battery of field artillery. Xavier's men were forced to retreat by the weight of the enemy firepower. The Germans, really believing that they had Xavier's men on the run, gave chase. Their field guns were highly manoeuvrable and the vehicles which drew them pursued the retreating *Maquisards* up a narrow side road into the hills. The going got rougher, but infuriated with the persistence of their attackers, the Germans pressed on.

The commander of the *Maquis* saw his chance. He sent a runner to Xavier who quickly deployed further forces in the rear of the advancing field guns. Within an hour the Germans were bracketed between two bands of *Maquisards*. The road was now a pitted track and the guns were tilting and bouncing over the uneven surface. There was complete silence. The German commander gave the order to halt and mopped his brow with a handkerchief, surveying the deserted landscape. Where had the enemy disappeared to?

'Now,' shouted Xavier. From the apparently deserted hedges, from behind boulders and crumbled shepherds' huts, the *Maquisards* poured out, levelling a deadly fire against the bemused gun crews. The Germans put up a brief defence and then surrendered. Their guns could not be manned and otherwise they were poorly armed.

For the first time, the *Maquis* were now in control of an artillery battery. It was a tremendous morale booster. Xavier saw to it that the advantage was military as well as moral. The field guns were manned by the *Maquisards* (after instruction by the German crews) and added to the fighting power of the secret army. The captured gun crews were employed at Xavier's headquarters – as mess waiters.

It was this action and the use of the guns by Xavier which led to the story current among the Germans that we were dropping artillery to the *Maquis*. We were in no hurry to disabuse them of this notion, but in fact it was not true. The belief that our men were more heavily armed than they were was also held by certain Allied commanders; on one occasion a small band of *Maquis* armed with light machine-guns was ordered to oppose a fully armed Panzer division. I was forced to point out that there were certain things that even the *Maquis* could not accomplish.

IV

The Panzer division which Roger's and Xavier's men had been harassing now came, like the Hermann Goering Division, to a full stop. The roads were impassable, even in the flat country of the Saône et Loire, where Tiburce and Guy D'Artois had organised a brilliant harrying force. The division was forced to turn and retire towards the south once again in order to try and find another, less trouble-ridden, route to the north and the distant battle area.

It now came into contact again with the forces under the command of Roger, whose men were dispersed once more along the lower stretches of the Route Hannibal. They found themselves in action against badly shaken Germans snaking about in an effort to shake loose from the unwelcome attentions of the evasive *Maquisards*.

Roger was well known throughout the south-east. He and his

men already had many battle honours and they had succeeded in closing the famous Route Napoléon entirely. The Germans had had so many casualties in their attempts to convoy troops along it that they had given up the attempt. Convoy after convoy had been sealed off and subjected to murderous Bren gun fire.

Now, as the plans for a landing along the Côte d'Azur went ahead in London, we were to put more and more work in Roger's way. He and his men stood up to it magnificently and the excellent *esprit de corps* which he had instilled in all his *Réseaux* now showed itself. The Simplon Railway was cut continuously and so were the lines which served the Rhone Valley. The Germans were in a frenzy of irritation: whole companies of field police were sent out by the Abwehr with orders to catch Roger, no matter what the cost. They were not to come back without him. In the event, they did not come back. Near Montélimar a complete company of them was ambushed and annihilated. In Valence, the railway line was completely blocked and freight cars were heaped, five and six on top of each other, across the line. Marseille was also partly under Roger, partly under the members of the 'Palestine Express', and there too the fighting grew hotter. The Germans had already destroyed the whole of the *Vieux Port* area with high explosives, but even this cataclysmic revenge had not deterred the men who lived there. They fought on from new streets, with new equipment but with the same objective: the elimination of the German forces of occupation.

Meanwhile Xavier was celebrating the expulsion of the Panzers from his zone by parading his men openly in the villages. On France's national day, he held a film show in which pictures of the Allied victories were shown in the cinemas of the Jura and the Ain. In this district, liberation was a mere formality: Xavier's men had completed it weeks before the arrival of Allied land forces.

Roger's task was only just reaching its fullest dimension. The Panzers were being engaged by his men, but their arms were incapable of destroying the Panzer heavy tanks. He appealed to us for harder hitting equipment. We dropped him bazookas, Brens and PIATs, but we could do no better than this. But even these arms needed trained operators, and Roger was faced with the harrowing spectacle of the Panzers, on the very edge of total destruction, making their escape. He appealed to us to arrange an air strike from North Africa where Allied troops were massing. The appeal was met.

While Roger's forces held the Germans pinned in the defiles of the Alpine foothills, bluffing them that his resources were stronger than they were, the RAF and American Tactical Air Force bludgeoned them, toppling tanks into the ravines, setting half-tracks on fire and finally immobilising a column of armour which might decisively have affected the fighting in the north or hampered the invasion in the south.

The invading Allied troops faced little opposition when they landed in August and began their swift advance through Provence to the north. Their comparatively easy progress was earned at the cost of many lives among Frenchmen and Frenchwomen who faced German tanks and armour with small arms, grenades and homemade bombs. In the Vercors, there was very heavy fighting. The Germans, savage and despairing, fought like demons.

Hatred and violence burst through the length of France as the *Maquisards,* indeed nearly the whole population, rose to pay off the score of four years of barbarism, terrorism and tyranny.

V

In the midst of this inferno, two days after the landing of the Allied force, Roger was caught by the Gestapo. It was desperately bad luck, for not only had he lived in constant danger for over a year without being caught, but he was badly needed to command his forces.

The only witness of his capture was his courier, Christine,[†] a Polish girl with a wonderful record in many of the German-occupied countries of Central Europe, who was hurrying to catch him up when she saw him taken. She followed as he was marched back to the local Gestapo commander. He was taken into the headquarters and the door shut behind him. Christine wondered what she should do. There was hardly time to collect help, for she knew that Roger might easily be taken away from the town by road towards the north. If the Germans knew how important their prisoner was (and descriptions of him had been circulated) they would not risk holding him so near the battle area. The Allied troops were moving too fast.

There was only one thing to do and Christine did it. She walked boldly up to the door of the Gestapo headquarters and addressed herself to the sentry.

'I want to see the chief of the Gestapo,' she said.

'You can't,' was the reply. 'He's busy.'

'I insist.'

'On what grounds?'

'I have some important information for him.'

'Wait here,' said the sentry. He was an elderly soldier and he went hesitantly inside to inform the Gestapo of their importunate

---

[†] Christine Granville (originally Krystina Skarbek), field name Pauline.

visitor. In a moment he returned. 'You can go in,' he reported doubtfully.

'Thank you,' Christine said politely, walking in.

'What is this information you have?' demanded a lieutenant behind a desk in the office.

'Are you in command here?' Christine asked.

'You can tell me your business, mademoiselle.'

'My business is with the Commandant.'

'He's occupied. I am authorised to take a message—'

'I must see the Commandant in person,' the girl insisted. She knew that her only hope was to deliver what she had to say to the man in supreme authority.

'What do you want to tell Colonel Schwarz?'

'Something that concerns him alone. Now, will you let me speak to him? It is to his advantage to hear me.'

The young officer rose unwillingly and went into the inner office. Through the open door, Christine could see Roger sitting in a chair with two thugs on either side of him. He looked through the door and saw her. His face was impassive. He gave no sign of recognition whatever.

The chief of the Gestapo returned with the lieutenant. 'What is it you want to tell me?' he snapped. 'I'm a very busy man.'

'What I have to say I must say to you alone.'

The chief nodded and the other officer left the room.

'Well?'

'I am here to speak to you on behalf of the *Maquis*,' Christine said.

'What? What?'

'You heard me, Colonel. You have a prisoner in there. I am here to ask you to give him up.'

'Are you mad? You've come here to waste my time…'

'I think not,' Christine interrupted. 'In a few hours the Americans will be here.'

'What? A few hours?'

'In a few hours,' Christine repeated. 'And when they finally arrive they will be very interested to hear the story I have instructed should be told about a Colonel Schwartz.'

'You know my name?'

'Of course.'

The use of his name seemed to impress the Colonel. 'What story have you told them?' the Colonel went on. 'That you have arrested and tortured an innocent man.'

'That is a lie.'

'That is the story, Colonel. The only way to save your skin is to release your prisoner.'

'Why? Why do you want this terrorist released?'

'My dear Colonel—' Christine said, shyly.

The Colonel looked down. 'In a few hours you say. How do you know they are coming so soon?'

'Everyone knows. If you don't release your prisoner, it will be your funeral. And I mean exactly that. Now then.' Christine was shaking from head to foot, though she seemed calm, for she knew that if the Colonel refused to release Roger she would herself be taken into custody and probably deported to Germany. 'American forces are already to the north of you,' Christine went on, seeing that the Colonel appeared undecided. 'In a matter of hours you will be cut off,' Christine ended.

The Colonel bit his knuckle. 'Bring the prisoner in here,' he shouted. 'Schnell.'

Roger was led in by the suspicious subaltern.

'You may leave,' the Colonel said to Roger.

Roger looked at Christine and blinked. Security could operate only to a certain point. Miracles were still rather outside the run of things.

'Herr Oberst—' began the subaltern in a shocked and angry voice.

'Silence,' barked the Colonel. 'Silence. Well, go on,' he said to Roger and the girl. 'Get out, both of you, get out.'

'Herr Oberst—'

'Come on,' Christine said.

In a daze, Roger walked down the corridor. The Colonel followed. At each sentry he gave orders for the two resisters to be allowed to pass. At the door of the headquarters he said: 'When the Americans come you will tell them what I have done?'

'We will tell them everything you've done,' Roger promised.

'Good, good,' smiled the German.

Roger and Christine walked slowly away down the street till they were out of sight. Then Roger turned and clasped Christine in his arms, roaring with laughter. Within an hour he was again in command of his *Maquisards*. It took the Americans somewhat longer than the threatened 'few hours' to reach Sisteron. In the command post, the Colonel waited for them impatiently. He was going to look rather a fool if they failed to turn up. Already the lieutenant was looking at him very suspiciously.

VI

The Hermann Goering Division was still in the toils. Aristide's men had chopped it into little pieces and now those shredded sections were being mopped up by the whole population of

France's south-west. This area had always been Resistance country and now, like Xavier's Jura, it virtually liberated itself, except for the big towns which were still strongly garrisoned by the Germans.

In fact, the Hermann Goering Division never did reach the battle front at all and those elements of it which escaped the full force of the *Maquisards'* fury were surrounded and pinned south of the Loire, where they finally surrendered. The delaying action so brilliantly engineered by SOE officers and so staunchly fought by the men under them had achieved far more than we in London had ever expected of it. It would have done all we had hoped of it if it had merely detained the enemy until Eisenhower's forces were securely lodged in France. It did much more than this: it so contained the Germans that they never fought on any front save that they least expected – in the country not yet reached by any invading force.

In the light of the final victory, so crushing and apparently so inevitable, it is difficult to recreate the tension we felt in London during those middle months of 1944. To invade the continent of Europe was an undertaking far more perilous, far less sure of success, than it now seems. Now it is the actions of the great armies which most commend themselves to the memoirs of Generals and the analyses of strategists; as time passes, the smaller strokes are lost in the admiration given to the overall effect. It was not always so: in that summer of 1944 many lives were saved by the exploits and the deaths of a few men. Great armies crossed bridges captured by a few irregulars under an English officer. Whole corps of German troops were diverted from the front by the bluff of a few hundred civilian riflemen.

At Romorantin, for instance, 400 Frenchmen armed with Stens and small arms managed to deny the Germans the use of the bridge over the Loire. The group was led by a British girl, Pearl Cornioley, whose maiden name was Witherington. A strong force of Germans were about to cross the Loire to join up with troops fighting east of Paris. SHAEF gave us the order to divert and hold them off. Pearl was short of trained men, so she armed all the civilians who would help her. She spread them out through the ripening cornfields on the banks of the river. When the Germans came up to the river a furious fusillade greeted them, apparently from troops occupying pre-arranged defensive positions along the far bank. The Germans approached the bridge, but the massed troops of their enemies drove them back. They faltered and retired, convinced that an American detachment had come up at fantastic speed (it would have been at the rate of about 200 miles in two days) and were entrenched against them. They moved farther up the river to find another crossing place. Most of the other bridges had been blown up and this particular corps never did manage to join the fighting in France. It only just was able to take part in the last battles of the war in Germany. By then the issue was beyond doubt.

It was this kind of holding action – in which considerable casualties could be inflicted – which made the *Maquis* so invaluable to Allied force commanders. In addition, German communications were hopelessly muddled and in many cases transport came to a halt. So efficient were the *Maquis* that the Allies were to have their work cut out to restore the facilities which had been so decisively denied to the Germans. I remember that one power plant at Creney near Troyes which Ben Cowburn had offered to blow up had been too well guarded to permit sabotage. It was just as well, for it was the only one in a wide area which was able to supply electricity to the liberated countryside. Ben Cowburn was, however, very irate at his failure.

On the whole we tried to limit the damage inflicted in the later stages to disruption, for we knew that total destruction of installations could embarrass us more than the Germans.

The only place where the Resistance was somewhat ineffectual (though this did not prevent individual acts of great bravery) was in Paris. In the capital, there were too many people eager to pay off old scores or to atone for old misdemeanours. The *Réseau* had been subject to continual waves of arrests and denunciations. As a result, their heads were hardly as well in control of Resistance groups as were their colleagues in other areas. There was too little organisation from the top, too little co-ordination and too little sense of timing. Paris fought the invader with courage (the plaques on the street corners are testimony to it) but with far less success than would have accrued with better discipline. The streets were crowded with armed men who attacked the Germans individually, as warriors might attack a pack of wolves.

Further, Paris rose rather sooner than wisdom should have permitted and the Resistance came near to suffering the fate of the Warsaw patriots, except that the Allies did not wait for them to be butchered before relieving the city. Any criticism which may seem to be implicit in what I am saying is not meant to be directed at anyone or any section in particular. The hazards in Paris were very great and unity harder to achieve: the outcome was not without its tragic side, but, as throughout the length of France, there was never any doubt of the patriotism of those who recklessly flung themselves upon the enemy. Of the civilian population of Paris in general (as indeed of that of London) no praise can be too high. I remember very clearly, on 26 August 1944, when I entered Paris for the first time since the war began, a small boy of six or seven walked solemnly up to me as I crossed the almost deserted Champs-Élysées. 'Permit me,' he said in faultless English, 'to shake hands with a gentleman. We have not seen any gentlemen for four years.'

Chapter 13

Aftermath

What then, in actual fact, were the achievements of the French section of SOE? In the last chapter I have made some attempt to outline the major successes which our men had during the invasion period. In the earlier ones I have tried to show the sort of difficulties, both administrative and personal, which they encountered and conquered. I hope that the increasing trust which the higher command came to place in the capabilities of SOE has emerged during the course of the narrative. In the beginning, the Generals were suspicious of our effectiveness and uncertain of our fighting qualities. By the end, neither was ever in doubt.

SOE finally came of age on D-Day plus fifteen. It was on that day that General Eisenhower's message came through to our office. It was Most Urgent.

This was the situation: our hold on the Normandy beachhead was far from secure; we had come up against very stiff resistance and we were pinned down; all our forces were fully committed; any reinforcement to the Germans might swing the balance and prove fatal to our cause. Those reinforcements were on the way. A Panzer corps was moving towards Normandy and was expected to cross the Eure near Évreux within the next twenty-four hours across the only remaining bridge. This bridge was the only one the RAF had failed to destroy. It had to be destroyed before the Panzers crossed it.

What General Eisenhower wanted to know was this: Could SOE destroy that bridge?

It was our chance to prove ourselves once and for all. My staff and I met in my office to consider the position. SHAEF was looking to SOE to save the balance of the battle. Could we meet the challenge?

'It boils down to this,' I said. 'Have we got someone who can get to that bridge and lay the charges under it before the Panzers get there? It's sure to be heavily guarded so it needs someone who's known locally and who can get across without too much difficulty – in other words, someone the guards will recognise as harmless.'

'Hervé's near there,' Vera Atkins said.

'Has he got any explosives left?' I said. 'That's the question.' I got through on the phone to our wireless station. 'When is Hervé's next sked?' I demanded. 'It should be tonight, unless he's changed it.' We waited while the man at the other end went to find out.

'Tonight at eight-fifty,' he reported at last.

'Take this message for him,' I said. '"BRIDGE AT ÉVREUX MUST REPEAT MUST BE DESTROYED NORMANDY BATTLE HINGES ON IT HAVE YOU EXPLOSIVES FOR JOB REPLY MOST URGENT MESSAGE ENDS."'

'I'll keep the line open for him,' the officer at the other end said. 'He'll be able to reply at once.'

'Good.' I put the phone down. 'If he hasn't got enough explosive,' I said, 'it's all up. It's too late to fly any in. Anyway the place must be crawling with Boches now.' The very outcome of the war seemed to us in that office to hinge on whether Hervé could do the job.

At eight-thirty we were all in my office, waiting for the result of Hervé's sked. We sat silently, staring at the phone. It rang at a quarter to ten.

I snatched it up. 'Yes?'

'This is Colonel Briggs here at SHAEF. Any news?'

'We're waiting to hear.'

'The RAF have failed again with the bridge. The Panzers will be there in three hours.'

'I can't tell you anything till I've heard from my man. I'm sorry.'

'Let me know at once when you hear something. The Supreme Commander's very anxious.'

We waited. Ten minutes later the phone rang. It was our wireless station.

'We have made contact with Hervé,' was the news. 'He understands the importance of the mission.'

'What about explosives?' I asked in as calm a voice as I could. 'Has he got sufficient?'

'I will read you his message. Here it is: "MESSAGE RECEIVED AND UNDERSTOOD WILL DO IMMEDIATELY EXPLOSIVES AVAILABLE VIVE LA FRANCE VIVE l'ANGLETERRE."'

I repeated it to the staff round my desk. Then I put the phone down and rang Colonel Briggs at SHAEF. 'The Supreme Commander's orders have been transmitted and will be carried out immediately,' I told him.

'I hope so,' Briggs said. 'If those Panzers get through, God knows what'll happen.'

'They won't get through,' I said.

What happened that summer night in Évreux we shall never

properly know. Immediately after receiving his orders Hervé went to see the local postman. From him he borrowed his uniform and his bicycle. He refused to say what he was going to do except to tell the postman that it was pour la France. From that time Hervé was never seen again by anyone who lived to tell the tale. My view is that he loaded the explosives into the postman's satchel and on the bicycle carrier. Then he cycled boldly up the bridge and past the guards who controlled it. As he reached the centre of it, before the guards could do anything to stop him, he flung the bike and himself to the ground and pressed the instantaneous detonators on the charges he was carrying, so blowing the bridge and himself to pieces.

The next morning an RAF reconnaissance plane flew over the Eure. There was no bridge standing. On the far side of the river, the wrong side, a Panzer corps was drawn up. That corps never crossed the Eure. That afternoon it was knocked out by a Typhoon squadron.

The next morning we had a short message of congratulation from the Supreme Commander.

From that day to the day when the last German was driven from French soil, SHAEF knew that it could rely on the bravery of our men to accomplish behind the enemy lines any mission short of meeting full German divisions in pitched battle. Our office was jammed with new battle orders for our agents, and the *Maquisards* who worked under them, and our wireless station worked night and day sending the orders to them and reporting back to us that mission after mission was completed, and that the *Réseau* in question was waiting eagerly for its next assignments. We were never short of them.

Sir Winston Churchill, in the dark days of 1941, gave us the order to 'set Europe ablaze.' After the war General Eisenhower was able to say that the operations of SOE, together with those of the *Maquis* with whom they were so closely associated, had shortened the war in Europe by nine months. In nine months a lot of towns are destroyed in a modern war, many millions of pounds of equipment are used and many lives are lost. If it is true that the war in Europe was shortened by nine months, SOE needs no further testimonial.

Books have been written since the war suggesting that the 'fifth column' is a much overrated weapon. I think such books are mainly concerned with the German fifth column in the Low Countries and in France during 1940, but the suggestion that what they say applies equally to Allied clandestine operations seems to me to be not without currency. Therefore I should like to point out once again that SOE was not a fifth column at all: it was a military organisation with strictly military objectives. For that reason it does not fall within the deprecated category of fifth columns.

The sabotage – and there was plenty of it, as I have pointed out – was ancillary to an overall military and economic end, the facilitation of Allied victory and the reconquest of Europe.

Ours was not a disjointed series of defiant and foolhardy acts, but a unified tactical and strategic operation. What made it so unusual – indeed there has never been anything like it before in the history of warfare – was that a large number of clandestine groups were welded together by a central direction which was immune from the hazards facing the individual members of the secret army and which yet was able vicariously to share in those dangers and often warn people of them, by the information which it was able to cull from many different sources and evaluate and sort out in London. At no time was SOE immune from disasters and, like most military commands, we had our share of them, but there can be no doubt that the constant dangers which the wireless operators ran in their efforts to keep us supplied with information were amply compensated by the advice and warnings we were able to give and the cohesion and sense of purpose we were able to create.

I emphasise the military nature of SOE because this appears to have become obscured in the scrutiny to which the events of the war have lately been subjected. I do not quarrel with those historians and politicians who criticise the running of wartime organisations, whether SOE or any other, but I do think that they should have some accurate perception of the status, nature and intention of those whom they are criticising. SOE has been treated by some writers as though it were a sort of glorified concert party into which men and women were inveigled by the London staff and then, inaccurately briefed and insufficiently trained, dropped into occupied France. This is so far from the truth as to demand a reply. In fact, all members of SOE were volunteers, carefully selected and weeded out, who knew exactly the sort of dangers into which they were going.

It has been suggested that women agents should never have been sent, that they were forced to undertake missions to which both by temperament and by nature they were unsuited and in physique and spirit inadequate. The dead cannot be revived by such accusations, they can only be dishonoured. Those of us who know of the work done by women like Violette Szabo, Noor Inayat Khan, Denise Bloch, among those who died, and by Lise de Baissac, the sisters Jacqueline and Eileen Nearne, and Nancy Wake among those who survived, can only feel anger and contempt for those who try to denigrate Baker Street by questioning the ability of women to fight alongside men and who impugn the efficiency of headquarters by doubting the readiness of brave women to face perils and, if necessary, to die for their countries. These women did an invaluable job and one for which, whatever people may say, they were admirably suited. Coolness and judgement were vital qualities; none lacked them. Courage was their common badge.

From the purely practical point of view, women were able to move about with far greater freedom than that accorded to men and they were less likely to be snapped up by German forced labour organisations. Also, I believe that their presence often had a steadying effect on the men who commanded them, while their resourcefulness more than once saved their less fortunate colleagues. For my part, I am inured to the attacks of those who, for reasons either personal or idealistic, doubt the competence no less than the striking power of SOE, but I cannot suffer in silence those who use the bravery of our women agents as a debating point.

During the last months of 1944, when France had been liberated, I was privileged to go the rounds of our *Réseau* and meet those who had fought with our men. I cannot think back to those days without a pang of nostalgia. How unified the Allies seemed! There was no town where we were not received with acclamation, no country village where toasts of undying friendship among the great nations were not drunk, no department which did not proudly display its battle honours gained in the defeat of the universal enemy. Everywhere Frenchmen looked forward to the resurgence of their country and to an era of peace and amity among all peoples.

The Resistance was a vital factor in this recovery of the French national spirit. The courage of the men who had fought in the *Maquis* typified what every Frenchman now wanted to believe to be the true essence of the nation. From the purely morale point of view, the *Maquis* was a tremendous fillip. It enabled the French to be proud of something. And they had something of which to be proud.

In many towns I visited the cemeteries where Frenchmen and their British colleagues were buried side by side in graves heaped with the tributes of those who fought with them and of those who did not dare to fight but could not forbear to honour. I saw more graves than there are names in this book and more ordinary men and women of France died for the Resistance than there are words in it.

As a triumph of human courage, as a tribute to the eternal hope which leads men to sacrifice everything in the defence of what they believe right, as an indication of the unity which can bind, for however short a time, men of different political, moral and religious views, the Resistance is never likely to be equalled. For in it every shade of opinion that cared for the dignity of man and for his freedom, every man who in the darkest hour yet believed that right would prevail, found its and his place. In it men and women were welded together in an unflinching and mighty confidence. All were heroes.

Appendix 1

Report of Sabotage and Guerrilla Warfare in Aristide's *Réseau* (gironde) as officially communicated by Aristide (Major R. Landes, MC) to SOE Headquarters in October 1944.

April 1944
GROUP 'PIERRE' (MÉRIGNAC)
Cut telephone line, sawed through telegraph poles situated on Avenue Bellevue 500 yards from Deux Poteaux (Mérignac-Centre). These twenty-five telephone and telegraph lines linked AA posts, also Staff HQ of Hitlerjugend. Telephone lines cut at various points at the sncaso aircraft works and within the camp. Destruction of telephone lines and electric current linking gun batteries and projectors at Cornier, on the Camarsac road near Bordeaux. Telephone lines cut at the Command Post at Quatre Pavilions near Bordeaux, linking the AA batteries on the coast. Telephone lines and railway signal lines cut 400 yards from the powder-factory at Bordeaux–Lacanau. Telephone lines linking the Peugeot factories at Mérignac with various enemy HQs cut: these lines were very important to the Germans; they were cut in several places over a section of 1,000 yards. Blowing up of a distributor post which supplied electricity to several AA batteries, also a radio detection-finder post situated at Mérignac.

May 1944
RAILWAYMEN'S TEAM
Sixteen electrically powered locomotives destroyed out of eighteen in the Monceaux Station.

GROUP 'PIERRE' (MÉRIGNAC)
Telephone lines linking marshalling yards of the Paris–Orléans Railway line and Bassens cut at Carbon Blanc. Underground telephone and electric current lines cut, linking the Hitlerjugend barracks and the Mérignac race-course, as well as the Mérignac general camp. Telephone and electric power lines linking the ten-gun battery of Chut at the Mérignac Aerodrome and the Command Post at the Château Laffargue at Mérignac, cut in

several places. Telephone lines on Pessac shooting range linking part of the Command Posts of Pessac–Alouette–Gazinet, cut 400 yards from Pessac: very important.

June 1944
GROUP 'PIERRE' (MÉRIGNAC)

Underground telephone lines cut between St Médard and several German Command Posts. Sabotage of nine electrically-powered locomotives and two electric 'Michelines' 400 yards from Pessac Station (100 yards from a German sentry box). Essential parts of locomotives completely destroyed, as confirmed by the head of the Depot at the principal Bordeaux railway station, by whom the debris was examined. Railway lines sabotaged between powder-factory and the Lacanau–St Louis line (results not confirmed).

GROUP 'DÉDÉ LE BASQUE'

Motorised convoy attacked on RN 157 on its way from Bordeaux:

Twenty-two trucks destroyed, 162 Germans killed, 182 wounded: the rest of the convoy retired to Bordeaux having been unable to get through ambush. Commando group losses: fourteen killed, forty-two wounded.

GROUP 'LÉON DES LANDES'

Railway line Dax–Bayonne cut at four points: 360,000 volt pylons blown up onto railway line. The 10,000 volt line feeding the stations cut in three places. Telephone and telegraph lines along the railway cut in five places. Underground cable on Dax–Bayonne road cut in ten places. Ten trees cut down as roadblocks on Dax–Bayonne road. All telephone and telegraph lines on main and secondary roads between Dax and Bayonne cut. German telephone lines cut, specially the one between German HQ at the Château d'Abesse and St Paul de Dax. German staff car attacked on Dax–Bayonne road: two officers killed, five wounded: our men were attacked by following truck but withdrew without loss.

At Nanosse, three teams blew four tall pylons carrying 150,000 volts – pylon across the railway track: the Dax–Mont-de-Marsan railway line cut in two places: the Dax–Orthez line pylon destroyed, cutting the 60,000 volt and the 10,000 volt lines feeding Dax and the railways.

German dispatch riders killed on Dax–Mont-de-Marsan road. All telegraph lines above ground on Dax–Mont-de-Marsan road and railway destroyed. The same team blew up Dax–Bordeaux line in six places. At Ponteux, Tartas, on Bordeaux–Dax line, five 150,000 volt pylons brought down across railway track, which is thus cut. The parallel line carrying 60,000 volts to the sub-stations cut in five places. Between St Lever and Ponteux an angle pylon blown up: the 30,000 volt and the 10,000 volt lines cut in several places. Ten trees cut down across main Dax–Mont-de-Marsan road. All overground cable lines destroyed on Dax–Mont-de-Marsan and Bordeaux–Dax main roads. Underground cable Bordeaux-Dax-Toulouse cut and 25 metres of it carried away at the Pont de Sort between Dax and Toulouse. Twelve trees cut down on second class road Dax–Montfort–Mont-de-Marsan. Traffic stopped. All overground cables cut at numerous points. Two pylons blown up so as to obstruct Orthez–Dax railway line near Mimbaste station. Telephone and telegraph cables on railway cut.

Dax–Peyrehorade: one angle pylon (60,000 volt) blown up on Bayonne line. Telephone and telegraph lines on Dax–Peyrehorade main road cut at numerous points and trees cut down across road. Sabotage of an enormous pylon on the Pau–Dax line; pylon blown up in fragments but remains standing. Angle pylon carrying 60,000 volts and 10,000 volts from St Lever blown up 300 yards from German watch-post. Pylon fell on and destroyed small transformer.

Four pylons blown up at Nanosse. Guerrilla fighting with ambushed Germans; two killed, three wounded: one of our men captured and killed. Another team attacked German formations, killing and wounding some (exact number unknown). One of our men wounded, but rescued.

Our Command Post attacked by 700 or 800 Germans armed with light tanks, mortars, field artillery and heavy automatic weapons. After vigorous resistance, the Commander orders withdrawal in good order. Germans were pushing a captured Frenchman in front of them, a revolver pressed into his back and forcing him to hold both hands above his head. Commander decided to blow up the Command Post so that it should not fall into enemy hands: prepared explosive charge and shouting to his men to retire, lit fuse. Enemy all round. Post exploded with detonation heard 24 miles away, but Commander had managed to get out of danger. Enemy stunned by vastness of explosion: forty-two Germans killed, numerous wounded by explosion and by murderous cross-fire partly from their own comrades. Three of our men killed, four captured and shot by Germans next morning, after refusing to divulge the name of their commander, despite a promise by the Germans of their lives if they did. They died heroically, singing the Marseillaise. Germans set fire to the farm where the Command Post was and arrested hostages from the civilian population.

Six rail-cuts between Misson and Pau. 60,000 volt line on railway cut. One cement pylon carrying the cable blown up between Misson and Puyoô, a second damaged. Underground cable Dax–Bordeaux blown between Dax and Castets (interruption of communications for many days). Underground cable between Dax and Bayonne blown up, interrupting all communications between Dax, Bayonne, Spain and Portugal. Underground cable blown up between Dax, Pau and Toulouse.

GROUP 'GEORGES'

Sabotage of: four 120,000 volt pylons near railway line; three 150,000 volt pylons near Grasignan; three 120,000 volt posts at Boir on St Genis road; three telegraph posts at St Fort. Electric line Hostenx–Bayonne cut. Eight 150,000 volt pylons near Ychoux. Twenty-four German telephone lines cut at La Souge. Three underground cables cut near Blaye. Two underground cables cut at the mouth of the Sauve. Points destroyed on railway at Clian. 100 yards of line at Villexavier destroyed. Two German trains derailed at Gennozac. Bordeaux–Bayonne line cut near Ychoux. Signals destroyed on Bordeaux–Dax line. Signals sabotaged at Bordeaux main station. Railway cut at Mosnac between Puy and Jonzac. Destruction of a bridge at Magnignas (RN 137). Destruction of a bridge on railway between Montendre and Chartresac. Destruction of a bridge on railway between Puy and Montignac. Destruction of a bridge near Puy (RN 137). Attack on a convoy near Saintes: result unknown. Two pylons blown up, denying electric power to railway. Three pylons blown up at Beychac.

COMMANDO GROUP 'DÉDÉ LE BASQUE'

Attack on *Milice* at Bordeaux: result unknown. Attack on German communications at Cenon: result poor. Second attack on German communications at Cenon: result satisfactory. Panzer Division's communications damaged at Monrepos. Attack on Bordeaux *Kommandantur*: serious damage; loss of German life unknown. German train cut in two and derailed on Bordeaux–Toulouse line. Three derailments of German trains near Jonzac. All German underground cables destroyed at Jonzac. Underground cable between Dax, Pau and Toulouse blown up.

'ARCACHON' GROUP

Two large HT pylons blown up, one line running along the railway and feeding the southern section. A third pylon is damaged by the fall of the other two. Twenty-nine workmen took three days to repair. Traffic partially stopped. Telephone and telegraph cables linking Arcachon with the outside world sabotaged.

'DÉDÉ LE BASQUE' GROUP

Three of our men attack German patrol thirty strong, without loss. German losses not known.

'FERNAND' GROUP

500 litres of petrol taken from Germans. Railway points attacked on metal bridge crossing the Garonne at Bordeaux, but without success owing to intervention of railway officials and, later, German sentinels and patrols. Operation

on the 60,000 volt electric line linking Chamberg, Le Bouscant, Couin: three pylons blown up, of which two completely destroyed. Operation on the 33 tonne crane at Caen and on a steam locomotive which was just leaving the repair shops. Crane completely destroyed. Engine rendered unserviceable for an unknown period owing to cylinder damage. Subsequent attempts at repairing crane abandoned after two months. Operation on two telegraph and telephone pylons on the Talence bridge. Trains delayed by twenty-four hours. German telephone communications cut in several places near Jonzac. Derailment of one German train near Pons. Derailment of one goods train near Fléac. Destruction of railway bridge near Fléac. Rail cut over 150 yards near Soulhac. Complete destruction of ammunition train near Fléac, numerous German casualties. Underground cables and HT pylons cut near Soulhac. A German express train derailed by sabotage, colliding with a petrol-tanker train north of Bordeaux. German car attacked at Bordeaux: one captain and one sergeant killed. A *Milice* car attacked at Bordeaux: four *miliciens* killed, two wounded.

July 1944
'FERNAND' GROUP

Attack on pylons near Arcachon: seven pylons destroyed; 600 yards of cable brought down; electricity cut, trains delayed seven hours. Damage unlikely to be repaired for forty-five days, despite round-the-clock work. Attack made in daylight, despite close guard by *Milice* and Germans.

Both railway tracks sabotaged for 250 yards 12 kilometres from Bordeaux on Bordeaux–Langon line, between Cadaujac and St Médard d'Eyrens: job done in broad daylight; delay of seventeen hours in normal traffic. Transformers sabotaged in railway repair shop of Bordeaux principal railway station: work stopped for three days.

'PIERRE DE MÉRIGNAC' GROUP

Two telephone lines cut at Anlac. Electric railway line sabotaged, imposing twelve hour delay on all traffic. Much sabotage of overhead telephone lines, including fifty linking the German HQ with an AA Post at Painvert. German counter-attack ineffectual. Four cables linking AA batteries and control posts at Alouette–Pessac–Gazinet destroyed. Five other cables linking AA batteries with control post at Beutre destroyed. Sabotage of communications in three places.

'ROLAND' GROUP IN BORDEAUX HARBOUR

All electric cables linking mines on the right bank of the Garonne cut; this was carried out from a canoe: the cuts were camouflaged so as to hide the damage. An attempt on the similar installations on the left bank failed. Electric cables linking mines destined to blow up Bastide Bridge cut, the work being camouflaged afterwards.

'DÉDÉ LE BASQUE' GROUP
Railway line on three bends of the Bordeaux–Le Verdon railway sabotaged for 144 yards at Soulhac. Five pylons and underground cables sabotaged near Soulhac. A German patrol encountered lost three killed and wounded, one of our group taken prisoner. Two cuts on permanent way 30 km. from Bordeaux on line to Toulouse: a semaphore destroyed: German pursuit ineffectual. Telephone-cable box destroyed at Lormont. Failure of an attempt to blow up a bridge on the Bordeaux–Libourne railway line at Ambarres: two of our men killed. No German loss. Cellulose factories at Facture attacked with much damage to machinery.

'GEORGE' GROUP
Powder-works at St Médard attacked: explosives placed on water-mains and conduits; factory out of action for fifteen days. Bridge destroyed between Pons and Jonzac. Bridge destroyed between Pons and Bougnon. Bridge partially destroyed at Hendaye. Bridge destroyed at Gars, forcing Germans to use road detour. Two pylons bringing power to German works at Soulhac destroyed.

'DÉDÉ LE BASQUE' GROUP
Railway sabotaged at St Germain de Lusignan (causing three-hour hold-up), at Coux (one locomotive destroyed: five-hour hold-up), at Tugenac (unsuccessful in one place, but munition train derailed, seventeen wagons overturned: two locos destroyed: four days' hold-up: German losses not known). Trees felled on Route Nationale 157: traffic held up twelve hours; German tank attacked, one German killed. Two large and one small pylon destroyed on Bordeaux–Libourne railway line. Railway sabotaged at Coux on Bordeaux–Paris line, 3 kilometres north of Montendre: traffic held up for four days. Munitions depot at Jonzac destroyed. Railway bridge destroyed at Bougneau, stopping traffic between Bordeaux and Saintes for more than forty-eight hours, after which only one track reopened. German requisitioning at Pons obstructed without retaliation from the enemy. Total destruction of Bougneau road-bridge, thus completing operation started some days previously: traffic completely stopped, necessitating detour of 45 miles. Points sabotaged at Pons station: considerable damage. Trees felled at Pas des Fenêtres prevent road traffic for twelve hours. Three pylons on line Pyrénées–Angoulême sabotaged at Clérac. Railway sabotaged at Coux on railway line Bordeaux–Saintes–Paris interrupts traffic for forty-eight hours. At the Latecouères aircraft factories at Toulouse, André Bouillard with two colleagues destroyed the two prototypes of the V4. Next day, photographs of the sabotage showing complete destruction of the

two prototypes were taken and sent direct to London by the Espagne route. Two armoured locomotives destroyed in Toulouse station.

THE 'ROCQUEFORT' GROUP

Though only lightly armed, attacked and seized a petrol depot. German train blown up near Riviere on Dax–Bayonne line: three coaches across the permanent way; four Germans wounded; no traffic for three days. Line blown up underneath German train on Dax–Bordeaux line at 6.30 a.m.: train stopped but not derailed; several hours' delay. On Dax–Pau line no train during night: Germans removed the explosives when patrolling. On Dax–St. Sever–Mont-de-Marsan line, no German train passed during night, so the team blew up three points at the exit of Montford station: twenty-two young people who were coming innocently to the Dax market were arrested; the Germans seized all the vegetables at the market; the population are highly amazed at this sign of German wrath. Underground cable Bordeaux–Dax blown up 6 miles from Dax. Germans, even angrier than at the railway sabotage, station troops at the point where the cable was cut and place automatic weapons all round; anybody using the road arrested: according to a German officer all the people of Dax are terrorists. Underground cable Dax–Toulouse blown up at Hinx S/Adour, cutting all telephone and telegraph contacts between Dax, Pau and Toulouse, also between Dax and Mont-de-Marsan. The same team were responsible for both operations. I am proud of them… Their Commander has lost all his property and personal possessions which have been seized by the Gestapo…

'LÉON DES LANDES' GROUP

Underground cables Dax–Bordeaux blown up between Dax and Castets (several days out of service): and at Gourbers near Dax, and at St Paul les Dax, and Montford: irreplaceable. Sabotage at Hendaye, but no full report available. At St Martin d'Oney, 300 yards of railway line blown up, cutting off Mont-de-Marsan airfield. Eight cement giant pylons blown between Puyoô and Dax, two between Puyoô and Bayonne, four between Orthez and Pau. Overhead cable cut, carried away and destroyed between Bayonne, Sabin, Orthez and Pau: traffic stopped for a number of days.

A particularly brilliant operation took place on 15 July 1944 at 9.10 p.m. All the petrol stored at St Paul les Dax was blown up. The seven tanks contained 456,000 litres of petrol and were totally destroyed. 200,000 more litres of oil were destroyed. The depot was guarded by three German watchposts and surrounded by AA batteries. The people of Dax were overjoyed, the Germans furious.

Railway bridge at Lucbardez on Mont-de-Marsan–Marmande line blown up: four days out of action (personally confirmed). 60,000 volt line from Licq blown up in mountain ravine, irreparable. The 60,000 volt line Sauveterre-de-Béarn–Baigts-Béarn blown up: six pylons destroyed. HT line blown at Lannemezan.

As a result of these acts of sabotage, electric power considerably reduced. We shall go on till we eliminate it altogether.

Cable linking France with Spain and Portugal cut at two points. German train blown up at Laluque: engine out of service at least two months.

On the Marmande line 350 yards of rail again blown up: Germans obliged to replace rails by using marshalling yard rails. Line from St Sever to Dax blown: several hours' delay. Fuse-boxes blown between Orthez and Dax, Orthez–Toulouse and Orthez–Pau. Points blown up in Bougue, Villeneuve de Marsan, Labastide d'Armagnac and Le Frède stations: traffic at a standstill. Complete munition train blown up in Laluque station when on its way to Normandy: twenty-two trucks containing shells and munitions of all kinds destroyed; first explosion at 8.30 p.m. followed by others throughout the night; forty-seven trucks carrying special German equipment reduced to matchwood and burned out; railway line and signalling apparatus destroyed; traffic totally stopped; trains from Toulouse, Pau, Bayonne, Dax, etc., had to be re-routed; no traffic between Bordeaux and Hendaye. The RAF had on several occasions tried without success to destroy this train.

August 1944
'DÉDÉ LE BASQUE' GROUP

German tanker-lorry blown up: 15,000 litres of petrol destroyed. German radio-detection van destroyed. Transmitting and receiving set captured and used by the group: two Germans killed. Trees felled at Pas des Fenêtres (RN. 157) stopping traffic throughout night. Two English parachutists coming from Normandy rescued. Sabotage on railway-line Bordeaux–Saintes–Paris: three points destroyed, as well as telephone lines.

Three and a half tonnes of flour destined for German Army taken from broken-down lorry at Crup: flour distributed to friendly bakers to provide bread for hungry population. Training and live shooting for recruits organised by English Corporal Owen Williams and CSM Leslie Jones of SAS. Coast protection sloop belonging to German Customs at Royan attacked by grenades while patrolling off Pauillac: six Germans killed; sloop sunk. German lorry attacked near Pas des Fenêtres: two Germans killed, four wounded. Another German convoy attacked near Mirambeau: four Germans, including an officer, lulled – several wounded. German convoy attacked on RN 137 near Plaine Selve: one lorry destroyed, two Germans killed. German truck attacked on RN 730 near St Cier du Taillon: seven Germans killed, two wounded. Telephone communications destroyed over

400 yards between Paris and Pons. (D 32 road). All telephone wires cut over 330 yards on RN 137. Two-hour attack at Murettes Fonceaux on RN 137 near Bellore: German car destroyed; one German killed, two wounded in first attack; one German killed, two wounded in second attack; one sidecar destroyed in third attack; two lorries destroyed, four Germans killed, several wounded in fourth attack. Telephone communications and posts destroyed between Plassac and Pons. HT pylon destroyed at St Cier du Taillon. Bordeaux–Saintes railway line cut for twenty-four hours. On RN 10 near Haut-Lieu, four Germans killed. One of our men wounded. On D 30 all telephone communications destroyed over 300 yards. Todt organisation material captured, including railway trucks, levellers and rails. On D 32 telephone communications destroyed over 200 yards: posts cut down. On RN 137, four attacks on German convoys, seven Germans killed, over ten wounded. Communications completely severed between Plassac and Pons. HT pylon destroyed at St Cier du Taillon. Bordeaux–Saintes railway cut at Carignac: traffic stopped for twenty-four hours. RN 10. German car attacked near Montlieu; four Germans killed, one member of our group wounded. A traitor P, who was responsible for the death by torture of two French men, was executed. Seven men and two cars patrolling road attacked strongly armoured German lorry. Patrols on RN 130 stopped vehicles going to Saintes in compliance with German requisition orders. Attack on watch-post at Coux. Telephone lines between Jonzac, Mirambeau, St Genes, St Fort and Mortange–viz all German circuits in the area destroyed by 4men. Telephone lines at St Thomas de Cognac, cutting all contact with Lorignac watch-post (repeated twice after repairs), two watch-posts destroyed by ten men at St Thomas de Cognac. German convoy attacked on D 2: two Germans killed, two wounded, German car made unserviceable. No French loss. German refuelling and munition truck attacked on D 2: five Germans killed, one wounded; no French loss.

Town of Montendre occupied: field gun and shells captured. Patrols made in forests of Bussac, Bédenac and Chatenet. Search for fleeing Germans in the forests: twenty-seven men captured. On Royan–Paris line 100 yards of rail destroyed: traffic stopped for twenty-four hours. Telephone wires cut on RN 137 on Jonzac road: German signs obliterated. Sabotage of track between Royan and Pons: results unknown. Telephone lines at watch-post at Souban-Mirambeau destroyed by three men.

Dédé le Basque (André Bouillard) with thirteen men attacked German convoy consisting of armoured cars, tracked vehicles and trucks. German force consisted of 435 men: action took place near Montendre, and lasted four hours; two armoured cars, sixteen trucks destroyed; Germans lost more than sixty men. André Bouillard, the head of the group, was killed and three men wounded. Germans were prevented from reinforcing their positions.

'FERNAND' GROUP
Two German lorries attacked: six Germans killed, five wounded. No French loss.

'PIERRE DE MÉRIGNAC' GROUP
Railway line blown at Arlac, and electric cables destroyed.

'GEORGE' GROUP
Round Bordeaux sixteen HT pylons blown up. Transformer in St Jean railway station destroyed. Three transformers at Pessac power-station blown up. Ten ammunition trucks sabotaged north of Bordeaux: five Germans killed. Six ammunition trucks sabotaged in Pessac station. German train attacked and sabotaged at Béliet; engine made unserviceable. Four 90,000 volt pylons blown up at Hosteins.

German car attacked on Bayonne road: officer killed: we lost one man killed. Unsuccessful attempt to sabotage Medoquine power-house. HT pylon sabotaged near Léognan: road blocked for two hours. German lorry blown up in front of Bordeaux Stock Exchange. Two Germans killed at Gravières. German lorry containing requisitioned bicycles blown up at Carbon Blanc: German guard killed.

Lorry trailer containing two aircraft engines, propellers and 100 litres of petrol set on fire. Tracked vehicle containing two machine-guns and petrol blown up in front of German HQ at Bordeaux. Two Germans killed at level crossing at Marcheprime: unfortunately the crossing-keeper was shot accidentally. Ammunition seized from German depot: one German soldier taken prisoner.

'ARCACHON' GROUP
German stores seized at Ychoux. Six pylons sabotaged between Ychoux and Lugos. German train derailed between Labouheyre and Ychoux. Numerous Germans killed and wounded. Track blown up during passage of train near Ychoux. Engine and five trucks derailed.

'LEON DES LANDES' GROUP
Three pylons blown up at St Paul les Dax near main transformer.

HT line blown up near Sauveterre de Béarn: three pylons brought down. Four pylons brought down at St Paul les Dax: traffic stopped completely. Near Mauléon, two pylons toppled into a ravine.

At Rivehaute three pylons, at Chéraute two, at Rivehaute two destroyed by explosives.

Underground cables Dax–Bordeaux blown up at St Paul les Dax, cutting telephone communication with Iberian Peninsula. German train blown up between Orthez and Baigts de Béarn: electric loco rendered unserviceable; five trucks derailed across track, traffic stopped. Train carrying heavy artillery blown up at Buglose: engine unserviceable, train stopped; traffic interrupted. Alas, trains don't go more than 12 miles per hour and it is difficult to bust everything up.

German military train blown up at Caudos; traffic paralysed. Train heavily laden with artillery blown up at Tarnos: engine overturned, numerous trucks blown to smithereens, traffic stopped for several days. A fifth train blown up. Sabotage of small metal bridge on Bayonne–Dax only partially successful at first attempt, completed at second.

Underground cables between Dax and Bordeaux, Toulouse and Bayonne blown up. All telephone communications in south-western France suspended. All HT cables in south-western France out of action: only steam trains can run. Sabotage kept on permanent twenty-four hour round the clock basis. All trains are blown up and traffic on railways is at a standstill. German troops are confined and requisition bicycles, horse-carts, wheelbarrows and try to flee: road attacks cost them dear: morale is very low; there is confusion in the ranks. Indescribable disorder reigns. The retreat resembles a rout of a band of gypsies rather than a withdrawal of troops.

Train towing 50 tonne crane, sent to lift previously sabotaged supply train, blown up: crane brought down across the track with numerous trucks; service completely stopped. On Bordeaux–Dax line a trainload of German railwaymen trying to escape and to get through despite the cost was blown up with great loss of life to the Germans (between Dax and Laluque). Military train blown up on Dax–Bayonne line. Pylons destroyed with result that traffic stopped for ten days. Underground cable cut as far as La Rochelle, in one direction, Spain in the other. All overhead circuits in south-west cut on 14 August and again on 18 August, as well as all HT lines: more than fifty pylons destroyed. No rail traffic in whole of south-western France. A German attempt to send an armoured train resulted in the latter being blown up with a record amount of PE. On 16 August another German attempt proved vain and contents of supply train were seized.

Group passes to open warfare in uniform on 20 August; 700 French attack German garrison at Mont-de-Marsan. The enemy, believing a full attack to be imminent retires precipitately without 'scorching the earth': much petrol abandoned: a seven hour fight with German reinforcements ensued; Germans had 1000 men engaged: they withdrew, leaving behind two field-guns, ten cars and a tanker containing 36,000 litres of petrol and a repair-shop lorry. One of our mortar shells scored a direct hit on a German ammunition truck which blew up, causing Germans heavy losses. Five Frenchmen and British Captain Mellows were assassinated by the Germans.

23 August. We attack Dax: violent fighting; fifteen German vehicles

destroyed, fifty German prisoners taken. At the same time, we attack Germans at Soustens, St Vincent de Tirosse and Bayonne, inflicting heavy losses and capturing ten tanks, twenty tracked vehicles, many field-guns and stores. Enemy in complete confusion – Germans at Bayonne, Hendaye and St Jean de Luz surrender without a fight.

ALL GROUPS

The Germans, having abandoned the whole of south-western France to the south of Bordeaux, withdrew on Bordeaux. I decided, in agreement with the Commissaire de la République, Monsieur Cusin, to give them an ultimatum, in order to save the port installations of Bordeaux. The Germans with thirty to 35,000 men are confined within the town, surrounded on all sides. They occupy the submarine base, guns are trained on the town from the heights round it. The ultimatum signed by the Commissaire de la République and the British Military Delegate, postulates unconditional surrender. On 17 August Germans announced provisional acceptance and promised not to 'scorch the earth'. French and British order population to remain calm (signed Triangle and Aristide (Major Landes)). Germans evacuate Bordeaux towards Libourne. They are attacked north of Bordeaux and lose many prisoners. Those at Soulhac and Royan are blockaded and retire to fortifications, whence we are not strong enough in arms to dislodge them. On 1–2 September 1,500 Germans armed with mortars attack near Lesparre, but after French counter-attack retire to Soulhac. A German sloop bombards Bordeaux. Our groups clean up the area of Blayes. On 6–7 September 600 Germans attack Mortange but are dislodged by French. Germans are still holding Gironde estuary.[†]

---

† NB: They held this territory until opening of 1945. – Ed.

Appendix 2

This list of all the agents known to have worked under Buckmaster has been compiled by David Harrison, who is a researcher specialising in the SOE French section. The list only includes those working under F Section direction who received SOE training in the UK before being sent into France or, if recruited locally in the field, were granted a commission. It should be noted that the names and details are not necessarily complete and that other names may yet emerge as new files are added to the National Archives at Kew.

SURNAME	FORENAMES	FIELDNAME	Operational Name	Name on Documents	Main CIRCUIT Main Mission (M)	ROLE	Arrival Date	Fate
ABBOTT	George William	Paul	MULBERRY	Georges Marie MARC	AUTOGYRO	Organiser	2/12/1942	Survived Capture
AGAPOV	Pierre	Raymond	-	-	JOCKEY	W/T Operator	Locally Recruited	Survived Capture
AGAZARIAN	Jack Charles Stanmore	Marcel	USHER	Jacques CHEVALIER	PROSPER-PHYSICIAN	W/T Operator	12/30/1942	Executed
AGAZARIAN	Françoise (Francine) Isabella	Marguerite	LAMPLIGHTER	Francine FABRE	PROSPER-PHYSICIAN	Courier	3/18/1943	Returned Safe
AGEE	Dr Fred B	Antonin	ANTAGONIST	-	SALESMAN 2	Medic	8/19/1944	Returned Safe
AISNER	Julienne Marie Louise (JuJu)	Claire	COMPOSITOR	Marie CLEMENCE	FARRIER	Courier	5/15/1943	Returned Safe
ALEXANDRE	Roland Eugène Jean	Astre	SURVEYOR	Roland Eugène Jean ESNAULT	SURVEYOR	Organiser	2/9/1944	Executed
ALLARD	Elisée Albert Louis	Henrique	MILLIONAIRE	Charles MONTAIGNE	LABOURER	Assistant	4/6/1944	Executed
ALLINGTON	Nicholas	Agrippa	AVENGER	Nicolas BARBES	HISTORIAN	Assistant	7/17/1944	Returned Safe
ALSOP	John DeKoven	Alonce	ADMINISTRATOR	-	FREELANCE	Instructor	8/8/1944	Returned Safe
AMPHLETT	Philip John	-	TAXIDERMIST	Philippe Jean CHIRAUX	Scullion 2 (M)	Saboteur	8/16/1944	Executed
AMPS	James Frederick (Jim)	Tomas	CHEMIST	Jean MARECHAL	PROSPER-PHYSICIAN	Assistant	10/2/1942	Executed
ANDRE	Georges	José	-	-	TREASURER	Assistant	Locally Recruited	Survived

SURNAME	FORENAMES	FIELDNAME	Operational Name	Name on Documents	Main CIRCUIT Main Mission (M)	ROLE	Arrival Date	Fate
ANTELME	Joseph France Antoine	Antoine	BRICKLAYER	Antoine RATIER Joseph DUMONTET	BRICKLAYER	Organiser	11/18/1942	Executed
APTAKER	Benjamin	Aléric	LIBRARIAN	Jean-Roger GAUTHIER	GARDENER	Instructor	3/6/1944	Returned Safe
ARCHAMBAULT	Jean Paul	Chico	APOTHECARY	-	DITCHER	Instructor	4/7/1944	Returned Safe
ARNAULT	Jean-Claude	Néron	HAIRDRESSER	-	WHEELWRIGHT	Assistant	1/6/1944	Returned Safe
ARON	Jean Maxime	Joseph	-	-	VENTRILOQUIST	Assistant	Locally Recruited	Escaped - 05/01/1944
AUBIN	Raymond	Alfred	AUDITOR	Jean Lucien de BREFEUIL	SCHOLAR	Organiser	7/7/1944	Returned Safe
AUDOUARD	Georges Henri	Martial	NOTARY	Georges Henri MASSON	STATIONER	Assistant	2/11/1944	Released
AUTOTTE	Joseph Roland	Alexander	AMATEUR	-	Helmsman (M)	W/T Operator	8/4/1944	Returned Safe
BAISSAC de	Claude Denis	David	SCIENTIST	Clement BASTABLE Michel ROUAULT Claude Marc BOUCHER	SCIENTIST 1 & 2	Organiser	7/30/1942	Returned Safe
BAISSAC de	Lise Marie Jeanette	Odile	ARTIST	Irène BRISSE Jeanette BOUVILLE	SCIENTIST 2	Organiser	9/25/1942	Returned Safe
BALTHAZAR	Edouard	Frascati	-	-	TINKER	-	Locally Recruited	Survived
BARDANNE	Jean Guépard	Hubert	-	-	CARTE	-	Locally Recruited	Released
BARRETT	Dennis John	Honoré	INNKEEPER	Charles MEUNIER	MINISTER	W/T Operator	4/12/1943	Executed
BARTHE la	Georges	Cyrus	-	-	BRICKLAYER	Assistant	Locally Recruited	Survived
BASEDEN	Yvonne Jeanne Thérèse de Vibraye	Odette	BURSAR	Marie BERNIER	SCHOLAR	W/T Operator	3/19/1944	Survived Capture
BASIN	François Marcel	Olive	URCHIN	François Marcel BASIN	URCHIN	Organiser	9/22/1941	Released - 29/11/1942
BASSET	Maurice Marie Roger	Ludovic	BEGGAR	-	BEGGAR	Organiser	4/11/1944	Returned Safe
BEAUCLERK	Charles Ralph	Casimir	BEADLE	-	DIGGER	W/T Operator	4/9/1944	Returned Safe
BEAUREGARD	Alcide	Cyrano	BURGLAR	André M BEAUREGARDE	LACKEY	W/T Operator	2/6/1944	Executed
BEC	Francis Eugène	Hugues	BORER	Raymond PERRIN Francisque Eugène LABROUSSE	HEADMASTER 2	Instructor	5/29/1944	Killed in Action
BEEKMAN	Yolande Elsa Maria	Mariette	PALMIST	Yvonne de CHAUVIGNY	MUSICIAN	W/T Operator	9/18/1943	Executed
BEGUE	George Pierre André	George 1	BOMBPROOF	Georges Robert MERCIER	AUTOGYRO	W/T Operator	5/6/1941	Escaped - 16/07/1942

SURNAME	FORENAMES	FIELDNAME	Operational Name	Name on Documents	Main CIRCUIT Main Mission (M)	ROLE	Arrival Date	Fate
BENOIST	Robert Marcel Charles	Lionel	CLERGYMAN	Daniel PERDRIDGE Roger Marcel Robert BREMONTIER	CLERGYMAN	Organiser	10/21/1943	Executed
BENOIT	Joseph Henri Armand	Boris	BARNSTORMER	-	SILVERSMITH	Saboteur	5/24/1944	Returned Safe
BENSTEAD	Walter Albert	Barbarousse	BUCANNEER	Albert BENISSET	Cut-Throat (M)	Saboteur	9/15/1944	Returned Safe
BERGE	Adrien Paul Léon	Tutur	STAYER	-	WRESTLER	W/T Operator	Locally Recruited	Survived
BERNARD	Ernest Paul	Jean	AUTOGYRO C2	Ernest JEAN	AUTOGYRO	Organiser	7/9/1941	Survived Capture
BERTHEAU	Louis Eugène Désiré	Pélican	-	-	AUTHOR	W/T Operator	Locally Recruited	Died in Captivity
BEUGNON	Raphael	Hugo	BILLSTICKER	Raoul BERGER	BEGGAR	Saboteur	4/11/1944	Returned Safe
BICHELOT	René François Marie	Alvar	BAGPIPER	René BERTRAND Raymond Jean BRIAND	SCHOLAR	Assistant	5/7/1944	Returned Safe
BIELER	Gustave Daniel Alfred	Guy	MUSICIAN	Guy MORIN	MUSICIAN	Organiser	11/18/1942	Executed
BIRCH	Charles	Charles	-	Charles DOULARD	Scullion 2 (M)	Saboteur	8/16/1943	Returned Safe
BISSET	Edward George Alfred	Adjacent	-	Jules LACROIX	Tilleul (M)	Saboteur	7/8/1944	Killed in Action
BLACKWELL	Thomas Geoffrey	Benedicte	BLOWER	-	SHIPWRIGHT	Instructor	8/25/1944	Returned Safe
BLANC le	Robert	-	-	-	DIPLOMAT	Assistant	Locally Recruited	Survived
BLOCH	André Georges	George IX	DRAFTSMAN	André Jean BERNARD	AUTOGYRO	W/T Operator	9/6/1941	Executed
BLOCH	Denise Madeleine	Ambroise	SECRETARY	Micheline Claude RABATEL	CLERGYMAN	W/T Operator	3/3/1944	Executed
BLOCH	Michel Georges	Boetie	BONESTTER	Michel BLOIS	FREELANCE	Instructor	8/31/1944	Returned Safe
BLOCH	Jean-Pierre	Gabriel	-	-	CORSICAN	Assistant	Locally Recruited	Escaped - 16/07/1942
BLOMFIELD	Vernon Elliot	Density	-	-	Bergamotte (M)	Organiser	7/1/1944	Returned Safe
BLONDET	Louis Alfred	Valerian	OSTLER	-	CLERGYMAN	Assistant	6/21/1944	Escaped - 05/01/1944
BLOOM	Marcus Reginald	Urbain	BISHOP	Michel BLOUNT	PRUNUS	W/T Operator	11/4/1942	Executed
BODINGTON	Nicolas (Nick) Redner	Jean	GAMEKEEPER	André ALCESTE André Edouard BRAND	PEDLAR	Organiser	7/30/1942	Returned Safe
BOISSIERE	Jacques François	Bocace	BIRDMAN	-	GLOVER	Instructor	9/12/1944	Returned Safe
BOITEUX	Robert René	Nicholas	SPRUCE GARDENER	René FIRMIN Roger LEGER	SPRUCE	Organiser	6/2/1942	Returned Safe
BORNEVAL	M.	Berthold	BREEDER	-	VENTRILOQUIST	Assistant	8/25/1944	Returned Safe

SURNAME	FORENAMES	FIELDNAME	Operational Name	Name on Documents	Main CIRCUIT Main Mission (M)	ROLE	Arrival Date	Fate
BOROSH	Henri	Marius	SILVERSMITH	Jean GOUMONT André TABASTE	SILVERSMITH	Organiser	1/21/1943	Returned Safe
BORREL	Andrée Raymonde	Denise	WHITEBEAM	Denise URBAIN	PROSPER-PHYSICIAN	Courier	9/25/1942	Executed
BOUCART	Robert Charles	Hors-Bord	-	-	Vaucluse (M)	Instructor	7/19/1944	Returned Safe
BOUCHARD	Henri	Noel	BANKER	-	DONKEYMAN 2	W/T Operator	5/7/1944	Returned Safe
BOUCHARDON	André	Narcisse	JOINER	André MICHEL	SACRISTAN	W/T Operator	8/19/1943	Escaped
BOUGUENNEC	Jean	Max	BUTLER	Francis Le GUEN	BUTLER	Organiser	3/24/1943	Escaped - 16/07/1942
BOUVIER	Armand	Tactful	-	-	WOODCUTTER	W/T Operator	Locally Recruited	Survived
BREEN	Arthur Vivien	Bruno	BEACHCOMBER	Jean BRIQUET	PEDAGOGUE	W/T Operator	7/31/1944	Returned Safe
BROOKS	Anthony Morris	Alphonse	PIMENTO	Antoine BREVIN,	PIMENTO	Organiser	7/2/1942	Returned Safe
BROUVILLE Comte de	Alain Jean Patrick René Maze-Sencier	Théodule	TREASURER	Marcel Jean SANGUIER	TREASURER	Organiser	4/11/1944	Returned Safe
BROWNE-BARTROLI	Albert James	Tiburce	DITCHER	-	DITCHER	Organiser	10/21/1943	Returned Safe
BRUCKER	Herbert	Sacha	BOATSWAIN	Robert BEAUMESTRE	HERMIT	W/T Operator	5/27/1944	Returned Safe
BRUHL	Robert George	Barnabe	BANDIT	Robert Gaston BAUMAN	PERMIT	Assistant	7/18/1944	Returned Safe
BURDEYRON	Noel Fernand Raoul	Gaston	AUTOGYRO C1	Fernand CAVALIER	AUTOGYRO	Organiser	7/9/1941	Survived Capture
BURNEY	Christopher Arthur Geoffrey	Charles	AUTOGYRO A YEW	Charles AG BRUNET	AUTOGYRO	Organiser	5/30/1942	Survived Capture
BUTT	Sonya Esmée Florence	Blanche	BIOGRAPHER	Suzanne Jacqueline BONVIE	HEADMASTER 2	Courier	5/29/1944	Released
BYCK	Muriel Tamara	Violette	BENEFACTRESS	Michèle BERNIER	VENTRILOQUIST	W/T Operator	4/9/1944	Died of Meningitis
BYERLY	Robert Bennett	Gontrand	BIOLOGIST	Robert Antoine BREUIL	SURVEYOR	W/T Operator	2/9/1944	Executed
CALSTAYUN	Alfred	-	-	-	SILVERSMITH	Assistant	Locally Recruited	Survived
CAMERON	Aylmer Evelyn	Cleon	CALCULATOR	-	FIREMAN	Saboteur	8/14/1944	Returned Safe
CAMMAERTS	Francis Charles Albert	Roger	JOCKEY	Charles Robert LAURENT	JOCKEY	Organiser	3/24/1943	Released
CAMPBELL	Alexander Peter Patrick	Clément	CHIROPODIST	Alexandre Pierre Georges CAMBIER	FIREMAN	Assistant	7/2/1944	Returned Safe
CAMPET	Louis	Lancelot	-	-	ACTOR	Assistant	Locally Recruited	Survived
CAUCHI	Eric Joseph Denis	Pedro	MESSENGER	Louis Jean CAUDRON	STOCKBROKER	Instructor	8/14/1943	Killed in Action

SURNAME	FORENAMES	FIELDNAME	Operational Name	Name on Documents	Main CIRCUIT Main Mission (M)	ROLE	Arrival Date	Fate
CAZA	Roger Mark	Emmanuel	PRELATE	Roger Marcel PILON	PIMENTO	W/T Operator	2/6/1944	Returned Safe
CHALMERS WRIGHT	Fergus Camille Yearman	Chalk	SOLICITOR	Camille CHAMALIERES	DONKEYMAN 1	PWE	10/2/1942	Returned Safe
CHARLET	Valentine Blanche	Christianne	BERBERIO	Sabine LECOMTE	DETECTIVE	Courier	9/1/1942	Escaped - 16/09/1943
CHARTRAND	Joseph Christian Gabriel	Dieudonné	MESMERIST	Claude CARTON	SALESMAN 1	Assistant	4/15/1943	Returned Safe
CHENE le	Henry Paul	Victor	PLANE	Henri Paul CHENET	PLANE	Organiser	4/23/1942	Returned Safe
CHENE le	Pierre Louis	Grégoire	ASPEN	Pierre LE FEVRE	SPRUCE	W/T Operator	5/3/1942	Survived Capture
CHENE le	Marie-Thérèse	Adèle	WISTERIA	Marie Thérèse RAGOT	PLANE	Courier	11/4/1942	Returned Safe
CHOREMI	André Constantin	Cresus	CONFECTIONER	André CLAVET	Cut-Throat (M)	Saboteur	9/15/1944	Returned Safe
CHURCHILL	Peter Morland	Michel	SPINDLE	Pierre Marc CHAUVET	SPINDLE	Organiser	1/9/1942	Survived Capture
CLECH	Marcel Remy	Bastien	GROOM	Yves le BRAS Marcel CORNIC	MONKEYPUZZLE	W/T Operator	4/21/1942	Executed
CLEMENT	Georges	Edouard	DRIVER	Georges Jean CLERMONT	PARSON	W/T Operator	7/25/1943	Executed
CLEMENT	Maurice Rémy	Marc	JURYMAN	René RIVIERE	FARRIER	Assistant	10/17/1943	Returned Safe
COHEN	Gaston Armand	Justin	WATCHMAKER	Jean Pierre DULAC Gaston RIGALE	JUGGLER	W/T Operator	6/13/1943	Returned Safe
COHEN	Albert	Camille	CABBY	-	FOOTMAN	Instructor	9/5/1944	Returned Safe
COLEMAN	Jean Henri	Victor	CHORISTER	-	ACOLYTE	Assistant	9/16/1943	Returned Safe
COLLETTE	Joseph Albert Howard	Carlos	COLLECTOR	Joseph Albert COLET	SALESMAN 2	W/T Operator	8/2/1944	Returned Safe
CONNERADE	George Auguste Joseph Louis	Jacquot	CALDER	Georges Auguste ARCHAMBAUD	Housekeeper (M)	Advance Party	6/22/1943	Returned Safe
CONUS	Adrien	Volume	-	André CUNOT	Eucalyptus (M)	W/T Operator	7/6/1944	Escaped when about to be shot
COOREMAN	Raoul Guérin	Felix	INNKEEPER	-	MINISTER	W/T Operator	Locally Recruited	Survived
COPPIN	Edward (Ted) Cyril	Olivier	BAY	Jean Pierre VIDAL	DONKEYMAN 1	Instructor	6/12/1942	Executed
CORBIN	Charles Henri Lucien	Allyre	CARVER	Camille Jean CRABOS	CARVER	Organiser	4/10/1944	Returned Safe
CORMEAU	Beatrice Yvonne	Annette	FAIRY	-	WHEELWRIGHT	W/T Operator	8/22/1943	Returned Safe
CORMIER	Robert Adrien Joseph Antonio	Bob	PEDLAR E	Robert CORMIER	PEDLAR	Saboteur	7/10/1944	Returned Safe
CORNIOLEY	Henri Charles Willy	Jean	-	-	WRESTLER	Assistant	Locally Recruited	Survived
COTTON-BURNETT	Roger Albert	Albert	AUTOGYRO B	-	AUTOGYRO	Assistant	5/14/1941	Survived Capture

THEY FOUGHT ALONE

SURNAME	FORENAMES	FIELDNAME	Operational Name	Name on Documents	Main CIRCUIT Main Mission (M)	ROLE	Arrival Date	Fate
COUNASSE	Emile René	Caton	CALLBOY	Emile René SOULLIER	VENTRILOQUIST	W/T Operator	5/27/1944	Survived
COUNET	André	Felix	-	-	DITCHER	Assistant	Locally Recruited	Survived
COWBURN	Benjamin Hodkinson	Benoit	BLACKTHORN	Jean François VILLENEUVE	TINKER	Organiser	9/6/1941	Returned Safe
CROIX de la	Jean	Delpech	-	Pierre CROIRE	Eucalyptus (M)	W/T Operator	6/29/1944	Returned Safe
CULIOLI	Pierre Urbain	Adolphe	-	Pierre LECLAIR	PROSPER-PHYSICIAN	Organiser	Locally Recruited	Survived Capture
CUNNINGHAM	William R	Paul	-	Paul de BONO	Dressmaker (M)	Saboteur	8/18/1943	Returned Safe
D'ARTOIS	Lionel Guy	Dieudonné	DECORATOR	Robert Guy D'ARTOIS	DITCHER	Organiser	5/23/1944	Returned Safe
DADA	René	Pagnon	-	-	MINISTER	Assistant	Locally Recruited	Escaped from captivity
DAMERMENT	Madeleine Zoe	Solange	DANCER	Jacqueline DUCHATEAU	BRICKLAYER	Courier	3/1/1944	Executed
DANE	Dr David M Surrey	Dodo	-	-	SHIPWRIGHT	Landing Grounds	8/14/1944	Returned Safe
DANIELS	William Hawk	Dick	DEALER	-	FOOTMAN	Saboteur	7/30/1944	Returned Safe
DARLING	George P	George	-	-	PROSPER-PHYSICIAN	Organiser	Locally Recruited	Killed in Action
DEDIEU	Gérard	Jerome	PERMIT	Gérard Louis DELESSE	PERMIT	Organiser	6/7/1944	Escaped - 05/00/1944
DEFENCE	Marcel Eusèbe	Dédé	WEAVER	Michel DELAPLACE Maurice DOARE	SCIENTIST 1	W/T Operator	5/14/1943	Executed
DEFENDINI	Alphonse	Jules	PRIEST	Ange DEFENDINI	PRIEST	Organiser	2/29/1944	Executed
DEFOURNEAUX	René Julien	Daniel	DAIRYMAN	René Jullian DELPEYRAUX	LICENCEE	Assistant	8/9/1944	Returned Safe
DEMAND	George W Hedworth	Edmonde	STEVEDORE	Pierre STRUBE	Scullion 1&2 (M)	W/T Operator	4/9/1943	Executed
DENISET	François Adolphe	Jean-Jacques	MARINER	François DUSSAULT;	SURVEYOR	W/T Operator	2/9/1944	Executed
DERICOURT	Henri Alfred Eugène	Gilbert	FARRIER	Marius FABER Henri GOGUENARD	FARRIER	Organiser	1/23/1943	Returned Safe
DESPAIGNE	Harry Marcel Richard	Richard	MAHOGANY ASSASSIN	Hughes Marcel DESGRANGES	DETECTIVE 2	W/T Operator	7/30/1942	Returned Safe
DETAL	Julien Théodore Joseph	Rodrigue	DELEGATE	Julien HAMONT	DELEGATE	Organiser	3/1/1944	Executed
DEVEREAUX-ROCHESTER	Elizabeth	Elizabeth	TYPIST	Denise Berthe ROQUETTE	MARKSMAN	Courier	10/19/1943	Survived Capture
DIACONO	Henry Louis-Antoine	Blaise	PLAYBOY	Henri GARNIER	SPIRITUALIST	W/T Operator	2/6/1944	Returned Safe
DORMER	Hugh Everard Joseph	Paul	OCULIST	Maurice DUPONT	Scullion 1&2 (M)	Leader	4/9/1943	Killed in Action

SURNAME	FORENAMES	FIELDNAME	Operational Name	Name on Documents	Main CIRCUIT Main Mission (M)	ROLE	Arrival Date	Fate
DOWLEN	Robert Roland	Richard	CHANDLER	François Antoine PERRIER	CHESTNUT	W/T Operator	3/18/1943	Executed
DUBOIS	André Jean Roger	Hercule	LIGHTERMAN	André DUBREUIL	DONKEYMAN 1	W/T Operator	4/15/1943	Executed
DUBOIS	Randall M	Charles			FREELANCE	Instructor	8/31/1944	Returned Safe
DUBOUDIN	Emile Jean Georges	Alain	PLAYWRIGHT	Jean Georges DEROY Jacques DUPRES	SPRUCE	Organiser	9/22/1941	Died in Captivity
DUCHALARD	Charles Joseph	Denis	STONEMASON	Charles DENISET	PRUNUS	W/T Operator	4/15/1943	Returned Safe
DUCLOS	Philippe Francis	Christian	STOCKMAN	Philippe MORVANT	DELEGATE	Assistant	3/1/1944	Executed
DUCLOS	Gustave	Charles	DUSTMAN	René LANDRAU	DIPLOMAT	W/T Operator	6/13/1944	Returned Safe
DUFFOIR	Pierre Roger	Amédé	DIVER		RACKETEER	Saboteur	4/16/1944	Returned Safe
DUFOUR	Jacques Auguste	Anastasie			STATIONER	Assistant	Locally Recruited	Survived
DUFOURNEL	Henri	Henri		Henri GARNIER	SILVERSMITH	Assistant	Locally Recruited	Survived
DUMONT-GUILLEMET	René Alfred	Armand	SPIRITUALIST	Jean CONTE	SPIRITUALIST	Organiser	2/6/1944	Returned Safe
DUNTON	Donald Jean William	Denis	CYPRESS		AUTOGYRO	W/T Operator	1/26/1942	Returned Safe
DUPONT	Maurice Maxime Leon	Abélard	DIPLOMAT	André GENESTRE	DIPLOMAT	Organiser	10/20/1943	Returned Safe
DUPRE	Louis	Léon	LICENCEE	Louis Jean DUGUET	LICENCEE	Organiser - W/T	7/8/1944	Returned Safe
DUSSAQ	René	Anselme	DRUGGIST	René DUFAYET	FREELANCE	Instructor	5/23/1944	Returned Safe
DUTHILLEUL	Maurice Paul	Champagne			BRICKLAYER	Assistant	Locally Recruited	Survived Capture
DUVAL	Raoul Richard	Dorsay	DWELLER	Richard DUMAIL	FREELANCE	Instructor	8/31/1944	Returned Safe
EDGAR	James	Cretois			Tilleul (M)	W/T Operator	7/8/1944	Returned Safe
ESKENAZI	Albert		FINANCIER	Albert DUBOIS	Dressmaker (M)	Saboteur	8/18/1943	Returned Safe
EXPERT	Marcel Alphonse Fernand	Marcel			ACTOR	Assistant	Locally Recruited	Survived
EYMOND	Jean	Estebán	ENVOY		VENTRILOQUIST	Organiser	8/31/1944	Returned Safe
FARMER	John Hind	Hubert	FREELANCE	Jean Emile FERANT	FREELANCE	Organiser	4/30/1944	Returned Safe
FAUCHER	Roger Louis	François	FOREMAN	Roger Louis FAUCHER	FREELANCE	W/T Operator	7/19/1944	Returned Safe
FEINGOLD	Adolph	Tutor	CLOWN	André GROSFILS	Tutor (M)	Assassin	3/10/1944	Returned Safe
FELDMAN	Léon	Fantin	FENCER	Léon FELGERES	WOODCUTTER	W/T Operator	9/10/1944	Returned Safe
FERNANDEZ	Leslie Percival	Rudolphe			Alpes/Maritime (M)	Saboteur	8/3/1944	Returned Safe
FIELDING	Alexander Wallace (Xan)	Cathédrale		Armand PONT-LEVE	Alpes/Maritime (M)	Liaison	8/9/1944	Released

SURNAME	FORENAMES	FIELDNAME	Operational Name	Name on Documents	Main CIRCUIT Main Mission (M)	ROLE	Arrival Date	Fate
FINCKEN	Jack Thorez	Jean	HORNBEAM		AUTOGYRO	Assistant	1/26/1942	Survived Capture
FINLAYSON	David Haughton	Guillaume	FRIAR	Daniel Henri GARCIE,	Liontamer (M)	W/T Operator	3/3/1944	Executed
FLOEGE	Ernst Friedrich	Alfred	SACRISTAN	Paul FONTAINE,	SACRISTAN	Organiser	6/14/1943	Returned Safe
FLORAS	Auguste Urbain Paul	Albert	SADDLER		JOCKEY	W/T Operator	10/27/1942	Returned Safe
FLOWER	Raymond Henry	Gaspard	MONKEYPUZZLE		MONKEYPUZZLE	Organiser	6/28/1942	Returned Safe
FONTAINE	Yvonne	Mimi	FLORIST	Yvonne CHOLET	MINISTER	Courier	3/26/1944	Returned Safe
FORSTER	John Francis Anning	Equerre	FREEMASON	Jean André FORESTIER	Bergamotte (M)	Medic	7/1/1944	Returned Safe
FOURNIER	Jean Maurice Charles	Autruche			Union III (M)	Liaison	8/12/1944	Returned Safe
FOX	Marcel Georges Florent	Ernest	PUBLICAN	Maurice René BEAUVAIS	PUBLICAN	Organiser	3/24/1943	Executed
FRAGER	Jacques Henri	Louba	ARCHITECT	Henri DUPRE	DONKEYMAN 1 & 2	Organiser	7/30/1942	Executed
FRASER	Edgar Lee		FURRIER		SALESMAN 2	Dakota Expert	8/2/1944	Returned Safe
FUCS	Henri	Abel	FLUNKY	Henri FOURNIER	HERMIT	Assistant	6/7/1944	Returned Safe
GAGLIARDI	David	Blond			Bergamotte (M)	W/T Operator	6/27/1944	Returned Safe
GAILLARD	Yvan Henri	Vincent	HOTELIER	Henri GALLON	VENTRILOQUIST	Instructor	6/7/1944	Returned Safe
GAILLOT	Henri Hubert	Ignace	DEACON	Jean Fernand MASSON	PARSON	Organiser	7/25/1943	Executed
GANAY de	Jean Louis	Rigobert	DIETICIAN	Jean GARCIN	DIETICIAN	Assistant	5/10/1944	Returned Safe
GARRY	Emile Auguste Henri	Phono	PHONO		CINEMA-PHONO	Organiser		Executed
GEELEN	Pierre Albert Hubert	Pierre	GRINDER	Pierre GARDE	LABOURER	W/T Operator	4/6/1944	Executed
GERSCHEL	Emile Marc	Gilbert	GLEANER		DIGGER	Instructor	7/2/1944	Returned Safe
GERSON	Haim Victor	René	TROPICAL		VIC (D/F)	Organiser	9/6/1941	Returned Safe
GILLETTE	Currenius	Guiseppe	GASTRONOMIST	Henri GILET	GLOVER	Instructor	9/12/1944	Returned Safe
GLAESNER	Pierre-Raimond	Alcide	LITIGANT	Raimond PERRIN	HEADMASTER 2	Instructor	5/29/1944	Returned Safe
GODARD	André						Locally Recruited	Survived
GOLDSMITH	John Gilbert	Valentin	TRAINER ATTORNEY	Jean DELANNOY	ATTORNEY	Organiser	10/2/1942	Escaped
GORODICHE	Jean	Granville	CURVILIGNE	Jean GRAVIER	Bergamotte (M)	Medic	6/27/1944	Survived
GRAHAM	Harry Huntingdon	Henri		Henri BERNEAU	Scullion 2 (M)	Saboteur	8/16/1943	Executed
GRANVILLE	Christine (Krystina)	Pauline		Pauline ARMAND	JOCKEY	Courier	7/7/1944	Returned Safe
GREEN	Donald Ernest Farrance	Progression			Union III (M)	Liaison	8/12/1944	Returned Safe

SURNAME	FORENAMES	FIELDNAME	Operational Name	Name on Documents	Main CIRCUIT Main Mission (M)	ROLE	Arrival Date	Fate
GRINBERG	Albert	Ibis	GOLDSMITH	Robert MARTIN	ACOLYTE	W/T Operator	Locally Recruited	Survived
GROVER-WILLIAMS	Charles Frederick William	Sebastien	CHESTNUT	Charles Frédérick LELONG	CHESTNUT	Organiser	5/30/1942	Executed
Guélis de	Jacques Théodore Paul Marie Vaillant	Théodore	FAÇADE	James Paul GILLIES	Tilleul (M)	Leader	8/6/1941	Returned Safe
GUERNE	Armel Eugène	Gaspard	-	Auguste PLANCHE	PROSPER-PHYSICIAN	Assistant	Locally Recruited	Escaped
GUIET	Jean Claude	Virgile	GUARDIAN	Jean GUYOT	SALESMAN 2	W/T Operator	6/8/1944	Returned Safe
GUIRAUD	René Jean André	André	GLOVER	René-Jean GUYON	GLOVER	Organiser	6/2/1944	Survived Capture
GUNN	Harvard John	Bambos	-	-	Alpes/Maritime (M)	Leader	8/9/1944	Returned Safe
GUNZBOURG de	Philippe	Philbert	-	-	WHEELWRIGHT	Courier	Locally Recruited	Survived
HAELLEBROUCQ van	Jean Marie Emmanuel	Yves	HAWTHORN	Jean Marie BOUSSAC	TINKER	Special Mission	5/14/1942	Escaped 05/01/1944
HALL	Virginia	Marie	HECKLER GEOLOGIST 5	Brigitte le CONTRE Marcelle MONTAGNE	HECKLER	Organiser	8/23/1941	Returned Safe
HAMILTON	John Trevor	François	TOBACCONIST	Jean Charles ROCHARD	SPRUCE	Liaison	12/30/1942	Executed
HAMILTON	James Alexander Stewart	Crosse	-	-	Toplink (M)	Leader	8/2/1944	Returned Safe
HARIVEL le	Jean Philippe Charles	Georges 25	HICCUP	-	CORSICAN	W/T Operator	10/10/1941	Escaped - 16/07/1942
HARRATT	Percy John	Peter	PEDLAR D	Pierre Jean DESANT	PEDLAR	Assistant	8/19/1944	Returned Safe
HASTINGS	Wendell Morse	Humbert	HAWKER	Maurice HAVART	Cut-Throat (M)	Organiser	9/15/1944	Returned Safe
HAYES	Jack Beresford E	Gilbert Eric	CORSICAN HELMSMAN	Jean Baptiste HERION André Jean GAUDIN	Helmsman (M)	Organiser	10/10/1941	Escaped - 16/07/1942
HAYES	Victor Charles	Yves	HOLLY PRINTER	Victor CHARLES	SCIENTIST 1	Instructor	5/14/1942	Executed
HAZAN	Victor Hyam	Gervais	CAMELIA	Raymond FAUVET	SPINDLE	Liaison	5/5/1942	Returned Safe
HEIMANN	Oscar	Anton	BOOKMAKER B	Oscar LECLERC	Bookmaker (M)	W/T Operator	12/30/1942	Returned Safe
HENQUET	Roger Robert	Roger	HERMIT	Roger Robert HENRIET	HERMIT	Organiser	5/27/1944	Returned Safe
HERBERT	Mary Katherine (Maureen)	Claudine	JEWELLER	Marie Louise VERNIER	SCIENTIST 1	Courier	11/4/1942	Released
HERBERT	René Louis Léon	Corvette	-	René Louis HEBRARD	Vaucluse (M)	Instructor	7/19/1944	Returned Safe
HESLOP	Richard Harry	Xavier	MAHOGANY MARKSMAN	René GARRAT	MARKSMAN	Organiser	7/20/1942	Released - 27/11/42 Survived 2nd Mission
HICKS	Whitmore George	Thomas	-	-	DITCHER	Assistant	Locally Recruited	Survived - Capture

SURNAME	FORENAMES	FIELDNAME	Operational Name	Name on Documents	Main CIRCUIT Main Mission (M)	ROLE	Arrival Date	Fate
HILLER	George Francois	Maxime	FOOTMAN	Georges François PRUDHON	FOOTMAN	Organiser	1/8/1944	Returned Safe
HINTON	Norman	Noel	JOURNALIST	Philippe LEMARE	Special Mission	Saboteur	11/17/1942	Returned Safe
HIRSCH	Jacques François Gustave	Arthur	-	-	SHIPWRIGHT	W/T Operator	Locally Recruited	Survived
HIRSCH	Pierre	Papaul	RAINCOAT	Pierre d'HAMBLEMONT	SHIPWRIGHT	W/T Operator	Locally Recruited	Survived
HOUDET	Maurice	-	-	-	SILVERSMITH	-	Locally Recruited	Survived
HOUSEMAN	John Vincent	Reflexion	-	-	Eucalyptus (M)	Assistant	6/29/1944	Returned Safe
HUDSON	Christopher Sydney	Albin	REDWOOD HEADMASTER	Jacques Etienne LAROCHE Michel PUISAIS	HEADMASTER 1 & 2	Organiser	9/25/1942	Escaped - 09/01/1944
HUE	André Hunter Alfred	Fernand	HILLBILLY	Alfred Marie HAVET	HILLBILLY	Organiser	6/6/1944	Returned Safe
HUMMEL	Alfred	-	-	-	DIPLOMAT	-	Locally Recruited	Survived - Capture
HUNTER	Cameron Bendey	Dalmatique	-	-	Union 111 (M)	Liaison	8/12/1944	Returned Safe
HYDE	Louis Gerald Varet	Frederic	HOSIER	Louis HAUMONT	GLOVER	W/T Operator	6/12/1944	Returned Safe
INAYAT KHAN	Noor-un-nisa (Nora)	Madeleine	NURSE	Jeanne-Marie REGNIER	CINEMA-PHONO	W/T Operator	6/17/1943	Executed
JANYK	Christopher	Georges	JUMPER	Georges CLAUDEL	JOCKEY	W/T Operator	3/1/1944	Survived - Capture
JAURANT-SINGER	Marcel André Louis	Flavian	SHAREHOLDER	Louis Marie JAUBERT	MASON	W/T Operator	3/3/1944	Returned Safe
JICKELL	Alan William	Gustave	LABURNUM PUBLISHER	Henri Jules FABRE	SPRUCE	Instructor	6/12/1942	Returned Safe
JOHNSON	Denis Owen	Gael	POET	Alfred JANSON	MARKSMAN	W/T Operator	10/19/1943	Returned Safe
JONES	George Donovan	Isidore	LIME	André VASSEUR	HEADMASTER 1 & 2	W/T Operator	9/25/1942	Escaped - 02/09/1943
JONES	Sidney Charles	Elie	INVENTOR	Jean-Marie TERBORRE Sylvain Charles LEJEUNE	INVENTOR	Organiser	10/2/1942	Executed
JULLIAN	Ginette Marie Hélène	Adèle	JANITRESS	Ginette Marie JOURDAIN	PERMIT	W/T Operator	6/7/1944	Returned Safe
JUMEAU	Claude Marc	Robert	REPORTER	André CHAMBON	CORSICAN	Instructor	10/10/1941	Died in Captivity
KALIFA	Simon	Paradiser	-	-	Toplink (M)	Saboteur	8/2/1944	Returned Safe
KERDRAU-HALSEY de	John A	Lutrin	-	-	Alpes/Maritime (M)	Instructor	8/3/1944	Returned Safe
KITCH	Darwin J	Carel	KIDNAPPER	Jean BOILEAU	GLOVER	Instructor	9/12/1944	Returned Safe
KNIGHT	William Barry	-	BAILIFF	Jean SIMON	Scullion 1 (M)	Saboteur	4/19/1943	Returned Safe

SURNAME	FORENAMES	FIELDNAME	Operational Name	Name on Documents	Main CIRCUIT Main Mission (M)	ROLE	Arrival Date	Fate
KNIGHT	Marguerite Diane Frances	Nicole	KENNELMAID	Marguerite Gisèle CHAUVAN	DONKEYMAN 2	Courier	5/7/1944	Returned Safe
LABELLE	Paul Emile	Nartex	-	Paul BOURGET	Vaucluse (M)	Instructor	7/19/1944	Returned Safe
LAKE	Peter Ivan	Jean-Pierre	LIFTMAN	Jean-Pierre LENORMAND	DIGGER	Instructor	4/9/1944	Returned Safe
LANDES	Roger	Aristide	ACTOR	René POL	ACTOR	Organiser	11/1/1942	Returned Safe
LANGELAAN	George	Langdon	UKELELE	Gérard TOUCHE	UKELELE	Leader	9/6/1941	Escaped - 16/07/1942
LANGMAID	Richard Robert	Viagodhe	-	-	Bergamotte (M)	W/T Operator	7/1/1944	Returned Safe
LANSDELL	Armand Richard	Oscar	PILGRIM	-	DONKEYMAN 2	Assistant	4/29/1944	Casualty
LARCHER	Georges Louis Jean	Albert	ACCOUNTANT	Jean MORET	Scullion 1 (M)	Saboteur	4/19/1943	Returned Safe
LARCHER	Maurice Louis Marie Aristide	Vladimir	LINESMAN	Maurice Louis LANGLADE	SCIENTIST 2	W/T Operator	2/10/1944	Killed in Action
LAROSEE	James Richard	Estephe	LAYMAN	Richard Le RICHE	DIPLOMAT	W/T Operator	6/13/1944	Returned Safe
LATOUR	Phyllis Ada (Pippa)	Geneviève	LAMPOONER	Paulette Janine LATOUR	SCIENTIST 2	W/T Operator	5/2/1944	Returned Safe
LAUSUCQ	Henri	Aramis	SAINT	Henri LASSOT	SAINT	Special Mission	3/22/1944	Returned Safe
LAVIGNE	Madeleine	Isabelle	LEVELLER	Mariette Henriette DELORMES	SILVERSMITH	Courier	5/24/1944	Returned Safe
LECCIA	Marcel Mathieu René	Baudouin	LABOURER	Georges LOUIS	LABOURER	Organiser	4/6/1944	Executed
LECOINTRE	Guillaume	Guillaume	LUMBERJACK	Gérard LAFARGUE	ATTORNEY	Organiser	5/14/1943	Returned Safe
LEDOUX	Jacques Paul Henri	Homere	ORATOR	Jacques LELONG	ORATOR	Organiser	2/9/1944	Executed
LEE	Lionel	Thibaud	MECHANIC	Jacques HERIAT	BRICKLAYER	W/T Operator	3/1/1944	Executed
LEE GRAHAM	Louis Pippin	Félix	SURGEON	Michel LEGRAND	REPORTER	N/K	4/13/1943	Survived - Capture
LEFORT	Cécile Margot (Cecily)	Alice	TEACHER	Cécile M LEGRAND	JOCKEY	Courier	6/17/1943	Died in Captivity
LEFROU de la COLOGNE	Louis Charles Maurice	Bernard	AUTOGYRO A2	Louis LEFROU de la COLOGNE	AUTOGYRO	Assistant	5/11/1941	Returned Safe
LEIGH	Vera Eugenie	Simone	ALMONER	Suzanne CHAVANNE	INVENTOR	Courier	5/15/1943	Executed
LEPAGE	Maurice	Colin	LIONTAMER	Maurice LANOIS	Liontamer (M)	Instructor	3/3/1944	Executed
LEROY	Robert	Louis	BUCKTHORN	-	Special Mission	Saboteur	9/22/1941	Returned Safe
LESAGE	Jules Eugène	Cosmo	LACKEY	Jules LEBRUN	LACKEY	Organiser	2/9/1944	Returned Safe
LESOUT	Edmond	Tristan	LENDER	Edmond LACROIX	Liontamer (M)	Instructor	3/3/1944	Executed

SURNAME	FORENAMES	FIELDNAME	Operational Name	Name on Documents	Main CIRCUIT Main Mission (M)	ROLE	Arrival Date	Fate
LEVENE	Eugene Francis	Boniface	LAWYER	Eugene André NIZET	Scullion 1 (M)	Saboteur	4/19/1943	Executed
L'HOSPITALIER	Robert	Marc	-	-	STATIONER	W/T Operator	Locally Recruited	Survived
LIEWER	Philippe	Clément	SALESMAN	Marcel BACKERT Charles BEAUCHAMP	SALESMAN 1 & 2	Organiser	4/15/1943	Escaped - 16/07/1942
LITALIEN	Joseph Gerard	Jacquot	LANDOWNER	Joseph LINTILHAC	DITCHER	W/T Operator	5/23/1944	Returned Safe
LODWICK	John Patrick Alan	Arsène	BOOKMAKER A	Robert MARTIN	Bookmaker (M)	Organiser	12/30/1942	Returned Safe
LONGE	Desmond Evelyn	Refraction	-	-	Eucalyptus (M)	Leader	6/29/1944	Returned Safe
LORD	Edwin	Leonce	LISTENER	-	FREELANCE	Instructor	8/31/1944	Returned Safe
LOSTRIE	Maurice Alexandre Adolphe	Alex	-	-	VENTRILOQUIST	Saboteur	2/25/1944	Returned Safe
LYON	Robert	Adrian	ACOLYTE	Georges Louis MARIONNET	ACOLYTE	Organiser	6/24/1943	Escaped - 16/07/1942
MACALISTER	John Kenneth	Valentin	PLUMBER	Jean Charles MAULNIER	ARCHDEACON	W/T Operator	6/16/1943	Executed
MACARTHY	Robert	Miguel	MALEFACTOR	-	SHIPWRIGHT	Instructor	8/25/1944	Returned Safe
MACKENZIE	Kenneth Yves Marcel	Baptiste	MISOGYNIST	Yves Marcel CHENARD	GONDOLIER	W/T Operator	3/22/1944	Returned Safe
MACKENZIE	Ian J	Thermometre	-	-	Tilleul (M)	Medic	7/8/1944	Returned Safe
MACOMBER	William Butts	Mederic	MATCHMAKER	-	FREELANCE	Instructor	8/31/1944	Returned Safe
MAETZ	Joseph Julien	Milou	MULETEER	Joseph MATHIS	STOCKBROKER	Assistant	8/26/1944	Returned Safe
MAINGARD	René Louis Amedée Pierre	Dédé	SHIPWRIGHT	Amedée MAIGROT	SHIPWRIGHT	Organiser	4/15/1943	Returned Safe
MAKOWSKI	Stanislaw	Dmitri	MACHINIST	Jean ROMIEU	VENTRILOQUIST	Instructor	4/9/1944	Killed in Action
MALOUBIER	Robert (Bob)	Clothaire	PORTER	Robert MOLLIER	SALESMAN 1 & 2	Instructor	8/16/1943	Survived - Capture
MALRAUX	Claude Raymond	Cicero	BEAUPERE	-	SALESMAN 1	Assistant	Locally Recruited	Executed
MANGOUX	Corbin de Gonzaque	Amict	-	Jean Bernard CHAILLOT	Vaucluse (M)	Leader	7/11/1944	Returned Safe
MANOLITSAKIS	John	Cyriel	PROPHET	Jean MANOT	ACTOR	Saboteur	4/11/1944	Returned Safe
MARCHAND	Joseph	Ange	NEWSAGENT	-	NEWSAGENT	Organiser	10/21/1943	Returned Safe
MARSAC	André	End	-	Philippe MURIEL	CARTE	-	Locally Recruited	Survived - Capture
MARTIN	Maurice	Adam	MAGICIAN	-	BEGGAR	W/T Operator	4/11/1944	Returned Safe
MARTIN	André Louis Henri	André	-	-	NEWSAGENT	-	Locally Recruited	Survived
MARTINEAU	Paul Victor	Felix	MERCER	-	VENTRILOQUIST	W/T Operator	7/4/1944	Returned Safe
MARTINOT	Pierre Maurice	Ulysses	MISSIONARY	Pierre DUVOISIN	JOCKEY	Instructor	3/7/1944	Survived - Capture

SURNAME	FORENAMES	FIELDNAME	Operational Name	Name on Documents	Main CIRCUIT Main Mission (M)	ROLE	Arrival Date	Fate
MATHIEU	René Marie A	Aimé	MANUFACTURER	René Marie MILLOY	STATIONER	W/T Operator	4/12/1944	Died in Captivity
MATTEI	Pierre	Gaëtan	HUNTSMAN	Pierre PAOLI	STATIONER	L/Grounds	2/11/1944	Survived - Capture
MAUGENET	André Adrien	Benoit	THATCHER	André Adrien Jules ROUVRAY	ACROBAT	Assistant	11/16/1943	Executed
MAURY	Jean Gerard	Arnaud	MINSTREL	Maurice FAURE	WIZARD	W/T Operator	4/6/1944	Returned Safe
MAYER	James Andrew John	Frank	SEXTON	Jacques André MALLET	ROVER	Assistant	2/12/1944	Executed
MAYER	Edmund Richard	Barthelemy	WARDER	Georges Richard MAIRE	FIREMAN	Organiser	3/8/1944	Returned Safe
MAYER	Percy Edward	Maurice	FIREMAN	Edouard Jacques GALLAND	FIREMAN	Organiser	3/8/1944	Returned Safe
MAYER	Roger	Jean-Pierre	-	-	SALESMAN 1	Assistant	Locally Recruited	Survived - Capture
McBAIN	George Basil	Cecil	RHYMER	Georges B BUISSONNIER	ARCHDEACON	Instructor	3/3/1944	Executed
MENDELSOHN	Dominique Armand Etienne	Benjamin	BROKER	Bernard Alain ARNAULT	DETECTIVE 1	W/T Operator	9/1/1944	Released - 09/09/1943
MENILGLAISE	Jean Guyon des Diguères de	Miguel	-	-	BRICKLAYER	-	Locally Recruited	Survived - Capture
MENNESSON	James Francis George	Henri	BIRCH	Jean François MARTINET	BIRCH	Organiser	4/23/1942	Executed
MEUNIER	Pierre	Edouard	MORALIST	Pierre MORNET	ACTOR	Instructor	4/11/1944	Returned Safe
MEUNIER	Jean Pierre Charles	Mesnard	-	-	DIRECTOR	Organiser	Locally Recruited	Survived - Capture
MICHEL	François Gerard	Jacques	DISPENSER	François Gerard MICHELET	ARCHDEACON	Instructor	9/22/1943	Executed
MILLAR	George Reid	Emile	CHANCELLOR	Georges Henri MAILLARD	CHANCELLOR	Organiser	6/2/1944	Returned Safe
MOMPEZAT	Roger	-	-	-	DETECTIVE 2	-	Locally Recruited	Survived
MONTALEMBERT de	Comte Arthur Franz	Bistouri	SATIRIST	-	SATIRIST	Organiser	Locally Recruited	Executed
MORAUD	M.	Bécassine	-	-	Vaucluse (M)	W/T Operator	7/16/1944	Returned Safe
MOREL	Gérard Henri	Paulot	LEVEE BARRISTER	Henri MOREL Jean François MAURY	Façade (M)	Liaison	9/4/1941	Escaped
MORGAN	William James	Miguel	MALEFACTOR	-	FIREMAN	Saboteur	8/14/1944	Returned Safe
MORPURGO	Mario	Michelange	MACEBEARER	Michel MARIE	JOCKEY	Assistant	8/11/1944	Returned Safe
MULSANT	Pierre Louis	Paul	MINISTER	Paul Henri MAUPAS	MINISTER	Organiser	3/4/1944	Executed

SURNAME	FORENAMES	FIELDNAME	Operational Name	Name on Documents	Main CIRCUIT Main Mission (M)	ROLE	Arrival Date	Fate
NEARNE	Jacqueline Françoise Mary Josephine	Jacqueline	DESIGNER	Josette NORVILLE	STATIONER	Courier	1/26/1943	Returned Safe
NEARNE	Eileen Mary (Didi)	Rose	PIONEER	Marie Louise TOURNIER	WIZARD	W/T Operator	3/3/1944	Escaped
NEWMAN	Isidore	Pepé	ATHLETE DIVIDEND	Pierre Jacques NERAULT Joseph NEMORIN	SALESMAN 1	W/T Operator	4/19/1942	Executed
NEWTON	Alfred Willie Oscar	Artus	GREENHEART	Alfred Georges DUSSERET	GREENHEART	Organiser	7/1/1942	Survived - Capture
NEWTON	Henry George Rodolfo	Auguste	ALMOND	Henri Marcel DUSSERET	GREENHEART	Organiser	7/1/1942	Survived - Capture
NONNI	Louis Antoine	Nicholas	NATURALIST	Louis Antoine NOURRY	SCHOLAR	W/T Operator	7/7/1944	Returned Safe
NORMAN	Gilbert Maurice	Archambaud	BUTCHER	Gilbert AUBIN	PROSPER-PHYSICIAN	W/T Operator	11/1/1942	Executed
NORNABLE	Gordon	Bayard	NAVVY	Guillaume NORMAN	MARKSMAN	Instructor	7/7/1944	Returned Safe
O'REGAN	Patrick Valentino William Rowan Hamilton	Chape	-	-	Toplink (M)	Instructor	8/2/1944	Returned Safe
O'SULLIVAN	Patricia (Paddy) Maureen	Josette	STENOGRAPHER	Micheline Marcelle SIMONET	FIREMAN	W/T Operator	3/23/1944	Returned Safe
OLSCHANEZKY	Sonia	Tania	-	-	JUGGLER	Courier	Locally Recruited	Executed
PARDI	Paul Baptiste	Philibert	PAWNBROKER	Paul B GIACOMMETTI	SCIENTIST 1	L/Grounds	11/16/1943	Died in Captivity
PARKER	Dr Geoffrey Edward	Parsifal	PASTRYCOOK	Henri Edouard MARTIN	MARKSMAN	Medic	7/7/1944	Returned Safe
PARSONS	Denis	Pierrot	FISHERMAN	-	WHEELWRIGHT	W/T Operator	4/10/1944	Returned Safe
PASCARD	Jean	Dudule	-	-	SCHOLAR	W/T Operator	Locally Recruited	Survived
PEARSON	David Morris	Philippe	PEDAGOGUE	Maurice GONZALES-PEYSSON	PEDAGOGUE	Organiser	7/31/1944	Returned Safe
PECQUET	André Edward	Paray	-	Armand Eugène PARENT	Eucalyptus (M)	W/T Operator	6/29/1944	Returned Safe
PERSONNIC le	André	-	-	-	SCIENTIST 2	Assistant	Locally Recruited	Survived
PERTSCHUK	Maurice	Eugene	PRUNUS	Gerard Henri PERREAU	PRUNUS	Organiser	4/23/1942	Executed
PEULEVE	Henri Leonard Thomas André	Jean	AUTHOR	Henri CHEVALIER	AUTHOR	Organiser	7/30/1942	Survived - Capture
PICKERSGILL	Frank Herbert Dedrick	Bertrand	ARCHDEACON	François Marie PICARD	ARCHDEACON	Organiser	6/16/1943	Executed
PINDER	Richard Francis	Willy	PROSECUTOR	Richard F PRIOLLET	FOOTMAN	Instructor	3/7/1944	Survived - Capture

SURNAME	FORENAMES	FIELDNAME	Operational Name	Name on Documents	Main CIRCUIT Main Mission (M)	ROLE	Arrival Date	Fate
PLEWMAN	Eliane Sophie	Gaby	DEAN	Eliane Jacqueline PRUNIER	MONK	Courier	8/14/1943	Executed
POIRIER	Jacques René Edouard	Nestor	DIGGER	Jacques René Edouard PERRIER	DIGGER	Organiser	1/29/1944	Returned Safe
POITRAS	Edwin W.	Paul	POSTMAN	-	TREASURER	W/T Operator	5/2/1944	Returned Safe
PURVIS	Robert William Berry	Manipule	-	-	Hautes Alpes (M)	Instructor	8/6/1944	Returned Safe
PUY du	Comte Jean Paul Marie	Camille	AUTOGYRO E	-	AUTOGYRO	Organiser	9/6/1941	Survived - Capture
RABINOVITCH	Adolphe (Alec)	Arnaud	CATALPHA	Guy LEBOUTON André RENAULT	SPINDLE	W/T Operator	8/29/1942	Executed
RAFFERTY	Brian Dominic	Dominique	AUBRETIA	Bertrand Dominic REMY	HEADMASTER 1	Organiser	9/25/1942	Executed
RAKE	Denis Joseph	Justin	JUNIPER RECEIVER	René DIEUDONNE Denis Joseph ROCHER	FREELANCE	W/T Operator	5/14/1942	Released - 27/11/1942
RAYNAUD	Pierre Jean Louis	Alain	LINKMAN	Pierre OGAPOFF	JOCKEY	Assistant	6/18/1943	Returned Safe
RECHENMANN	Charles Théophile	Julien	ROVER	Claude ROLAND	ROVER	Organiser	3/21/1944	Executed
REDDING	Gustave Claude Brooks	Georges 30	WATERWORKS	Charles Robert RENARD	AUTOGYRO	W/T Operator	2/12/1942	Survived - Capture
REE	Harry Alfred	César	STOCKBROKER	Henri REHMANN	STOCKBROKER	Organiser	4/16/1943	Escaped
REEVE	François William Michael	Olivier	CARDINAL	Michel Louis DUCHESNE	FARMER	Assistant	6/14/1943	Escaped
REGIN	Christian	Christian	GOLDSMITH	-	NEWSAGENT	W/T Operator	Locally Recruited	Survived
REGNIER	Jean-Marie	Porthos	MASON	Noel CALVE	MASON	Organiser	3/5/1944	Returned Safe
RENAUD	Jean	Jean	-	-	DITCHER	Assistant	Locally Recruited	Died in Captivity
RENAUD-DANDICOLLE	Jean Marie	René	VERGER	Jean Marie DEMIREMONT	SCIENTIST 2	Organiser	1/29/1944	Died of wounds in captivity
ROBERT	Jacques	Molecule	-	-	Bergamotte (M)	Leader	6/27/1944	Returned Safe
ROCHE	Raymond Bruce	François	AUTOGYRO D2	-	AUTOGYRO	Saboteur	9/22/1941	Escaped - 16/07/1942
RODRIGUE	Georges	Philippe	-	-	SCIENTIST 2	Assistant	Locally Recruited	Survived
ROE	Herbert Maurice	Maurice	PEDLAR B	Maurice ROLLARD	PEDLAR	W/T Operator	7/10/1944	Returned Safe
ROLFE	Lilian Vera	Nadine	RECLUSE	Claudie Irene RODIER	HISTORIAN	W/T Operator	4/6/1944	Executed
ROPER	John Charles Abercromby	Retable	-	-	Haute Alpes (M)	Instructor	8/6/1944	Returned Safe
ROSENTHAL	Jean Pierre	Cantinier	APOTHEME	Jean Pierre DEBLAY	MARKSMAN	Organiser	9/22/1943	Returned Safe
ROUNEAU	Maurice Henri	Adolphe	RACKETEER	Henri Robert MANGUY	RACKETEER	Organiser	4/16/1944	Returned Safe

SURNAME	FORENAMES	FIELDNAME	Operational Name	Name on Documents	Main CIRCUIT Main Mission (M)	ROLE	Arrival Date	Fate
ROUSSET	Marcel Joseph Louis	Léopold	BARBER	Roger François Marcel DOUCET	BUTLER	W/T Operator	3/24/1943	Escaped - 08/06/1944
ROWDEN	Diana Hope	Paulette	CHAPLAIN	Juliette Thérèse RONDEAU	ACROBAT	Courier	6/17/1943	Executed
RUDELLAT	Yvonne Claire	Jacqueline	SOAPTREE	Jacqueline VIALLET	PROSPER-PHYSICIAN	Courier	7/30/1942	Died in Captivity
SABOURIN	Romeo Roger	Leonard	SORCEROR	Guy Robert DESJARDIN	PRIEST	W/T Operator	3/3/1944	Executed
SAILLARD	Philippe	Touareg	–	Georges LANCIEN	Eucalyptus (M)	W/T Operator	7/6/1944	Returned Safe
SANSOM	Odette Marie Celine	Lise	CLOTHIER	Odette METAYER	SPINDLE	Courier	11/4/1942	Survived - Capture
SARRETTE	Paul François Marie Charles William	Louis	GONDOLIER	Paul SAULIEUX	GONDOLIER	Organiser	12/20/1943	Killed in Action
SAVY	William Jean	Alcide	WIZARD	Michel RICHOU	WIZARD	Organiser	3/3/1944	Returned Safe
SCHLEY	Reeve	Samson	SANDWICHMAN	–	FREELANCE	Instructor	8/8/1944	Returned Safe
SCHWATSCHKO	Alexander	Olive	POLITICIAN	Albert POULNOT	STATIONER	L/Grounds	2/29/1944	Killed in Action
SERENI	Antoine Guillaume	Casimir	–	–	JOCKEY	W/T Operator	5/11/1944	Returned Safe
SEVENET	Henri Paul	Rodolphe	DETECTIVE	Henri DAGOBERT	DETECTIVE 1 & 2	Organiser	8/26/1942	Killed in Action
SHANNON	Jack Thomas	Taux	–	–	Bergamotte (M)	Saboteur	6/27/1944	Returned Safe
SHEARN	Charles Ronald	Septime	STRAGGLER	René SARRONT	PERMIT	Assistant	8/8/1944	Returned Safe
SHEPPARD	Robert Marceline	Patrice	PALM	Jacques Robert DEROUE	SPRUCE	Saboteur	6/2/1942	Survived - Capture
SIBREE	David Whytehead	Morand	–	David MORAND	Scullion 2 (M)	Saboteur	8/16/1943	Executed
SILLITO	Hugh Davidson	Sylven	SCOUT	Georges CHAUVET	GONDOLIER	Liaison	8/31/1944	Returned Safe
SIMON	André Louis Ernest Henri	Diastique	–	André LOFFET	Tilleul (M)	L/Grounds	5/6/1942	Released - 09/07/1942
SIMON	Octave Anne Guillaume	Badois	SATIRIST	Guillaume Octave SABATIER	SATIRIST	Organiser	3/7/1944	Executed
SIMON	Jean Alexandre Robert	Claude	–	–	STOCKBROKER	–	Locally Recruited	Killed in Action
SINCLAIR	Jack Andrew Eugene Marcel	Adalbert	SHOPKEEPER	Jacques André Eugéne BERTIER	MONK	Assistant	3/6/1944	Died in Captivity
SIROIS	Allyre Louis Joseph	Gustave	SATYR	André Louis SIROIS	CARVER	W/T Operator	3/3/1944	Returned Safe
SKEPPER	Charles Milne	Bernard	MONK	Henri TRUCHOT	MONK	Organiser	6/17/1943	Executed
SONGY	Guy S	Sostene	SUBSCRIBER	–	FOOTMAN	Saboteur	7/30/1944	Returned Safe
SORENSEN	Christian	Chauble	–	Christian Marcel SEVAIN	Alpes/Maritime (M)	Leader	8/3/1944	Released

SURNAME	FORENAMES	FIELDNAME	Operational Name	Name on Documents	Main CIRCUIT / Main Mission (M)	ROLE	Arrival Date	Fate
SOSKICE	Victor Andrew	Solway	-	-	Scullion 2 (M)	Saboteur	8/16/1943	Executed
SOUTHGATE	Maurice	Hector	STATIONER	Robert MOULIN	STATIONER	Organiser	1/26/1943	Survived - Capture
SOWDEN	Alfred Claude Brinton	Claude	PEDLAR C	Alfred Claude SAUNIER	PEDLAR	W/T Operator	7/10/1944	Returned Safe
St.GENIES de	Marie Joseph Gonzagues	Lucien	SCHOLAR	Georges Henri HOLLENEAU	SCHOLAR	Organiser	3/19/1944	Killed in Action
STAGGS	Arthur Albert George	Guy	BAKER	Albert FOULON	FARMER	W/T Operator	11/18/1942	Released
STARR	John Ashford Renshaw	Bob	ACROBAT	Jean-Pierre DUMONTAY / Jean-Pierre MEUNIER	ACROBAT	Organiser	8/29/1942	Survived - Capture
STARR	George Reginald	Hilaire	WHEELWRIGHT	Serge WATREMEZ	WHEELWRIGHT	Organiser	11/4/1942	Returned Safe
STEELE	Arthur	Laurent	WAITER	Arthur SAULNIER / Arthur CLERMONT	MONK	W/T Operator	6/20/1943	Executed
STONEHOUSE	Brian Julian Warry	Célestin	JAPONICA	Michel CHAPUIS	DETECTIVE 1	W/T Operator	7/1/1942	Survived - Capture
STRATON Van der	André Henri	André	VENDOR	André VALLON	ACROBAT	Assistant	9/6/1944	Returned Safe
STUDLER	André	Sylvain	SQUATTER	-	HISTORIAN	Assistant	4/6/1944	Escaped
SUTTILL	Francis Alfred	Prosper	PHYSICIAN	François DESPREE	PROSPER-PHYSICIAN	Organiser	10/2/1942	Executed
SYBILLE	Alphonse	Sanche	SQUEAKER	Louis SICAMBRE	WOODCUTTER	Assistant	9/10/1944	Returned Safe
SZABO	Violette Reine Elizabeth	Louise	SEAMSTRESS	Corinne Reine LEROY	SALESMAN 1 & 2	Courier	4/5/1944	Executed
TABOURIN	Jean	-	-	-	DITCHER	-	Locally Recruited	Survived
TASCHEREAU	Leonard Jacques Thomas	Thomas	TOUT	-	DIPLOMAT	Assistant	6/13/1944	Returned Safe
TESSIER	Paul Raymond Elie	Theodore	COMEDIAN	Paul TERRIER	MUSICIAN	Assistant	8/18/1943	Killed
THIBEAULT	Paul Emile	Gervais	TATLER	-	DIPLOMAT	Instructor	6/13/1944	Returned Safe
TROTOBAS	Michael Alfred Raymond	Sylvestre	FARMER	Joseph RAMPAL	FARMER	Organiser	9/6/1941	Escaped - 16/07/1942
TURBERVILLE	Daniel	Daniel	DIVINER	Jacques DORMOY	CORSICAN	Instructor	10/10/1941	Escaped
TURCK	Gilbert Charles Georges	Christophe	-	Gerard Emile TAMBON	Special Mission	W/T Operator	8/6/1941	Escaped
UGET	Marcel	Paquebot	-	-	CHESTNUT	Assistant	Locally Recruited	Survived - Capture
ULLMANN	Paul Eugène Bertron	Alceste	UPHOLSTERER	Paul P LORAINE	STOCKBROKER	Mortar Expert	4/15/1944	Killed in Action
VALLEE	François	Oscar	PARSON	Jacques André DELORME	PARSON	Organiser	6/18/1943	Executed
VEILLARD	Roger	Vulcain	VALUER	-	DIETICIAN	Assistant	8/18/1944	Escaped Gestapo

SURNAME	FORENAMES	FIELDNAME	Operational Name	Name on Documents	Main CIRCUIT Main Mission (M)	ROLE	Arrival Date	Fate
VEILLEUX	Marcel	Yvello	VAGABOND	-	MARKSMAN	W/T Operator	7/7/1944	Returned Safe
VOMECOURT de	Pierre de Crevoisier	Lucas	AUTOGYRO	-	AUTOGYRO	Organiser	5/11/1941	Survived - Capture
VOMECOURT de	Philippe Albert de Crevoisier	Gauthier	VENTRILOQUIST	Philippe Robert COURCELLES	VENTRILOQUIST	Organiser	4/10/1944	Escaped - May 1942
WAKE	Nancy Grace Augusta	Hélène	WITCH	Lucienne CARLIER	FREELANCE	Courier	4/30/1944	Returned Safe
WALTERS	Anne-Marie	Colette	MILKMAID	Anne Marie ROUX	WHEELWRIGHT	Courier	1/5/1944	Returned Safe
WATNEY	Cyril Arthur	Eustache	FORGER	Michel André PONTLEVE	FOOTMAN	W/T Operator	1/8/1944	Returned Safe
WATT	Adher Pierre Arthur (André)	Geoffroi	SWINEHERD	André Pierre DAMIDEAU	FARRIER	W/T Operator	10/17/1943	Returned Safe
WEIL	Jacques	Jacques	-	-	JUGGLER	Organiser	Locally Recruited	Survived
WILEN	Odette Victoria	Sophie	WAITRESS	-	LABOURER	W/T Operator	4/11/1944	Returned Safe
WILKINSON	Edward Mountford	Alexandre	PRIVET	Edmund Paul MONTFORT	PRIVET	Organiser	6/1/1942	Executed
WILKINSON	George Alfred	Etienne	HISTORIAN	Georges Alfred VERDIER	HISTORIAN	Organiser	4/5/1944	Executed
WITHERINGTON	Cécile Pearl	Marie	WRESTLER	Geneviève TOUZALIN	WRESTLER	Organiser	9/23/1943	Returned Safe
WOERTHER	Albert Victor	Justin	WOODCUTTER	-	WOODCUTTER	Organiser	7/18/1944	Returned Safe
WOOLF	Ivan Justin (Ian)	Jean Paul	WANDERER	Jean Paul ROUSSEL	SHIPWRIGHT	Dakota Expert	8/26/1944	Returned Safe
WORMS	Jean Alexandre	Robin	JUGGLER	Jules WARRENS	JUGGLER	Organiser	1/23/1943	Executed
YOUNG	John Cuthbert	Gabriel	JUDGE	Charles CAMUS	ACROBAT	W/T Operator	5/20/1943	Executed
ZEFF	Edward (Ted)	Georges 53	EBONY	Etienne Pierre PASCAL	SPRUCE	W/T Operator	4/19/1942	Survived - Capture

Index

Agazarian, Jack Charles Stanmore (Marcel) 172
Aimé, Jean 103, 105, 192, 205, 217
Alexandre 114
Anjou, Madame 124–5
Antelme, Joseph (Antoine) 231
Arpiège, Monsieur 26–7
Atkins, Vera 17, 62, 81, 174, 263
Audubon de Charbonnier, Monsieur 143–4

de Baissac, Claude 118–19, 121–3, 129, 181, 184–7
de Baissac, Lise 267
Barjou, Monsieur 207
Baseden, Yvonne (Odette) 229, 235, 247
Beekman, Yolande (Mariette) 138, 238
Belgium 76
Bertrand 29
Bieler, Gustave (Guy) 238
Blanc, Gerard 98
Bleicher, Sergeant Hugo 228, 231
Bloch, Denise 267
Borrel, Andrée 226, 229
Bourne-Paterson, Major 75, 79–81, 103, 136
Briggs, Colonel 264
Brigitte 147–9
British Broadcasting Corporation (BBC) xii, 65–6, 100, 122, 163, 166, 198, 218, 240–41
French Service 63, 100, 164–5

British Expeditionary Force (BEF) 4, 76
Browne-Bartroli, Albert (Tiburce) 88, 251
Buckmaster, Maurice ix–xii, 3–5, 9–10, 13–15, 42, 61, 67–8, 179
Specially Employed (1952) xii, 1
Burdeyron, Noël (Gaston) 21, 23–9, 42–3, 62

Cambridge University
St Peter's College 125
Cammaerts, Francis (Colonel Roger) 236
Canada 226
Canaris, Admiral Wilhelm 150
Carre, Monsieur 129–30
Chaperon, Martial 247
Churchill, Peter (Raoul) 57, 76, 95, 122, 143, 158, 174, 192, 215, 229–30, 235
Churchill, Winston 12, 67, 265–6
Clément 85, 88–9, 96–8, 102
Corbin, Charles 211, 218
Cornioley, Pearl 259
Cowburn, Ben (Benoit) 16–19, 76, 93–4, 99, 158, 260
Culioli, Pierre 209

D'Artois, Guy 251
Denivelle, Gaston 248
Denvers, Colonel 9–11
Déricourt, Henri x
Dhose, Commandant 211, 223

Dufour, Jacques (Anastasie) 245–6
Dumont-Guillemet, René (Armand) 140–42, 147, 172–3, 210–11

Eisenhower, Dwight 258, 262–3, 266

Farmer, John (Hubert) 248
First World War (1914–18) 248
Foot, M. R. D.
    SOE in France x
Ford Motor Company ix, 3, 8
Fragonard (Le Chef) 118, 129, 188, 193, 196, 207, 209, 211, 213–14, 216–24
France ix, 3–4, 6–7, 13–18, 21, 24, 28, 33, 41, 46, 48, 50, 52, 55–6, 60, 72, 78, 83, 97, 116, 132, 142, 150, 177, 181, 202, 225, 227, 236–7, 241–3, 249, 259, 268
    Ain 236, 253
    Annecy 94
    Antibes 76, 84–5, 88–9, 91, 96, 122
    Ardennes 241
    Belin 191
    Bergerac 196–7, 199
    Besançon 171, 173, 241, 250
    Blois 184
    Bordeaux 18, 94, 118, 129, 181, 184–5, 187, 189, 191, 195, 207, 223, 241
    Calais 240
    Cambrai 65, 146, 158
    Chartres 241
    Chateauroux 175
    Clermont-Ferrand 174–5, 178–80, 202, 241
    Corrèze 245
    Côte d'Azur (Riviera) 19, 30, 48, 242, 252
    Creuse 245
    Dijon 241
    Dordogne 241, 245
    Douai 146–8
    Dunkirk 18
    Gironde 245
    government of xii
    Grenoble 241
    Jura 236, 241, 243, 247, 253, 258
    Le Havre 18, 95
    Le Mans 182, 241
    Lille 95, 136–7, 139, 144, 146–7, 149–50, 152, 158, 241
    Loire 258–9
    Lyons 59, 81, 94, 96, 103, 178
    Marseilles 18–20, 30–31, 39, 75, 87, 94, 178, 180, 241
    Massif Central 237, 241, 248
    Meaux 140, 142, 147
    Moret 143
    Narbonne 40
    Nevers 15
    Nice 94
    Normandy 239
    Orléans 241
    Paris 22–4, 28–9, 43, 57, 74, 95, 104, 107, 115, 124, 127, 129, 136, 139–40, 142, 146, 155, 181, 226, 228–30, 241, 259–61
    Pau 129–31
    Perpignan 116
    Provence 253
    Pyrénées 41, 133
    Rennes 241
    Roquefort 129–30
    Rouen 95, 233–5
    St Jean de Losne 247–8
    St Tropez 30
    St Quentin 137, 238
    Saone et Loire 251
    Seine, River 10, 233
    Toulon 241
    Tours 184
    Troyes 93, 95, 134

Franck, Thomas 159
Frédéric 172
Free French ix, xii, 14, 31, 50–51, 76, 94
French Foreign Legion 130
French Resistance ix, 40, 70, 86–7, 95–6, 135–7, 139, 147, 157, 170, 175, 190, 195, 206, 208–9, 221, 223, 269
  Maquis/Maquisards xii, 56, 93, 174, 191–2, 224, 236–7, 242, 244–8, 250–52, 254, 256–60, 265–6, 269
  members of 40
  Réseaux 51–6, 67, 70, 98, 132–3, 137–8, 162, 171, 173–4, 181, 185, 187–8, 192, 196, 200, 204, 207, 211, 222–3, 226–30, 233, 236, 238, 260, 265, 268
Fuller, Jean Overton x

de Gaulle, Charles ix, 2, 9, 50–52, 95, 120–21, 138
Gelin, Francois 145
Gendarmerie 204
Georges 19, 219–21
Germany 147, 162, 202–3, 246, 257, 259
  borders of 93
Gibraltar 19–20, 83–4
Gielgud, Major Lewis 19, 77, 81
Goering, Hermann 235, 242, 244–6, 251, 258
Granville, Christine (Pauline) 254, 256–7
de Gua, Colonel Henry 248
Gubbins, Chief Colin xi
de Guélis, Major 18–20, 22, 26, 81, 119

Hambro, Sir Charles 11–13, 15–16
Harrison, David xiii

Herbisse, Monsieur 207–8
Hervé 263–5
Heslop, Richard (Xavier) 95, 103, 109–13, 115, 236–7, 243, 247, 250–51, 253, 258
Hitler, Adolf 67, 108
Hoare, Sir Samuel 117
Huot, Major 134

Igor, Monsieur 215
Intelligence Corps ix, 7–8
Inayat Khan, Noor (Madeline) xi, 231–2, 267
Italy
  Turin 178–80

Jouas, Colonel 196–7
Judaism 31
Jules 143–6
Juller, George (Maxime) 54–5

Landes, Roger (Aristide) 181–6, 188, 196–7, 204–6, 208–13, 216, 219–20, 222–3, 229, 243, 251–2, 254–5, 257
Legros, Monsieur 175, 179
Leroux, Max 138, 140, 146–7, 155
Lévy, Doctor 87–8, 90–92, 96
Libya 1
Liewer, Philippe 233–4
Low, Nigel 45–6, 48–9

Maingard, Amédée 174–5, 179
Malin, Monsieur 189
Maloubier 233–4
Maquis xii
Marc 219
Marks, Leo xi
  From Silk to Cyanide xi
Morel 111–12
Morgan, Harry 20, 30–33, 37–41, 75–6, 87, 119–24, 127, 130–31,

136, 164, 166–7, 169–72, 190, 196, 198–203

Nearne, Eileen 267
Nearne, Jacqueline 174–5, 267
Netherlands
   Holland 124
Newton, Henry George Rodolfo (Auguste) 206
Nicholas, Elizabeth x
Noble, George 15
Norman, Gilbert (Archambaud) xi, 181–3, 227, 229
Nornable, Gordon 237
Nulli, Monsieur 30–31, 37

Palestine Express 31
Parker, Dr Geoffrey (Parsifal) 236–7
Paul 152–3
Peugeot, Robert 162–6, 169
Peulevé, Harry 132–3, 188, 195, 205
Poirier, Gustave 197–201
Portugal
   Lisbon 73
Poulain, Jacques 20

Raczynski, Stanislaw 34–5
Rake, Denis 76–8, 83–5, 87, 89–92, 96–7, 99, 102–17, 132–4, 172, 200, 236–7, 248–9
Raymond 123–4, 126–9, 188–90, 192–4, 196
Rée, Harry 162–3, 167, 169, 175
Renée (Virginia Hall) 96–9, 102, 108–9
Rex 190–92

de St Genies, Marie Joseph Gonzagues (Lucien) 247
Schwartz, Colonel 256–7
Second World War (1939–45) ix
   20 July Plot (1944) 151

Battle of Dakar (1940) 2–3
Battle of Dunkirk (1940) 4, 76
belligerents of 243, 251, 259–60, 266, 268
Fall of France (1940) 28, 132
Normandy landings (D-Day) (1944) ix, xi, 45, 56, 133, 137, 174, 192, 224–5, 228, 233, 235–7, 239, 241–4, 262–3
Ravensbrück 246
Secret Intelligence Service 67, 129, 150–51
Smee, Colonel 42–3
Socialist Party 197
Southgate, Maurice (Hector) 174–5, 177
Soviet Union (USSR) 73, 202, 217–18, 248
Spain 41, 103, 131
   Barcelona 124
   borders of 54, 117, 133
   Civil War (1936–9) 117, 124, 190
   Figueras 117
   government of 124
   Madrid 117
   Portbou 117
Special Operations Executive (SOE) ix–xi, 9, 11, 14–16, 35, 45, 52, 61, 72, 78, 93, 96–7, 134, 138, 151, 175, 178, 232–3, 235, 249, 258, 263, 266–8
   Belgian Section 15
   French Section ix–xii, 6–7, 16, 57, 225, 261
   Head Office 47–8
Starr, George (Hilaire) 132–3, 136, 242, 244
Supreme Headquarters Allied Expeditionary Force (SHAEF) 225, 239, 259, 264
Suttill, Major Francis (Prosper) 95, 181, 226–31

Switzerland 172
    borders of 171–3
    Sainte-Croix 172
Szabo, Violette 232–4, 245–6, 267

Templer, General 4–6
Theophile, Abbé 130–31
Third Reich (1933–45) x, 2, 9, 12, 17, 21–2, 24, 26, 30, 43, 45, 53–4, 66, 72–6, 87, 99–101, 116, 123, 129, 137, 144, 148, 169–70, 173, 187, 193, 199, 214, 220–21, 236, 252, 259, 263
    Abwehr 58, 87, 151, 228
    Gestapo 29, 38, 44, 47, 67, 82, 87, 115, 129, 141, 151, 156, 158, 160–61, 171, 199, 201, 210–16, 218, 230–32, 239–40, 254–5
    Schutzstaffel (SS) 86, 107–8
    Sicherheitsdienst x
    Todt 192
Timken Ball Bearing Factory 10
Trotobas, Michael (Sylvestre) 137–9, 143–5, 147, 150, 152–5, 158–61, 244

United Kingdom (UK) 1, 36, 73, 127, 190, 249–50
    Air Ministry 140
    Bletchley Park xii
    Cambridge 125, 128
    Coventry 114
    First Aid Nursing Yeomanry (FANY) 60–61, 65, 68–9
    government of 246
    Guilford 78
    London ix, xi–xii, 3–4, 6–7, 11, 16–17, 19, 28, 35–6, 54, 63, 67–71, 81–3, 95, 100, 103, 118, 133–4, 138–9, 155, 164–5, 177, 182, 185–8, 200, 210, 218, 220, 223, 226–7, 229–30, 234, 239, 252, 258, 261, 267–8

    Ministry of Economic Warfare 7, 41, 134, 174, 225
    Portsmouth 76
    Royal Air Force (RAF) 43, 53, 60, 66, 77, 94, 118–19, 124–6, 135, 141, 147, 157, 162, 166–7, 177–8, 189, 209, 253, 262, 264–5
    Bomber Command 149, 151, 155–7, 177
    Scotland Yard 46, 82
    Treasury 165
    War Office 3, 10–11, 77, 118
    Whitehall 4
United States of America (USA) 73
    American Tactical Air Force 253

Vichy French 2, 49, 114, 116, 204
    Milice 22, 30, 32–3, 37, 40, 84, 86, 90, 96, 98, 102, 110, 112–13, 158–60
de Vomécourt, Pierre (Félix) 20–21, 23–7, 32–6, 42–4, 75

Wake, Nancy 248, 267
Warsaw Patriots 260
Watney, Cyril (Eustache) 54–5, 160
Wilkinson, Edward (Alexandre) 109–16
Wilkinson, George 117
Wilma, Princess 107

Yveline 81–2, 88, 91
Yvette, Pierre Embrasse 66